D1756271

Plagiarism in Early Modern England

Plagiarism in Early Modern England

Edited by

Paulina Kewes
Senior Lecturer
Department of English
University of Wales, Aberystwyth

First published 2003 by
PALGRAVE MACMILLAN
Houndmills, Basingstoke, Hampshire RG21 6XS and
175 Fifth Avenue, New York, N.Y. 10010
Companies and representatives throughout the world

PALGRAVE MACMILLAN is the global academic imprint of the Palgrave Macmillan division of St. Martin's Press, LLC and of Palgrave Macmillan Ltd. Macmillan® is a registered trademark in the United States, United Kingdom and other countries. Palgrave is a registered trademark in the European Union and other countries.

ISBN 0 333 99841–3

This book is printed on paper suitable for recycling and made from fully managed and sustained forest sources.

A catalogue record for this book is available from the British Library.

Library of Congress Cataloging-in-Publication Data

Plagiarism in early modern England / edited by Paulina Kewes.
    p. cm.
    Papers from a conference on 'Plagiarism in history and theory' at the Institute of English Studies in November 1999.
    Includes bibliographical references and index.
    ISBN 0-333-99841-3 (cloth)
    1. England–Intellectual life–Congresses. 2. Plagiarism–England–Congresses. 3. English literature–History and criticism–Congresses.
1. Kewes, Paulina.
DA110 .P56 2002
942–dc21   2002072841

10   9   8   7   6   5   4   3   2   1
12   11   10   09   08   07   06   05   04   03

Printed and bound in Great Britain by
Antony Rowe Ltd, Chippenham and Eastbourne

To the memory of Don McKenzie

Contents

vii

List of Figures

Notes on Contributors

Paul Baines is Senior Lecturer in the Department of English Language and Literature, University of Liverpool. His recent publications include: *The House of Forgery in Eighteenth-Century Britain* (1999); *The Complete Critical Guide to Alexander Pope* (2000); and *Five Romantic Plays 1768–1821* (co-edited with Edward Burns, 2000). In 2001 he was awarded a British Academy Research Readership to work on Edmund Curll.

Ian Donaldson is Grace I Professor of English and Director of the Centre for Research in the Arts, Social Sciences, and Humanities at Cambridge University, and a Fellow of King's College. He has published widely on Jonson, Shakespeare and Renaissance drama. He is a general editor of *The Cambridge Edition of the Works of Ben Jonson*, and is currently completing a life of Ben Jonson.

Bertrand A. Goldgar is Professor of English at Lawrence University. He is the author of *Walpole and the Wits: The Relation of Politics to Literature, 1722–1742* (1976), has edited or co-edited three volumes of Henry Fielding's works for Clarendon Press, and is currently editing *The Grub-Street Journal*.

Nick Groom is Senior Lecturer in Post-Medieval English Literature at the University of Bristol. He is the author of *The Making of Percy's Reliques* (1999), editor of *Thomas Chatterton and Romantic Culture* (1999), and edits two scholarly series for Routledge Research. His most recent books are *Introducing Shakespeare* (2001) and *The Forger's Shadow: How Forgery Changed the Course of English Literature* (2002). He has now returned to his work on the English ballad tradition.

Brean S. Hammond is Professor of English at the University of Nottingham. He is the author, most recently, of *Professional Imaginative Writing in England, 1670–1740: 'Hackney for Bread'* (1997); and essays on James Thomson, literature and politics in the eighteenth century, Swift, and, in collaboration with the editor of the present volume, on Rochester. His latest project has been an edition of five plays by Vanbrugh for the OUP World's Classics series.

Andrew Hope most recently taught history at Newstead Wood School, Kent. He worked with the University of Leuven to prepare the 'Tyndale's Testament' exhibition at Antwerp, which opened in September 2002, and contributed articles on the history of the English Bible to the exhibition catalogue. He has also published articles on Lollardy.

Paulina Kewes is Senior Lecturer in English at the University of Wales, Aberystwyth. Her publications include *Authorship and Appropriation: Writing for the Stage in England, 1660–1710* (1998) and essays on Shakespeare, Dryden, Renaissance, Restoration and eighteenth-century drama. She is completing a book on theatrical representations of history in early modern England.

Harold Love holds a personal chair in English at Monash University, Melbourne. He is the author of *Scribal Publication in Seventeenth-Century England*, and has edited the works of Thomas Southerne (with R. J. Jordan) and John Wilmot, Earl of Rochester.

Stephen Orgel is the Jackson Eli Reynolds Professor in Humanities at Stanford. His most recent book is *The Authentic Shakespeare* (2002), and he is the author of *Impersonations: The Performance of Gender in Shakespeare's England* (1996); *The Illusion of Power* (1975); *Inigo Jones* (in collaboration with Sir Roy Strong, 1973), and *The Jonsonian Masque* (1965). His many editions include Christopher Marlowe's poems and translations, Ben Jonson's masques, *The Tempest* and *The Winter's Tale* in The Oxford Shakespeare, and *Macbeth, King Lear, The Taming of the Shrew, Pericles* and *The Sonnets* in the New Pelican Shakespeare, of which he is general editor.

Barbara Ravelhofer is a Research Fellow at the Istituto di Studi Avanzati, University of Bologna. She has published on English Renaissance drama, dance history and European spectacle culture of the early modern period. She is currently writing a book on dance and costume in the Stuart masque.

Lisa Richardson is working on the use and imitation of classical and other literary models in early modern English historiography. She was formerly Julia Mann Junior Research Fellow at St Hilda's College, Oxford.

Christopher Ricks is Warren Professor of the Humanities at Boston University and co-director of the Editorial Institute. He has taught at

Boston University since 1986; he was formerly King Edward VII Professor of English Literature at the University of Cambridge. His numerous books include *Keats and Embarrassment* (1974); *T. S. Eliot and Prejudice* (1988); *Beckett's Dying Words* (1993); *Essays in Appreciation* (1996); and *Allusion to the Poets* (2002). He has edited the poems of Tennyson and the early poems of T. S. Eliot, as well as the *New Oxford Book of Victorian Verse* (1987) and *The Oxford Book of English Verse* (1999).

Richard Steadman-Jones is a Lecturer in the School of English at Sheffield University where he is responsible for promoting interdisciplinary work spanning the departments of English Language & Linguistics and English Literature. He has a particular interest in language study undertaken within contexts of cultural and colonial encounter, and his PhD dissertation, which he is currently preparing for publication, deals with Romantic-period accounts of the South Asian language, Urdu.

Richard Terry is Reader in Eighteenth-Century English Literature at the University of Sunderland. His publications include *Poetry and the Making of the English Literary Past, 1660–1781* (2001) and essays on numerous aspects of eighteenth-century literature, especially on burlesque poetry. He has edited a collection of essays on James Thomson to mark the tercentenary of the poet's birth, as well as co-authoring an introductory book on poetry. He is currently at work on a study of mock-heroic poetry, *The Mock-Heroic Moment*.

Preface

This book originates in controversy. In recent years disagreements – or perhaps confusions – over the meaning of the term plagiarism, its applicability in individual cases, and its position *vis-à-vis* the related concepts of appropriation, allusion, imitation, intertextuality, copyright infringement and forgery have become more heated than ever. For some, plagiarism is a moral transgression.[1] Others view it as a venial offence and rank plagiarism alongside such morally neutral modes of composition as collage, parody and pastiche.[2] There are also those who promote plagiarism as a revolutionary practice subversive of ruling ideologies and power structures.[3] 'Pragmatic plagiarism', 'creative plagiarism', 'perceptive plagiarism', 'virtuous plagiarism'[4] – however playful, these phrases drawn from recent studies of the subject evince tolerance or approval of plagiarism.

So what is plagiarism and how strongly should it be reprobated? How have the meaning of plagiarism and attitudes towards it changed over time? The opportunity to discuss these and related questions came when Professor Warwick Gould invited me to organize a conference on 'Plagiarism in History and Theory' at the Institute of English Studies in November 1999. The thematic and chronological scope of the conference was broad, the presentations covering a variety of literary forms from the premodern to the postmodern. *Plagiarism in Early Modern England* seeks to meet the need for a discussion of plagiarism both tighter in its contextual focus and more extensive in the range of genres, topics and disciplines covered. It is informed, too, by a concern to address questions about definition and methodology. The book spans three centuries, from the sixteenth to the early nineteenth, individual contributors focusing more narrowly on particular historical moments. It does away with the traditional distinction between 'literary' and 'non-literary' plagiarism and emphasizes the significance of contextual and material dimensions of acts of theft or alleged theft.

Our prime aim is at once to theorize and to historicize plagiarism. The first part of the book launches a debate about the ethical, philosophical, artistic and legal implications of plagiarism. Individual essays in Part II provide historical case studies. Variously centred on translations of the Bible, historiography, drama, poetry, commonplace books, dance treatises, sermons and colonial grammars, they attest to the diversity of practices and perceptions of plagiarism in English cultural and intellectual life of the early modern period.

Inevitably a book of this nature raises more questions than it answers. We hope that its interdisciplinary programme, and its combination of archival research with theoretical approaches, will encourage further thinking about plagiarism and about the concepts related to it, in other genres, cultures and periods.

*

This book owes its inception to many people and institutions. Generously sponsored by the British Academy and hosted by the Institute of English Studies, the conference on which this volume is based greatly benefited from the liberal patronage and enthusiasm of Warwick Gould and the assistance of Michael Baron. Josie Dixon of Palgrave Macmillan who attended the conference was warmly supportive of a collection on the subject of plagiarism in early modern England.

I have incurred further personal and institutional debts in preparing the volume for publication. Clare Hall, Cambridge; the Folger Shakespeare Library, Washington D.C.; and the University of Wales, Aberystwyth, have all provided wonderfully congenial work settings and institutional support. To Helen Cooper, Paul Hammond, Bill Sherman, William St Clair, Blair Worden and Steven Zwicker I am grateful for their conversation, advice and hospitality. Special thanks are due to my contributors for their grace, efficiency and professionalism. Throughout the process of readying *Plagiarism in Early Modern England* for the press, the support and advice of Rob Hume have been invaluable. The suggestions of the anonymous reader, too, have made this a better book. At Palgrave Macmillan, the editorial counsel and care of Eleanor Birne and Becky Mashayekh have been a great boon. Finally, for help with tracking down the elusive Rembrandt painting which appears on the cover I owe thanks to Moira Vincentelli and Mike Franklin.

My greatest personal and intellectual debt is expressed in the dedication. It was Don McKenzie with whom I first discussed the early modern preoccupation with plagiarism and it was on Don's recommendation that Warwick Gould invited me to organize the Conference on Plagiarism at the Institute of English Studies, a conference which Don himself sadly did not live to attend. This volume is but a small tribute to the memory of the best and most generous of teachers and friends.

*

I am grateful to Professor Christopher Ricks and the British Academy for permission to reprint Professor Ricks's 1998 British Academy Lecture on 'Plagiarism' from *Proceedings of the British Academy*, vol. 97 (1998).

1
Historicizing Plagiarism

Paulina Kewes

The idea of plagiarism, like all ideas, has a history. To earlier generations it had semantic inflections and resonances different from those we recognize today. Plagiarism has been subject to condemnation on at least three grounds. The first is moral or ethical: plagiarism is dishonest and deceitful, bringing unearned credit (and often profit) to its perpetrator. The second is aesthetic: plagiarism can debase the object or objects from which it steals, and there are those who hold that '[t]he plagiarist is simply the bad borrower'.[1] The third is forensic or legal: although unlike copyright infringement, a much later development with which it is sometimes confused, plagiarism is not an offence punishable by law,[2] it is often denounced as criminal, and calls are periodically made for punitive legislation to be put in place. The conflicting impulses behind those perspectives, which have themselves evolved in response to commercial circumstances, new theories of artistic creation and developments in copyright law, have repeatedly complicated judgements of plagiarism and shaped the rhetoric used to condemn or exculpate it. Despite an abiding sense that plagiarism is morally wrong, there has been much fluidity in the way the charge has been applied, and virtually identical acts of illicit appropriation have been sometimes denounced, sometimes excused and sometimes praised.

The historical approach that generally characterizes this volume will not please everyone. Indeed one of its contributors, Christopher Ricks, in the seminal essay reproduced here, is suspicious of historical approaches to ethical issues. To him, emphasis on change across generations produces an extenuating moral relativism which shields the evil of plagiarism from its due obloquy. But there are historical approaches and historical approaches. Ricks is rightly dismissive of the 'construction industry', that is, the post-Foucauldian investigations into the 'construction' of the author, the subject, and the like.[3] It is true that, as Ricks alleges, there has been some shoddy scholarship which anachronistically projects modern-day ideologies to do with gender, race or class on to historically remote controversies.[4] It is also true that some interpreters get their history wrong.[5] None of the contributors to this volume, I think, would wish to endorse the blanket assertion made by another of the writers challenged by Ricks that 'our basic sense of plagiarism came to be born in the seventeenth century'.[6] Yet bad history is no argument against history itself. To reconstruct the attitudes of the past, moreover, is not necessarily to vindicate them. It is merely to acknowledge that whatever *we* might think is the correct way of apprehending plagiarism – and even today, as this book demonstrates, there is hardly a consensus on the matter – our predecessors may not have shared, and in fact often did not share, our perspectives.

Continuity and change in thinking about plagiarism can be assessed only through a detailed investigation of the contexts in which accusations of theft were made, or in which we would expect them to have been made. There are questions about definition, practice and reception. Has the understanding of plagiarism changed over time? What has been its relation to such concepts as imitation, borrowing, adaptation, allusion, intertextuality, appropriation, copyright infringement? To what extent have ethical and aesthetic judgements of plagiarism coincided or conflicted? How has the rhetoric of condemnation and apology developed? The principal aims of an historical account of plagiarism are to recreate the outlook that prevailed at particular moments; to examine if and how that outlook changed; and to explain why the change occurred.

The question of approach

There are two ways of situating plagiarism in historical perspective. First, there is the broad-sweep approach that traces the practices and perceptions of plagiarism from the earliest times to the present day. Second, there is the period-specific approach that focuses on a particular era which it explores in detail. Both have their strengths. The first usefully highlights large-scale conceptual shifts such as, for example, the decline in the cachet of imitation in favour of creative originality. It also allows for cross-cultural comparisons of attitudes towards unacknowledged copying in, for instance, classical Antiquity, the medieval world, the Renaissance, and so on. The second provides for a detailed reconstitution of the often contradictory views of appropriation at a particular time. Given the extensive chronological span and propensity towards generalization that characterize the transhistorical approach, some contextual complexities are bound to be overlooked. The period-specific approach, which is more sensitive to local developments, is less well equipped to assess the implications of long-term cultural change. Although distinct, the two approaches are complementary and interdependent.

The most recent scholarly study of plagiarism, Marilyn Randall's thoughtful and thought-provoking *Pragmatic Plagiarism: Authorship, Profit, and Power* (2001), adopts the transhistorical approach. The present volume, as both its title – *Plagiarism in Early Modern England* – and the titles of the individual essays make clear, opts for contextual particularity. What are the interpretive consequences of these choices? By exploring the rhetoric and the social and cultural circumstances of the reception of plagiarism from classical Antiquity to the present, Randall charts the development of plagiarism as an aesthetic concept which, although mostly seen as negative, has been occasionally promoted as a desirable mode of composition. Working within the theoretical framework of pragmatics and reader-response criticism, she shifts the discussion of intentionality of plagiarism from author to reader, pointing out that it is the reader's 'authority that invests him with the capacity for *recognition* of the repetition, for *naming* it, thereby constructing it as fraudulent or otherwise, and for *judging* the repetition and the perpetrator as being condemnable, excusable, or in some instances praiseworthy'.[7] These are points well taken. Unfruitful attempts to prove the author's fraudulent intent even when evidence of such intent has been wholly lacking have long bedevilled critical accounts of plagiarism, and Randall is right to stress that, over the past two millennia, readers have often invented intentions for authors. Given the monumental timeframe of her book, Randall admits that her 'sporadic approach...will of necessity be selective, non-linear, and far from exhaustive' (p. xii), relying as it does on a series of case studies. 'My method attempts to be transhistorical,' she explains, 'while avoiding ahistoricity: in crossing vast stretches of time, I endeavour to uncover, despite the historical specificity governing differences in judgments about plagiarism, the transhistorical constants that inform them' (p. 10).

Plagiarism in Early Modern England differs from Randall's monograph – as well as in being a volume of essays by several hands – in its chronological span, in its coverage, and in many of its findings. It is chronologically narrower, covering approximately three centuries, from 1500 to 1800, but it is broader in its thematic range. Unlike Randall who restricts her enquiry to literary plagiarism, it cuts across the distinction between literary and non-literary writings – a distinction which was itself a product of the early modern – and explores manifestations of plagiarism in poems, plays, historiography, sermons, dance treatises and grammar books. Finally, where Randall stresses the historical stability of both the perceptions of plagiarism and the criteria by which they have been informed, *Plagiarism in Early Modern England* evinces diversity and change. To some extent this divergence is a function of legitimate differences in approach. A study of a discrete phenomenon (literary plagiarism) over an extended period will naturally tend towards recognition of transhistorical constants, while an enquiry into roughly contemporary practices and beliefs (manifestations of plagiarism in early modern England) will be likely to reveal multiplicity and contradiction. There are, however, specific problems with Randall's account. First, her decision to exclude non-literary forms of plagiarism is open to challenge, for the idea of literature as a distinct field of intellectual activity is itself a historical construction. By separating the 'literary' from the 'non-literary', moreover, Randall forgoes the opportunity to address broader questions about the cultural proprieties of appropriation. Second and more important, she overlooks the role of the material forms of the textual evidence of literary plagiarism. Yet, as I hope to show in the following pages, to understand plagiarism and its reception we need to examine not only the verbal content of the allegedly plagiarized or plagiarizing texts, and of the responses to them by successive generations of readers, but also the physical medium through which that content has been communicated.

So far I have looked at the criteria for delimiting the chronological span of an historical account of plagiarism. Now I want to address questions about evidence, medium and context.

The evidence

What sort of evidence can be used in tracing the views of plagiarism and other forms of appropriation? First, there are statements made by authors that either deny any kind of textual debt or contrast their open borrowings with unacknowledged copying. Second, there are the pronouncements made by critics and readers that classify specific cases of textual appropriation as plagiaristic or else exonerate them from the charge. Third, there are the theoretical accounts of plagiarism and its legitimate counterparts such as translation and imitation. To recover the historical inflections of plagiarism, we have to consider not only *what* was said about plagiarism, but also *how* and *where* it was said. In other words, we need to examine the evolution of languages in which intellectual theft has been identified and judged, and the material forms of their transmission, a point to which I shall return. To illustrate: among the most prominent tropes used to justify plagiarism has been the metaphor of conquest. 'He invades Authours like a Monarch,' Dryden famously said of Ben Jonson, 'and what would be theft in other Poets is onely victory in him.'[8] Once uniformly positive, in the postcolonial era the connotations of military, economic or cultural subjection of one nation, race or state by another have become intensely pejorative. That semantic change, in turn, has drained the conquest metaphor of its rhetorical power to excuse plagiarism, turning the traditional trope of vindication into one of condemnation. Gendered metaphors, too, have undergone a parallel process of reinterpretation. In the early seventeenth century, John Florio thought it natural to contrast an ambitious task of compiling a dictionary, the *World of Words*, with the less taxing project of translating Montaigne's *Essays*, by figuring the former as masculine – 'my last Birth, which I held masculine (as are all mens concepts that are their owne, though but by their collecting...)' – and the latter as feminine: 'this defective edition (since all translations are reputed females), delivered at second hand'.[9] Nowadays such a distinction would be unthinkable. The transformation of these and other metaphors is symptomatic of plagiarism's shifting cultural value.

To the *what* and the *how* we must add the *where*. For the textual sites in which views of plagiarism have been articulated are themselves significant for the interpreting of those views. It matters, for example, whether a given statement was designed to be public, having been made through the medium of print, or private, appearing in a diary or a letter. If it was public, what form did it take? Was it expressed in a preface, review, critical essay, scholarly study, biography, letter to the editor, prologue or epilogue? Or was it conveyed metatextually as when literary or intellectual theft is thematized in a play or a novel or when it is made the subject of an epigram or of satirical verse? Finally, the frequency with which accusations of plagiarism have been made is a telling index of plagiarism's importance as a cultural concern. What sets the early modern period apart from previous eras is the accumulation of evidence that attests to the mounting anxieties about illicit copying. Whether designated as 'plagiary' (a native recension of the Latin *'plagiarius'* that made its appearance in the 1590s)[10] or whether defined in more descriptive terms, covert appropriation of the intellectual or artistic labours of another came under unprecedented scrutiny. Charges of theft, sometimes of ideas, sometimes of words, proliferated in a variety of literary, artistic, religious and political contexts from which they had hitherto been absent. The profusion of documentary evidence that bespeaks a change in both thought and practice is precisely what makes the early modern period an exciting one to study, and why it is the focus of this book.

Medium and access

As I have begun to suggest, in tracing the reception of plagiarism we must examine not only the transmission of textual commentary about specific instances of copying, but also the material forms of the appropriated and appropriating texts. For those material forms have been instrumental in shaping both appropriative practices and the rating of individual acts of appropriation as legitimate or illegitimate. There is a qualification to be made here: plagiarism does not always require actual copying – writing down passages of text, or taking notes or drawing a sketch. The recollection of a book, a musical theme or a picture may inspire a new work, and it may also make the author of that work liable to accusations of plagiarism. It is the theft of the general idea that authors sometimes complain of, not the exact reproduction of the original. The role of memory raises the grey area of influences that are half-remembered or even forgotten, and that sometimes produce what might be called – however oxymoronically – unintentional plagiarism.

This book is mainly about textual copying. In earlier discussions of plagiarism little attention has been paid to the physical medium of the text. And yet various technologies of text production and transmission – manuscript, print, electronic media – make possible, indeed invite, certain forms of appropriation while precluding others. Plagiarism routinely involves not only an act of writing but also an act of reading, so the material form of what is being read – and copied – determines how it is done: reading a messy manuscript and copying it by hand is onerous; by contrast, reading a printed text, scanning it and editing it on one's own computer is easy. One more caveat, however: there are broader issues of cultural outlook and religious doctrine which complicate any attempt to chart simple linear 'progress' from oral to literate cultures, from manuscript to print, from epochs when there was no notion of individual authorship and hence no concern about attribution, originality, plagiarism and forgery to ones where such issues were paramount. Classical Antiquity provides examples of sophisticated attribution studies, of denouncements of literary theft, of scrupulous detection and condemnation of forgeries.[11] By comparison, in the medieval period individual authorial identity mattered a lot less, and copying and repeating were seen as legitimate tools of disseminating the truth. The Renaissance doctrine of imitation made manifest the links between old texts and new ones, inviting comparisons between contemporary writers and their classical models. Questions were raised about acceptable levels of verbal indebtedness to earlier works, whether ancient or recent, sometimes very recent. At the same time, however, the Renaissance culture of *sententiae* and teaching by *sententiae* was posited on a large public fund of thought, tropes and phrases. The oral, the aural and the written remained in close proximity, as did manuscript and print.

Historically, transitions from one form of scribal (or print) publication to another – for example, from the roll to the codex – created different opportunities for, and imposed different constraints upon, appropriation. 'Plagiarie had not its nativitie with printing,' noted Sir Thomas Browne in the mid-seventeenth century, 'but began in times when thefts were difficult, and the paucity of books scarce wanted that invention.'[12] Browne was right in saying that plagiarism pre-dates the invention of print, but he was unaware that it also pre-dates the invention of the material objects he refers to as books. Until the second century AD when the manuscript book – the codex – made its appearance, texts had been stored on papyrus rolls (*volumina*).[13] The roll and the codex provide very different kinds of reading experience. In order to read a roll, one has to hold it in both hands, unfolding it with the right hand and rolling it up with the left. With the arrival of the codex, the reader's hands are needed only intermittently to turn the pages, and are now free to copy. Not only have reading and writing become natural allies, the reading process itself has become far more user-friendly through the emergence of such pointers and marking techniques as indices, marginal annotations, chapter and section headings. To go back and scan the text once again requires far less effort than with the papyrus roll. The opportunities for both appropriation – whether licit or illicit – and its detection have grown substantially.

The reading praxis in the ancient world contrasts sharply with the modern practice of personal private reading. Much reading from rolls was done aloud by slaves or with slaves turning the roll. Slaves were also employed in copying rolls. Even so, the contrast between reading (and copying) from a roll as opposed to a codex has serious implications for the study of appropriative practices. So do the possibilities opened up by the spread of movable type from the fifteenth century onward which made books cheaper and more easily available. Humanist reading was predicated upon the taking of notes for use: extracts from multiple-printed books were copied by hand into personal commonplace books, frequently with little attention to attribution.[14] Originally compiled for private use, many commonplace books such as Ben Jonson's *Timber* found their way into print with or without the collector's knowledge or cooperation. As Anne Moss has observed, '[t]he commonplace-book mode of rhetorical production had been haunted by the bogey of plagiarism ever since Petrarch'.[15] Surprisingly, the implications of textual commonplacing for the understanding of plagiarism have been little studied. Was commonplacing perceived as theft when the compilation was passed on for further circulation either in manuscript or printed form? Perhaps the sources from which specific passages had been drawn were meant to be recognized by the knowing readers? Harold Love explores these questions in his contribution to this volume.[16]

From the practice of excerpting passages from a variety of books for personal use there was only a short step to copying from several sources for publication. In one sense this mode of appropriation, which grew rapidly after the advent of print, must have made recognition of the borrowings, allusions or thefts difficult as the reader would have needed access to the same books – six, seven, eight, or more – that the appropriator had used. In another sense, however, it brought unacknowledged copying into the open: with all kinds of printed matter flooding the market and with the levels of literacy rising steadily, the likelihood of readers perceiving affinities between and among texts expanded. Like the invention of printing in the late fifteenth century, the invention of the photocopying machine, the computer and the scanner in the twentieth has further facilitated eclectic appropriation of all sorts of materials. Indeed, the development of information technologies and the surge of desktop publishing could be said to have produced a new breed of appropriator, one who surfs the net, scrolls down the computer screen and downloads stretches of text while taking advantage of the multiplicity of search options, engines and databases. In the twenty-first century plagiary-hunters, or merely academic instructors wishing to check the self-sufficiency of their students' essays, avail themselves of the same opportunities.

The changing technologies of textual transmission have had a decisive role in shaping the practice of plagiarism. They have also affected the judgement of particular kinds of illicit copying, for example from manuscript, as distinct from printed or, more recently, electronic, texts. As Harold Love has demonstrated, from the sixteenth to the early nineteenth century – the period covered by this book – scribal and print publication existed side by side in England. The spectrum of scribally published materials included not only what we might term imaginative literature – poems, plays, songs – but also newsletters, political pamphlets, sermons and music.[17] To this list might be added translations of politically or religiously sensitive works that would have been dangerous to print such as, in the sixteenth century, Niccolò Machiavelli's *Discourses* and *The Prince*.[18] This continued interaction between manuscript and print influenced both the forms and the perceptions of plagiarism. Theft from manuscript sources attracted increasing opprobrium even when the stolen text was not intended for print publication. In the case studied by Barbara Ravelhofer, one dancing master stole from an unfinished treatise by a colleague in order to present an elegant copy to his patron.[19] The thief did not 'publish' the plagiarised text in the sense of seeking to achieve circulation among a larger audience; so far as we know, his text existed in only one scribal copy. Even so the injured author, who had himself planned to use the work to solicit aristocratic patronage, cried thief. He publicized his colleague's dishonesty in the preface to a revised, enlarged and lavishly printed version of his composition. Clearly, materiality mattered to him and he assumed that it would matter to his audience.

As the fracas between the two choreographers shows, moreover, in analysing the impact of various textual media on the reception of plagiarism, we confront the problem of access. People have always been alive to the value of circumstantial evidence in ascertaining textual debts. For example, the notebook of Thomas Gibbons records his disappointment with George Ruggle's *Ignoramus* (1615), a play whose satire of the legal profession delighted the Jacobean court. Having found in the Clare Hall library not just the foreign source of the skit, but the very copy the appropriator had annotated in the process of turning it into English, Gibbons indignantly disparaged Ruggle's authorial credentials: 'The comoedie of Ignoramus so abusiue against Lawyers and supposed tobe made by Mr Rug of clare hall in Cambridg is but a translation of a comedy in Baptist porta out of Italian intituled Trapulario as may be seen by the comedy it self extant in clare hall library with notes of Mr Ruggells theron of his contriuing & Altering therof.'[20] The concern to demonstrate that the thief did have access to the purloined text, and, whenever possible, to exhibit the material object bearing the marks of the culprit's pen, prefigures a similar concern of modern-day courts which routinely throw out copyright infringement suits where the accused can have had no opportunity to read the work he or she is charged with having copied.

An historical account of plagiarism, then, needs to assess not only the relative ease of access to the source-text, but also the distribution of attitudes towards theft from texts circulating in various forms. Is it more reprehensible to steal from a manuscript, a printed book or an on-line publication? Ever since the invention of printing, and more recently, since the advent of the Internet, attitudes towards illicit copying varied depending on the medium of the text. In the Renaissance, many genteel and aristocratic amateurs confined the circulation of their writings to scribal copies in order to avoid the 'stigma of print'.[21] Their professional rivals who hoped to make a living by selling their work to theatres or booksellers might well have thought that if a poem circulated with such apparent insouciance was purloined, its author got no more than he deserved. The professional's scathing view of the genteel contempt for the press is explicit in Michael Drayton's '[O]f Poets and Poesie'. The poem sets out to delineate a canon of English literature from Chaucer and Gower to Shakespeare and Ben Jonson. Strikingly, Drayton excludes from his account all contemporary writers who eschew print and hence avoid submitting their works to the scrutiny of the reading public:

> . . . be inform'd that I
> Only my selfe, to these few men doe tye,
> Whose works oft printed, set on every post,
> To publique censure subject have bin most;
> For such whose poems, be they nere so rare,
> In private chambers, that incloistered are,
> And by transcription daintyly must goe;
> As though the world unworthy were to know,
> Their rich composures, let those men that keepe
> These wonderous reliques in their judgement deepe,
> And cry them up so, let such Peeces bee
> Spoke of by those that shall come after me . . .[22]

It does not seem too fanciful to conjecture that Drayton would have felt scant sympathy for those genteel amateurs whose scribally circulated work got seized by others. The sense that a text published on the Internet – for instance, on the author's web-site – is somehow fair game is the modern equivalent of the early modern proclivity towards recycling manuscript texts. In contrast to the aristocratic preference for scribal publication, however, the motives for putting one's work on-line may range from a genuine lack of concern about financial profit to disagreement with one's publisher to plain inability to secure a contract, in which case the on-line text is probably not worth plagiarizing anyway.

It is one thing when the plagiarized text is in the public domain – whether in scribal, printed or electronic form. It is another when it exists only as a private manuscript or a file on a personal computer. As Christopher Ricks has noted, to liken plagiarism to theft is misleading because in contrast to other forms of stealing which palpably deprive the victim of some sort of property – whether money or goods – literary 'theft' does not in fact deprive the plagiarized author of anything.[23] The credit for the work is still his, even if the plagiarist also lays claim to it. But in the case of plagiarism from texts that can only be accessed by stealth, metaphorical theft may be compounded by literal theft – of a manuscript, a computer print-out, a floppy disk. 'I missed my booke one day,' wrote Thomas Newman in the dedication of his translation of *The Two First Comedies of Terence called Andria, and the Eunuch* (1627), 'and then found it againe gelded of the three Latter Acts of the third Comedie. Shortly after I met the Copie thereof in the hands of a Stationer.' Not only did the unnamed perpetrator – 'this thiefe, this plagiarie' – make wrongful 'use' of Newman's 'labour' by selling it to a bookseller.[24] He also violated the privacy of Newman's lodgings where he seized the latter's work-in-progress. As the example of the two Jacobean dancing masters illustrates, plagiarism from a text which exists in a single manuscript copy often involves a breach of trust, friendship or professional integrity. Newman's predicament testifies that it can also entail an infraction of privacy and property.

So far we have considered plagiarism from texts which have been written down and which existed in some material form, whether as manuscripts or printed books or computer files that can be read, downloaded or printed out. But what about orally transmitted texts such as plays, songs or sermons? Again, the orality of the appropriated or appropriating text serves as an important guide to changing sensibilities. In Shakespeare's lifetime, when many if not most theatrical scripts were kept out of print, we find few charges of theft against dramatists. By the later seventeenth century, when publication of new plays became the norm, such charges multiplied. The proliferation of printed drama was not the only reason for this change, but it was an important one. So while it would be wrong to take the paucity of negative comment as a sign that in the earlier period plays had been exempt from the contumely that attaches to plagiarism, we can certainly detect a connection between the increased availability of printed play-texts and the mounting intensity of public disapproval directed at unacknowledged copying.[25]

What, then, are the methodological implications of these remarks for the historical study of plagiarism? Until well into the twentieth century, literary criticism and textual editing and bibliography ran parallel courses. Editors, bibliographers and textual critics prepared 'authoritative' texts; literary scholars studied them. No one asked how interpretation might be affected by the arrangement of the words on the page, the format of the book or its transmission. Now, in the aftermath of the pioneering contributions by D. F. McKenzie and Jerome McGann, no self-respecting literary scholar would dare ignore the consequences for interpretation of the interdependence between what McKenzie referred to as 'typography and meaning' and McGann as the 'linguistic and bibliographic codes'.[26] Cultural critics and historians, however, still have much to learn from those recent developments in the study of textual transmission, a discipline designated by McKenzie as the sociology of texts.[27] The historical study of plagiarism cannot remain oblivious to the changing forms in which texts were published, read, copied and returned to the public domain, for the medium of the plagiarized or plagiarizing text provides evidence that can be used in reconstructing the context or contexts in which an act of copying occurred and was judged.

Contexts

The contexts of plagiarism are various and can be variously reconstituted. In most cases, the nature and amount of available evidence will dictate the primary context for its analysis: for instance, the profusion of late seventeenth-century commentary on plagiarism in drama points to the importance of a generic context. But other contexts – aesthetic, commercial, political – might be usefully invoked in explaining the cultural implications of this and other kinds of plagiarism.[28]

In terms of selecting materials for contextual analysis, the study of plagiarism has been impaired, I believe, by the concentration on 'literary' manifestations of plagiarism to the exclusion of other forms of writing, such as historiography, scientific tracts, sermons, philosophical and political writings, commonplace books, scholarly works, criticism, journalism, financial and economic publications,[29] and of non-verbal forms of artistic creation such as music and the visual arts. To focus on forms and genres which modernity has labelled literature is not only to impose anachronistic categories on the past, it is also to produce a partial and distorted picture of the early modern period. Although this volume does not purport to be comprehensive, its range of case studies, which are centred variously on translations of the Bible, historical writings, drama, poetry, dance treatises, sermons and colonial grammars, reveals the complexities and discrepancies in contemporary outlook.

To document the range of opinions held at a particular time can be an end in itself. In the case of early modern attitudes towards plagiarism, moreover, an illustration of diversity provides a much needed corrective to earlier critical presumptions. As Harold Love has observed, what might be acceptable in one context would be inappropriate, indeed illegitimate, in another.[30] Love adduces evidence from the history of the commonplace book and the sermon. For the seventeenth-century Puritan and Anglican divines, he shows, the status of the sermon as inspired or made up of materials copied without acknowledgement was a matter of religious conviction, not an aesthetic or a moral concern.[31] Whereas the Anglicans, especially those in the Laudian tradition, refused to see preaching as a species of authorship and defended even covert reuse of earlier texts on the ground that those might enhance the didactic efficacy of the sermon, the Puritans derided derivative sermonizing and called for inspiration in elucidating the word of God. The Puritan notion of inspiration thus prefigures the subsequent secular demand for inspired creation and originality.

Natural philosophy as it developed after the Stuart Restoration was another realm in which the threat of plagiarism was a source of considerable unease. That unease, and the manner in which it was expressed, were substantially different from the bickerings, with which they coincided, among professional playwrights and poets. As Adrian Johns has shown, for the highborn authors associated with the Royal Society, plagiarism and piracy signified a loss of honour that was essential to their social identity. Hence the genteel members of the Society made efforts to control the dissemination of their findings in order to guarantee that their priority could not be questioned.[32] Johns relates the repeated usurpations visited on Robert Boyle, the most renowned of Restoration *virtuosi*.[33] Exasperated by 'the subtil practice of several Plagiarys' who republished accounts of experiments he had conducted as their own, or stole his papers from his laboratory so as to get into print first, or made unfair use of the discoveries he had generously shared with them, Boyle grew bitter, distrustful and reclusive. He started to hide his notes, keeping them in separate bundles, and resorted to publishing his research piecemeal to protect it from seizure and corruption. He related his injuries in *An Advertisement of Mr. Boyle, about the Loss of many of his Writings* (1688), and repeatedly stressed the need for scholarly solidarity in the face of 'yᵉ prejudice, such Plagiarys must naturally do to yᵉ Commonwealth of Learning'.[34] Boyle would have no doubt endorsed his continental contemporary's diatribe against dishonest scholars: Jacob Thomasius' *Dissertatio philosophica de plagio literario* (1673).[35] In one sense seventeenth-century debates about the proprieties of preaching and of scientific research are worlds apart. Yet – contrary to the professional writers of whatever stripe – neither for the divines nor for the natural philosophers was economic profit a consideration, something that an enquiry exclusively into literary theft would fail to point up.

When we move from illustration of attitudes to explanation, a contextual study of plagiarism provides a useful safeguard against the allure of overarching narratives. Why did plagiarism become such a pressing concern in early modern England? Recent scholarship has attributed this development to the emergence of the market for print that enabled enterprising individuals to earn a living by writing for publication.[36] The growth of the literary marketplace boosted the stature and economic standing of professional authors, but it also produced ruthless competition, professional rivalries and pressure of deadlines. In their search for profit, writers routinely recycled the works of others and their own earlier productions. With the volume of printed matter rising steadily and standards of literacy improving, the intertextual links between and among texts came under increasing public scrutiny. This scenario, while not incorrect, is seriously incomplete. It does not explain, for example, why views of appropriation should have varied and fluctuated at any one time. Nor does it have the capacity to account for short-term variation and local change.

Whether to do with scientific enquiry or religious instruction, the intellectual context in which an act of appropriation occurred was crucial in shaping its public perception. We encounter similar diversity of opinion in respect to literary genres and forms. For example, in the late sixteenth century, with the theatre still thought of as live entertainment rather than an art-form with cultural pretensions, it was easier to borrow in drama – a predominantly oral form – than in poetry. A poet would not have ventured to copy as extensively from a predecessor as Shakespeare and his fellow playwrights did when they drew on translations, history books, popular romances, ballads and pamphlets. Furthermore, when we consider attitudes towards plagiarism in relation to the three major literary modes – poetry, drama and prose fiction – we find a significant repositioning of those attitudes in response to the changing status of each of them. Early debates about the proprieties of literary borrowing centred on the drama. By the mid-eighteenth century the focus of controversy over literary theft shifted from drama to poetry, both native classics such as Milton and towering moderns such as Pope being arraigned for their alleged covert appropriation of the work of their predecessors.[37] Whereas late seventeenth-century discussions of plagiarism such as Gerard Langbaine's preface to *Momus Triumphans; or, The Plagiaries of the English Stage* (1688) illustrated their claims by citing examples drawn from plays, eighteenth-century critical treatises centred on poetry: Joseph Warton's *Essay on the Writings and Genius of Pope* (1756), Edward Young's *Conjectures on Original Composition* (1759), William Duff's *Essay on Original Genius; and its Various Modes of Exertion in Philosophy and the Fine Arts, Particularly Poetry* (1767) and his *Critical Observations on the Writings of the Most Celebrated Geniuses in Poetry. Being a Sequel to the Essay on Original Genius* (1770), and Alexander Gerard's *Essay on Genius* (1774). In these enquiries into the ethics and psychology of artistic creation, Shakespeare was usually represented as a poet rather than a dramatist, his involvement with the theatrical marketplace being quietly overlooked. The focus on poetry evinces a decline in the value of imitation and the corresponding valorisation of creative originality. As Richard Terry has argued, poetic works which a generation earlier would have been praised for their skilful imitation of time-honoured models now came to be denounced as plagiaristic.[38]

With the bulk of debates about literary plagiarism concentrating first on the drama and later on poetry, our period provides few instances of prose fiction coming under scrutiny. This is not to say that writers of novels, novellas, romantic fiction, and the like, were wholly exempt from censure if their work was perceived to be derivative; however, given the relative generic novelty of such writings, there seems to have been greater scope for 'novelty' of subject-matter, language and style. Certainly, no novelists suffered accusations of plagiarism on a scale comparable to those visited on the poets Milton and Pope, though Laurence Sterne did earn posthumous opprobrium for his inclusion of passages from Robert Burton's *Anatomy of Melancholy* in *Tristram Shandy*. By contrast, in the modern world, the majority of plagiarism charges involve novels. This is because prose fiction is much the most profitable and popular of literary forms.

To the aesthetic, social, religious and economic contexts which foreground the variety of views of plagiarism in early modern England we must add another. The problem of illicit appropriation became entwined, especially from the time of the Civil Wars, in the developments which enhanced the nation's self-esteem and its interest in its own identity. Samuel Sorbière's excoriation, in his *Relation d'un Voyage en Angleterre* (1664), of English writers as plagiaristic, and hence inferior to their continental, especially French, counterparts, sparked a fierce row over the integrity of England's national culture.[39] Sorbière did not restrict himself to any particular form or genre; rather, he was making a general point about insular culture, which he saw as derivative and excessively dependent on influences from abroad. Englishmen felt they had to vindicate their country's international reputation. Sorbière's attack and the controversy it provoked point to the broader cultural implications of what is typically seen as a conflict between the plagiarist and his (or her) victim. The canonization of Shakespeare in the eighteenth century is a case in point.[40] By the 1760s Shakespeare was hailed as Britain's greatest original genius. Characteristics of his work which had troubled earlier generations – and which indeed still alienated some people in the eighteenth century – also became a source of attraction. The unruliness, the naturalness, the spontaneity of his writing, its indifference to classical rules of dramatic form, stood in contrast with the formal artifice and imitative bent of French dramatists, especially Corneille and Racine. Shakespeare came to epitomize the free and independent spirit of the British nation and Britain's cultural ascendancy over its European rivals. The eighteenth century did not want to know about his extensive – and unacknowledged – appropriations.[41] The Bard could not be a plagiarist.

Contrary to the standard narrative, 'print culture' and 'professionalization of writing' were not the only impulses behind the mounting preoccupation with illicit copying and the increased incidence of public acknowledgements of sources, models and influences. In addition to long-term developments in aesthetics, culture and the literary marketplace, we find more local and contingent factors too. When political or commercial circumstances changed, so did the proprieties of appropriation. Not all genres and forms of writing, however, were affected in the same way. To identify short-term, context- and genre-specific patterns of change is to go beyond both the approaches that are not sufficiently sensitive to historical developments and the current vogue for providing general explanations in terms of the evolution of print culture and the rise of the author. Lisa Richardson's revisionist account of formal historical writings from the sixteenth century to the eighteenth is instructive here.[42] Political upheaval, Richardson demonstrates, had a decisive impact on the conventions of the genre. At the start of her period, unacknowledged transcription in formal historiography went unchallenged and unremarked; by its end, to acknowledge and reproduce one's sources had become the norm. Yet this is no tale of steady progress towards modern standards of scholarly accuracy and integrity. The shift, Richardson argues, can be more precisely dated and accounted for. It occurred against the backdrop of political divisions and the polarization of public opinion in the middle decades of the seventeenth century, the time of the English Civil War, Cromwellian Protectorate and Stuart Restoration. Contemporary historians, most of whom had polemical ends in view, felt compelled to cite, even reproduce, the documents and materials on which their own narratives were based as a means of staking a claim to objectivity and factual truth. This was a strategy designed to avoid charges not of plagiarism or shoddy scholarship but of partisan bias. *Plagiarism in Early Modern England* furnishes many examples of such contingent and unexpected developments which shaped the practice of appropriation in specific forms and genres.

Our book demonstrates, moreover, the dynamic relation between text and context, that is, the power of a single textual 'event' (J. G. A. Pocock's phrase)[43] to transform the mental landscape of an era. Several contributors – Nick Groom, Paul Baines, Richard Terry – discuss the fraudulent charges of plagiarism against Milton that were manufactured by William Lauder and publicized by him with the unwitting assistance of Samuel Johnson in the mid-eighteenth century. The upshot of the Lauder affair was that, as Terry puts it, 'for a time . . . the motive of detraction inherent in alleging plagiarism [came to be] more vilified than plagiarism itself'.[44] An earlier example of a similarly influential textual intervention into widely shared beliefs was the publication, in 1688, of Langbaine's *Momus Triumphans*, a comprehensive arraignment for theft of Restoration dramatists, which listed sources and analogues of all of the English plays published to that date. Although derivative and plagiaristic plays did not disappear in the aftermath of Langbaine's diatribe, it was no longer possible to pretend that appropriation in drama is not a problem or deny its scale. So an historical account of plagiarism should not only ask how context shapes cultural practices and perceptions but also identify the moments when aesthetic, economic or intellectual circumstances are themselves altered by textual events.

*

To acknowledge the effect of a series of variables – the technologies of text production, genre, the social and economic status of both the original author and the alleged plagiarist, the commercial viability of the stolen product, and the cultural and political universe in which the theft occurs – upon the understanding and application of the term plagiarism is not to deny the moral dimension of the act. Rather, it is to recognize that at certain moments in the past one or more of those factors were of crucial importance in shaping the judgement of illicit appropriation and the rhetoric used to denounce or exculpate it. Why did that scourge of Renaissance plagiarists, Ben Jonson, come to be denounced as a thief within decades of his death? Why did the eighteenth century overlook in Shakespeare transgressions against textual property and propriety virtually identical to those for which it castigated Dryden? Why did allegations of plagiarism in the mid-eighteenth century become, at least for a time, more objectionable than the act itself? If the picture of the early modern period that emerges from this volume is one of diversity and contradiction, this is not a sign of the moral relativism disliked by Christopher Ricks, but an outcome of rigorous – and verifiable – historical scholarship which marshals archival evidence and invokes a variety of specific contexts to interpret it. Marilyn Randall's *Pragmatic Plagiarism* has recently reminded us of the many transhistorical continuities in the reception of plagiarism. This book reveals the complexities and discontinuities of the reception of plagiarism in early modern England.[45]

Part I
Approaches to Plagiarism

2
Plagiarism*

Christopher Ricks

When the President – the previous President – of the British Academy invited me to give this lecture, I took up the terms in which he had written, and proposed the subject of plagiarism: 'It relates to "scholarly debate"; it has "general public interest"; and I even like the dark thought that it's something "the Academy exists to promote"...'. Judge then of my pleasure when, in his Presidential Address for 1997, the President announced that the lecture would be 'on "Plagiarism"', not a subject which the Academy exists to promote, but one in which we all have an interest'.[1]

'Sir, – I am concerned to see your able correspondent W. H. throwing away his valuable time on so threadbare a topic as Plagiarism': Thomas De Quincey, or probably he,[2] in 1827. 'Of plagiarism, little new can be written': Hillel Schwartz, *The Culture of the Copy* (1996).'[3]

The news this very day (10 February 1998) in *The Times* is of a student's going to the High Court

> to try to force Cambridge University to award him a degree after he was accused of cheating. Kamran Beg is believed to be the first student to challenge the university in court over allegations that he plagiarised part of an essay in his postgraduate finance degree at Trinity College. Mr Beg's solicitor denied his client acted dishonestly and said he had inadvertently omitted attributions or footnotes to passages he had quoted.

Plagiarism is perennial – and annual. 1997 saw the publication here of Neal Bowers' pained book, *Words for the Taking*, the words of which were taken up in many a long review. Subtitled *The Hunt for a Plagiarist*, it told how some of Bowers' published poems were republished by another, a pathological tinkerer who had many a name and a squalid criminal record. To Bowers may be added other continuing attentions. In almost every issue, *Private Eye* takes pleasure in exposing plagiarisms, and not only as the regular feature 'Just Fancy That!' The *Sunday Telegraph* of 3 August 1997 carried a column by Jenny McCartney on the romance novelist Janet Dailey, her plagiarism and psychological problems. A very recent film, *Good Will Hunting*, currently triumphant in the cinemas of Boston, Massachusetts (where the film is set), shows in an early scene the hero securing a woman's tender notice by accusing his rival of being about to plagiarize, and the closing words of the film are the retort of rueful friendship, 'He stole my line!'

So much is plagiarism in the air that when the *New Yorker* (22–29 December 1997) printed a cartoon about it (by Joseph Farris), I saw or imagined the cartoon's own doubleness: in a bookstore where there can be seen a section headed HISTORY, a man browses in the section headed PLAGIARISM. Books that are plagiarisms, I take it; but those shelves could as well consist by now of books on PLAGIARISM.

I choose this subject because it combines the enduring and the current, with a further twist: I shall argue that this dishonesty is too often exculpated by dishonesties, by evasive banter and by slippery history.

Definition, first. The *Oxford English Dictionary* rules:

> **plagiarism** The wrongful appropriation, or purloining, and publication as one's own, of the ideas, or the expression of the ideas (literary, artistic, musical, mechanical, etc.) of another.

Notice 'wrongful', as constitutive within the definition, and add, constitutive too, that – as Peter Shaw has put it (into italics) – 'Throughout history the act of using the work of another *with an intent to deceive* has been branded as plagiarism'.[4]

Marcel Lafollette, in *Stealing into Print: Fraud, Plagiarism, and Misconduct in Scientific Publishing* (1992), has said of plagiarism that 'Its definition is simple'.[5] If he is, as I believe, right, why does Peter Shaw grant – too concessively – that 'There will always remain certain gray areas resistant to definition'? Because it is easy, even for someone as morally alert as Shaw, to let one thing slide into another. That the supporting evidence for the accusation of plagiarism may on occasion be elusive, insufficient or uncertain is not the same as thinking that the definition of plagiarism is uncertain. The grey areas may remain resistant to adjudication without being resistant to definition. It may be perfectly clear what constitutes plagiarism ('using the work of another *with an intent to deceive'*) without its being clear that what faces us is truly a case of this. In his lasting book of 1928, *Literary Ethics*, H. M. Paull admits what we should all admit on occasion, 'the difficulty of deciding what is plagiarism and what is legitimate borrowing',[6] but the difficulty of deciding is not the same as the difficulty of defining. That it may in some cases be very hard to make this accusation – like many another accusation – stick, does not entail there being about the accusation anything loose.

Far from there being, as it suits some people to maintain, insuperable problems of definition, there aren't even any superable problems. The morality of the matter, which asks of us that we be against deceit and dishonesty, is clear, and is clearly defined. Those of us who believe, as to plagiarism, that nothing is more important than *not making excuses* should be more than usually careful not to permit the easy excusing that slides in with the misguided concession that the world has never been able to decide what it means by plagiarism.

One of the most adroit of the exculpators, Professor James Kincaid, wrote of plagiarism in the *New Yorker* (20 January 1997): 'As for defining it, we leave that to the officials – in this example, Northwestern University.' Quizzing Northwestern's sentence on the responsibilities of 'a conscientious writer', Kincaid asked: 'But how do I distinguish what I have "learned from others" from what I am "personally contributing"? If I subtract everything I have learned from others (including Mother?), what is left?'[7] These are good questions – essential questions for anyone whose profession is teaching – but only if they are genuinely questions, only if jesting Kincaid were to stay for an answer. For him, though, they are rhetorical questions, inviting abdication. Distinctions the conscientious making of which is crucial are guyed as naive nullities.

Kincaid on occasion has recourse to putting the word *original* within quotation marks, 'original', though not exactly quoting it. He does the same with 'plagiarism'. This is the usual intimation that a particular concept is a coercion by power, acquiesced in by naivety. The hermeneutics of suspicion avails itself of this punctuation of suspicion. Some of us at least, it implies, are aware that this concept – like every other concept – is implicatedly problematic; aware, too, that it is moreover not problematic at all, being nothing more than a construction, as they say, imposed by the powers that be or that were.

Not plagiarism, then (something that people mistakenly suppose they understand); rather, 'plagiarism'. But the prophylaxis of quotation marks has itself come under suspicion lately, so the new thing is to announce that one both may be and may not be availing oneself of the nicety.

I do not put the word 'plagiarism' in quotation marks most of the time, but perhaps those quotation marks should be imagined.... I have been interested, then, in cultural distinctions between legitimate and illegitimate forms of appropriation. For this reason, I may have used the term 'plagiarism' to describe a wider range of transgressive appropriations than perhaps the word ordinarily signifies.[8]

Laura J. Rosenthal, in *Playwrights and Plagiarists in Early Modern England: Gender, Authorship, Literary Property* (1996). But what may perhaps be more widely transgressive is assuredly narrower in one way: in that it eschews moral considerations. For what could be less morally open to scrutiny than the transgressive? Professor Rosenthal tells us that her purpose is 'to question differences between plagiarism, imitation, adaptation, repetition, and originality'. But rhetorical questioning leads to the required answer: that there is no difference between these things other than that power uses the opprobrious term plagiarism when the work emanates from those whom power dislikes. Appropriation of appropriations, saith the Preacher, appropriation of appropriations, all is appropriation.

The objection to such arguments is not that they are strongly political but that they are weakly, wizenedly, political. Professor Rosenthal's book is itself animated by a political fervour that is clearly and duly moral, but her undertaking then requires her to write as if a political reading – in her case, a reading *à la* Foucault – had to extirpate from a discussion of plagiarism all moral considerations. What would have to be in moral terms a matter of honesty or dishonesty (plagiarism being dishonest) is replaced – not complemented – by a matter of power, necessity, the tyrant's plea. The 'cultural distinctions between legitimate and illegitimate forms of appropriation' become a matter of nothing but 'the cultural location of the text and the position of the author',[9] instead of being among several aspects each of them germane. Rosenthal is convincing on particular injustices and prejudices, but her setting does an injustice to politics, in that the room it leaves for conscience is in the animating of the inquiry, not within the inquiry proper.

The consequence of an investigative determination that 'denaturalizes the distinction between imitation and plagiarism'[10] is that the prefix de- becomes a virus, working to demean and to degrade moral thought. That no moral position is natural does not of itself entail that moral positions are nothing but the insistences of power. Moral agreements, though not natural, may be valuable, indispensable, worthy of the respect that they have earned. That plagiarism may valuably be seen under the aspect of politics, and that politics may in turn be valuably seen under the aspect of power at the time, need not and should not issue in the denial that plagiarism asks to be seen too under the aspect of ethics. The extirpation of ethical or moral considerations by such political history is a sad loss, to political history among other needful things.

Plagiarism is a dishonesty. This can be swept to one side, leaving not the dishonest but the culturally conditioned and exclusively power-ruled illegitimate. Or it can be swept to the other side, leaving not the dishonest but – assimilating plagiarism now to copyright – the illegal.

It is natural to move to infringement of copyright when thinking of plagiarism, but crucial that one should be aware of moving. For as Paul Goldstein says in *Copyright's Highway* (1994): 'Plagiarism, which many people commonly think has to do with copyright, is not, in fact a legal doctrine.'[11] In a review article on Goldstein's book and two others (*Times Literary Supplement*, 4 July 1997), James Boyle, a professor of law, pondered 'Problems of defining the limits of copyright in the age of the Internet – and of pop-music parody'. His thoughts on intellectual property are germane to plagiarism, since intellectual property may be seen not only under a legal aspect but under a moral one. Boyle observes that 'there is considerably more dispute about the desirability, role and extent of intellectual property – even among defenders of the free market – than there was about the desirability of private property in general', and he concludes with the justified asseveration that 'intellectual-property law has become the boundary line, or perhaps the hinge, between art and commerce, between "free speech" and economic monopoly, between public culture and private property'.

The subtlety and tenacity of Boyle's thinking discredit James Kincaid's condescension to the law, setting it right; some of us, Kincaid is confident, have learnt from recent literary theory the complexities of intellectual property: 'Still, the law lumbers on as if nothing more complicated than cattle rustling were involved.'[12]

Far from lumbering, intellectual-property law is limber, well aware of the complications. But, to moral considerations the law must always offer a handshake at arm's length. For although the law is a moral matter, being distinguishable from but not distinct from justice, the law acknowledges that there is a moral world elsewhere. A pity, then, that the legal-eyed Alexander Lindey, in *Plagiarism and Originality* (1952), on occasion grants too much to the legal. 'Since any discussion of plagiarism is, from a realistic standpoint, meaningless without reference to the legal consequences, I've devoted quite a bit of space to court cases.'[13] Granted, legal consequences have a remarkable realism, reality even, but it is misleading to speak as if opprobrium or disapproval, such as should be incurred by plagiarism, is from a realistic standpoint meaningless. Again, Lindey writes, truly, that 'Plagiarism and infringement are not the same thing, though they overlap', but he goes on at once to infringe the moral sphere: 'Plagiarism covers a wider field; infringement involves more serious consequences.'[14] It would be wrong to acquiesce in this implication that the legal is of its nature more serious than the moral. That gambling debts may be legally irrecoverable but are honourbound was and is a social reality of entire seriousness. The consequences of dishonourable behaviour have been, and fortunately still sometimes are, no less serious than legal proceedings.

Lindey's momentary lapse has its literary counterpart, when Donald Davie writes that 'the hymn-writer did not have copyright in his work as other authors did; and so plagiarism is a concept that does not apply'.[15] But plagiarism is distinguishable from infringement of copyright, and if it were *tout court* the case – which I doubt – that plagiarism is a concept that does not apply to hymns, this would have to be a consequence of something other than the hymn-writer's not owning copyright. The same slide can be seen, not this time in a lawyer or a critic but in a literary theorist. In *Hot Property: The Stakes and Claims of Literary Originality* (1994), Françoise Meltzer sometimes lets her attention slip. 'A good example of how originality and, therefore, plagiarism are governed more by the character of the community than by immutable notions of right and wrong is to be seen in the U.S. Copyright form.'[16] The legal rights and wrongs may be manifest in the copyright form, but there are other rights and wrongs. So it is a pity that in her firm account of the accusation of plagiarism levelled at Paul Celan, plagiarism from Yvan Goll, Meltzer should assimilate the moral question of plagiarism to the legal question of copyright.

> So was the widow Goll right about the most notorious of her charges? That is, did the phrase 'black milk' belong to her husband? The answer, of course, must be no. First, for a simple reason: even the American copyright form states that one cannot protect 'titles, names and short phrases'. It is impossible to claim the invention of so few words.[17]

This is muddled, muddied. That no one can legally protect short phrases is perfectly compatible with someone's justifiably claiming to have created a short phrase, and this is in turn compatible with someone else's being guilty of plagiarizing a short phrase. 'Black milk' – 'schwarze Milch' – may be insufficiently remarkable as a short phrase for the charge of plagiarism to be substantiable, but there are equally short phrases which it would be worse than imprudent for me, say, to accommodate in a poem of mine without acknowledgement or allusion. T. S. Eliot offers many: 'maculate giraffe', 'sapient sutlers', 'beneficent spider', 'forgetful snow'. One could grant that none of these could be copyright while at the same time believing that the appearance of them outside Eliot might form the *prima facie* basis of a plagiarism charge.

To the exculpations of plagiarism that rest upon a limiting of the necessary judgement to legal judgement (breach of copyright then being the only breach that we need ponder), there have been added the exculpations that seek to call, as a witness for the defence, history. Simply: plagiarism is a recent construction in need of demystifying. For a reminder that the construction industry is booming, see *The Construction of Authorship* (1994), in a very up-to-date series called 'Post-Contemporary Interventions'.[18]

This recency claim has at once to deal with an unwelcome witness for the prosecution. Call Marcus Valerius Martialis. Martial's testimony is perfectly clear, is not at all recent, and is notarized in seven poems about plagiarism. Added to which, there is the further inconvenience, for the revisionist historian of plagiarism, that it is to Martial that we owe the very application to literary deception of the word *plagiarius*, the abductor of the child or slave of another.

> Th'art out, vile Plagiary, that dost think
> A Poet may be made at th'rate of Ink,
> And cheap-priz'd Paper; none e'er purchas'd yet
> Six or ten Penniworth of Fame or Wit:
> Get Verse unpublish'd, new-stamp'd Fancies look,
> Which th'only Father of the Virgin Book
> Knows, and keeps seal'd in his close Desk within,
> Not slubber'd yet by any ruffer Chin;
> A Book, once known, ne'r quits the Author; If
> Any lies yet unpolish'd, any stiff,
> Wanting it's Bosses, and it's Cover, do
> Get that; I've such and can be secret too.
>   He that repeats stoln Verse, and for Fame looks,
>   Must purchase Silence too as well as Books.[19]

The half-dozen other epigrams by Martial take an equally though differently sardonic tack in their contemptuous rebuking of the dishonesty of the plagiarist.

Since copyright is in hock to the cash-nexus and is a relatively recent invention, it would suit a certain political slant if plagiarism were a recent invention too. But what about Martial? He may get reluctantly acknowledged, but will then find himself labelled a distinctly unusual case. Revisionism knows that there is some wresting to be done, some wrestling, the Newest Laocoon. Thomas Mallon, in *Stolen Words* (1989), his study – in detail – of some central plagiarism cases, noticed that 'scholars will tie themselves up in knots exonerating Coleridge. In one book Thomas McFarland sees his thefts as being not plagiarism but "a mode of composition – composition by mosaic organization".'[20]

But then the older historians of plagiarism were sometimes off guard. H. M. Paull, for instance, after substantiating the stigma of plagiarism in classical times and thereafter, slips into misrepresenting the history that he himself tells. 'All this shows that such practices now needed an apology'; 'But perhaps the best proof that direct plagiarism was becoming discredited . . .':[21] yet Paull had shown that such practices had always needed an apology, that plagiarism had always been discredited. What, then, moved him to put such a gloss upon the history he had given? His progressivism. For Paull was committed, as his closing pages announce, to the conviction that 'on the whole there has been a distinct progress towards an unattainable ideal: unattainable whilst human nature remains unchanged. Forgery, piracy and plagiarism, the three most considerable literary crimes, have sensibly diminished.'[22] The closing words of his book are 'contribute to the advancement of the race'. Paull's liberal progressivism is the fitting converse, obverse, of the prelapsarian revisionism which claims that, until the invention of the author, *circa* some time like the seventeenth century, there was no such thing as plagiarism and the deploring of it. In pious times, ere Authors did begin, before to plagiarize was made a sin . . .

Exculpations, then, have long been at work. Harold Ogden White, *Plagiarism and Imitation During the English Renaissance: A Study in Critical Distinctions* (1935), opened with a fervid denunciation of 'modern critics' for imposing the concept of plagiarism upon the past;[23] but despite his insistence that 'Englishmen from 1500–1625' were 'without any feeling analogous to the modern attitude toward plagiarism', his book is full of indictments of plagiarism, from classical and Renaissance times, that are entirely at one with what he deplores as the modern attitude toward plagiarism.[24] How does White effect this? By the simple expedient of substituting for the word plagiarism the word piracy.

When the poetaster Bathyllus piratically claimed the authorship of an anonymously issued poem of Virgil's – so runs the apocryphal anecdote – Virgil retorted: 'I made the verses, another has stolen the honour.' But Martial's protest at the piracies of which he had been the victim is probably the most famous in all literature, because in it he first used the word *plagiarius*, literally 'kidnapper', for a literary thief.[25]

White quotes Florio on fellow writers: 'What doe they but translate? perhaps, usurpe? at least, collect? if with acknowledgement, it is well; if by stealth, it is too bad.'[26] Is this not the deploring of plagiarism? As so often, a distinction kicked out of the door comes back in through the window. Call all plagiarisms piracy and you have rendered plagiarism non-existent. White certainly shows that imitation was greatly valued in classical times and in the Renaissance, but he does not show that there was no distinction then between imitation and plagiarism, no disapprobation of plagiarism, for he himself reports such disapprobation of unacknowledged, secret or furtive borrowings. For Donne, White says, and substantiates, 'borrowed matter is to be thankfully acknowledged, not ungratefully purloined by stealth'.[27]

Thomas Mallon acknowledges, as everyone must, that something happened in the seventeenth century, but is it true that 'our basic sense of plagiarism came to be born' – *born*, that exactly – 'in the seventeenth century'?[28] Printing had changed something, yes – but 'it was printing, of course, that changed everything'?[29] Everything? Not the nub dishonesty, the claiming credit for a poem someone else has written.

In *Crimes of Writing* (1991), a book that oddly does no more than mention plagiarism, Susan Stewart has a passing comment: 'plagiarism of course arises as a problem at the same time that other issues of writing's authenticity come to the fore.'[30] But 'problem' there has to cover a lot of ground; it is not the case that condemnation of plagiarism arose as late as the new commodification would like to believe. We are assured by Stewart that in medieval times there was no such thing as plagiarism (reprehensible), and yet the assurance, from Giles Constable, does waver rather: 'the term plagiarism should indeed probably' – indeed probably – 'be dropped in reference to the Middle Ages, since it expresses a concept of literary individualism and property that is distinctly modern'.[31] And Martial, was he distinctly modern? He lacked a distinctly modern concept of literary property, no doubt, but he certainly had – and named – the concept of plagiarism.

As with other prelapsarian history, as with any telling of the Fall itself, the moment is elusive, contested, often gets pushed further back. Brean Hammond, in *Professional Imaginative Writing in England, 1670–1740* (1997), makes a good case for dating the 'originality' debate earlier than usual, retrieving it from the eighteenth century: 'there is, I would contend, an earlier cultural formation, that of dramatic writing in the 1670s and 1680s, wherein the problematic nature of borrowing from earlier works was already under heated negotiation'.[32] But why stop there, when it comes to negotiating the problematic nature of borrowing? Best, moreover, for Hammond to tread carefully on this 'original composition' ground, since there have been heavy investments in the eighteenth-century allocation. So Hammond prudently claims less than he might and should: 'In this period therefore, earlier than is sometimes supposed . . . there was the *beginning* of an *attempt* to define "originality" in writing and the *ur-conception* of proprietary authorship' (italics supplied).[33]

Stephen Orgel makes a similar move in his influential article on 'The Renaissance Artist as Plagiarist'. He claims that the charge of plagiarism did not appear significantly until after the Renaissance. One may grant a premise of his, as to 'different ages', without granting the elisions and assimilations that accompany it. Was Inigo Jones a plagiarist?

> Jones's practice may legitimately raise certain questions about the validity, function, philosophic implications of imitation; but such questions will also be profoundly time-bound. Different ages give very different answers to the basic question of what, exactly, it is that art imitates: for example, nature, or other art, or the action of the mind. Modern critics grow uncomfortable when it proves to be imitating other art too closely.[34]

Yes, such questions will be time-bound. But what exactly is Orgel's dissent from modern critics here? 'Imitating other art too closely' might be a matter of the servile, the inability to add anything at all – but then on this the modern critic would be at one with the ancient and the Renaissance critic. Or 'imitating other art too closely' ought to apply, given that Orgel's context is plagiarism ('The Renaissance Artist as Plagiarist'), to plagiarism. But here too the modern critic is not shown by Orgel to be at odds with the ancient and the Renaissance critic. Such modern critics as equate even very close imitation with plagiarism are unthinking, yes; but that the accusation of plagiarism is often foolishly and ignorantly levelled has no bearing on whether it can be, and could be back then, responsibly and justly levelled. There was, Orgel concedes, 'a long history of discomfort with Jonsonian borrowing';[35] nevertheless, if Jonson's borrowings were scarcely ever deplored as plagiarism (it was Jonson who did the deploring, launching in *The Poetaster* the missile 'plagiary' in English: 'Why? the ditt' is all borrowed; 'tis Horace's: hang him plagiary'), this need not be because the concept of plagiarism was scarcely present to people's minds, but because the distinction between the furtively dishonest (plagiarism) and the openly honourable (imitation) existed and was well understood, with Jonson then judged to be practising not the unhappy former but the happy latter.

But Orgel needs a more dramatic history, a moment to identify, cultural history being one long identification parade. 'By the time Dryden was writing *Of Dramatic Poesy*, however, Jonson's borrowings required a defense': 'He invades authors like a monarch, and what would be theft in other poets, is only victory in him.' Orgel says of Dryden's aphorism: 'This was written only forty-five years after [Inigo] Jones's praise of Jonsonian "translation", and thirty years after Jonson's death. In that short time translation, imitation, borrowing, have become "learned plagiary", "robbery", "theft".'[36]

Now it may well be that the elapsing of the half-century brought about an exacerbation that ministered to ill-judgement in accusations of plagiarism; that it often became an easy, unjust, and uncomprehending charge. But this is not the same as maintaining that what had earlier been understood as translation and imitation, without reference even to the possibility of the accusation of plagiarism, was succeeded by a world in which the honourable terms 'have become' replaced by opprobrious terms understood as posited of just the same practices, now without reference even to the possibility of praiseworthy translation and imitation. It is, to me, impossible to credit Orgel's insistence that 'The question of the morality of literary imitation, then, starts to appear significantly in England only after the Renaissance, and on the whole in reaction to it.'[37] Many of Orgel's most telling instances tell a story that is not the one he retails. Thomas Browne sees in plagiarism a great human failing, 'the age-old desire "to plume themselves with others' feathers"'. Orgel remarks: 'It is a vice, as Browne continually laments, that has always been with us: plagiarism is the Original Sin of literature.'[38]

It is when, *à propos* of plagiarism, Orgel turns to allusion that the gaps in the argument yawn. 'We might want to argue that there is a vast difference between adopting the role of a classic poet and copying his words, but is there? The adoption of roles by Renaissance poets involved a good deal of direct imitation and allusion.'[39] Well, we might admit that there is not a *vast* difference between adopting a role and (without acknowledgement, since Orgel is discussing plagiarism) copying out words, while still believing that there is a crucial difference. And is not allusion incompatible with plagiarism? 'So, to stay for the moment with simple cases, how would a Renaissance audience have responded to blatant plagiarism? Sometimes, obviously, simply as an allusion: a great deal of Renaissance art offered its patrons precisely the pleasures of recognition.'[40] Hearing 'Come my Celia', did the Renaissance reader 'condemn Jonson for plagiarizing Catullus? or did he, on the contrary, admire a particularly witty adaptation of the art of the past to the designs of the present?'

The latter, for sure. But this is because the Renaissance audience well understood that what it was responding to here, what 'Renaissance art offered' here, was *not* 'blatant plagiarism', was not plagiarism. Allusion, plainly; and the defence that the poet is alluding is one that, should it be made good, must exculpate the poet. That the defence is sometimes unconvincing is a different story. Thomas Mallon is right, I should judge, not to accept the defence of Laurence Sterne that maintains that those moments of his are never plagiarisms but always allusions. But allusion has to be the contrary (Orgel's 'on the contrary') of plagiarism, since allusion is posited upon our calling the earlier work into play, whereas the one thing that plagiarism hopes is that the earlier work will not enter our heads. T. S. Eliot said, in an interview in August 1961:

> In one of my early poems ['Cousin Nancy'] I used, without quotation marks, the line 'the army of unalterable law...' from a poem by George Meredith, and this critic accused me of having shamelessly plagiarised, pinched, pilfered that line. Whereas, of course, the whole point was that the reader should recognise where it came from and contrast it with the spirit and meaning of my own poem.[41]

The fame of Meredith's line, and the conclusive placing of it by both poets, leave me in no doubt that Eliot tells the truth here; but even those who suppose him being wise after the unfortunate event would grant that, if credited, allusion is a defence that must stanch the accusation of plagiarism. And one reason why plagiarism in, for instance, scientific research is importantly different is that it is not at all clear there what it would mean to claim that one was not plagiarising but alluding to (as against, say, referring to) earlier work.

That such-and-such wording, being an allusion, is not plagiarism, would not have to mean that there could not be any infringement of copyright. Paul Goldstein begins *Copyright's Highway* with the copyright conflict in 1990 when the rap group 2 Live Crew issued their derisive parody of the Roy Orbison/William Dees hit, 'Oh, Pretty Woman'. Parody, being allusive, cannot be plagiaristic, but it may still violate someone's rights – among them, copyright. The lawyer, though, needs to be sensitive to the judgments germane to literary allusion. Alexander Lindey, whose book on *Plagiarism and Originality* I value, ends up on one occasion agreeing amiably to overlook (as an authorial inadvertence) a moment that, contrariwise, solicits the reader's advertence:

> A reviewer of Evelyn Waugh's *Scott-King's Modern Europe* praised the following excerpt as a 'burst of stylish writing':
>
>> He was older, it might have been written, than the rocks on which he sat; older, anyway, than his stall in chapel; he had died many times, had Scott-King, had dived deep, had trafficked for strange webs with Eastern merchants. And all this had been but the sound of lyres and flutes to him.
>
> 'Stylish, indeed!' cried a reader with a long memory. The passage, he said, was obviously a paraphrase of the celebrated description of La Gioconda in the chapter on Leonardo in Walter Pater's *The Renaissance*:
>
>> She is older than the rocks among which she sits ... she has been dead many times, and learned the secrets of the grave; and has been a diver in deep seas ... and trafficked for strange webs with Eastern merchants ... and all this has been to her but as the sound of lyres and flutes.
>
> John K. Hutchens, the book critic who published this intelligence, did not take it too seriously. It was the sort of thing, he felt, that could have happened to anybody. He was right.[42]

Oh no, he wasn't right. Nor is Mr Lindey. Waugh was not covertly plagiarizing, but this is because he was overtly alluding. Not waiving, but waving.

An honest misunderstanding, this, on Lindey's part. It is the insufficient honesty with which the particular dishonesty that is plagiarism is so often treated that is the increasingly sad business. Samuel Johnson wrote of plagiarism as 'one of the most reproachful, though, perhaps, not the most atrocious of literary crimes'.[43] The reproach has to be for dishonesty, and yet how remarkably unreproached plagiarism usually goes.

The dishonesty is furthermore a point of dishonour. For honour is doubly at issue: the plagiarist hopes to gain honour from a dishonourable practice. 'His honour rooted in dishonour stood.' Peter Shaw, in his essay 'Plagiary', showed how kid-gloved the handling or fingering of plagiarism often is; he limned the psychology or psychopathology of plagiarism, including the embarrassment that so often overcomes those who find themselves faced by its two-facedness. His plea for responsible reproof strikes me as compelling, but it has not slowed down the manufacture of excuses. The usual dealings with this double-dealing are less than ever honest.

Yet then this, too, has a long history. William Walsh opened his entry on plagiarism, in his *Handy-Book of Literary Curiosities* (1909), with a question inviting the answer No: 'Is plagiarism a crime?' He duly arrived at the conclusion from which he had started: 'On the whole, as between the plagiarist and his accuser, we prefer the plagiarist. We have more sympathy for the man in the pillory than for the rabble that pelt him.' Even the case of Neal Bowers (that notable recent victim of one David Jones) incited in reviewers a need to dissociate themselves from his moral urgings. Mark Ford, in the *London Review of Books* (21 August 1997), expressed sympathy with Bowers in some ways (his plight 'considerably intensified by the difficulties he experienced trying to persuade others to take these thefts as seriously as he did'), and yet Ford is moved to mock Bowers ('Bowers assumes the mantle of heroic vigilante defending the integrity of poetry against potentially overwhelming forces of evil'), and proffers an insufficiently vigilant argument: 'It's hard to be as appalled by Jones's poetic kleptomania as Bowers insists one ought to be. This is perhaps partly because the two poems stolen from the 1992 issue of *Poetry* are not in themselves mind-blowingly original.' But a judgement on how appalled we should be by the conduct of the plagiarist (and Jones's continuing behaviour was diversely appalling) need not be commensurate with the degree of originality in the poems dishonestly laid claim to. The calculated indecorum of Ford's phrase 'not in themselves mind-blowingly original' gives vent to something, something that is not the same as finding Bowers's book tonally imperfect. Again, one might concur with James Campbell, in his review of Bowers (*Times Literary Supplement*, 28 February 1997), as to failures of tone in Bowers's wounded account ('a sanctimoniousness about his way of telling' the story, Campbell finds) while still judging it unjust of

Campbell to deprecate the fact that 'Bowers frowns at colleagues who dare to smile when they hear about it'. As well Bowers might, I should have said. But then this too is continuous with the long history of casting as priggish those who, with a straight face, deplore plagiarism. For one of the touching moments in Bowers's book tells of how he too used to reach for evasive levity, giving his students what he called his 'thou-shalt-not-steal-spiel', 'mocking myself', staging 'my wise guy presentation'.

If I now refer to the demoralising of plagiarism, I refer to such discussion of it as evacuates morals as well as morale. One form of this might be politics as impervious to individual conscience, with plagiarism 'a cultural category defining the borders between texts and policing the accumulation of cultural capital'.[44] (Policing, in the mode, being a much scarier thing than theft.) Another form might be the genial throwing up of hands, as when a discussion of plagiarism glides from cake-recipes to cooked books and then to not living by bread alone:

> To an equally folk-anonymous tradition [as a recipe] belonged Dr. Martin Luther King, Jr., who in his Boston University thesis quietly integrated a few lines from theologian Paul Tillich and fifty sentences from another's thesis even as he would smoothly merge the rhetoric of evangelical preachers to emerge with his own voice in Montgomery.[45]

Even as? There is a lot of smooth merging going on there. As who should say, *Relax*. '– sure they are unsure. When a young historian, shown to have plagiarized his first book, becomes a Program Officer at the National Endowment for the Humanities, is a high school girl to blame for reworking a magazine piece on who was to blame for Pearl Harbor?'[46] Yes, she may well be. How many wrongs exactly *does* it take to make a right?

The essay that I take as most thoroughly colluding with the greatest number of wrongs is one from which I quoted earlier, that by James Kincaid in the *New Yorker* (20 January 1997). His title was 'Purloined Letters' (once more unto this breach), and his subtitle was 'Are we too quick to denounce plagiarism?' (No, this question does not expect the answer No.) Reviewing Neal Bowers' book, Kincaid speaks roundly ('no doubt about it') and then proceeds to get round it. To follow the moves, one needs an extended quotation.

> Sumner/Compton/Jones [Bowers' plagiarist] is a cheat, no doubt about it; and now and then we run across other cases of plagiarism

that shut before they are open. For instance, one of my own students turned in a paper on 'Great Expectations' which was an exact copy of Dorothy Van Ghent's essay – an essay so celebrated that I recognized it right off and, at the first opportunity, raised the issue with my student. 'Shit!' she said. 'I paid seventy-five dollars for that.' It did seem a cruel turn of the screw to have term-paper companies selling plagiarized essays for students to plagiarize; but ethics are ethics, I told my student.

I could speak loftily on the subject because the ethical issues in her case were so clear-cut. They aren't always.[47]

The exculpatory bonhomie is unremittingly at play and at work. There is the reassuring assurance that Van Ghent's essay was so celebrated that Kincaid really isn't seeking any credit for recognising it right off. There is the unmisgiving little thrill of ' ''Shit!'' she said' (Tina Brown's *New Yorker* wouldn't be printing a stuffed shirt) – Kincaid is a robust man from a robust university where the women students are robust and no professor would take amiss their being so. There is the syntactical *plaisanterie* of 'but ethics are ethics, I told my student'. And then, at the move into the next paragraph, there is the endearingly disparaging adverb 'loftily', disparaging oneself in the nicest possible way and making it clear that, even in the most clear-cut case, to take a moral tone would be a lapse: 'I could speak loftily on the subject because...' Not that we have been given the chance to hear Kincaid speak loftily on the subject; rather, 'ethics are ethics' came across, as it was meant to, as calculatedly mock-pompous. A low move, 'loftily'.

I find this repellent, and not only professionally (professorially), in its combination of failure of nerve with nerve. 'The ethical issues in her case were so clear-cut': and was there any clear-cut dealing with the ethical issues? Nothing is said of what the exposure of her dishonesty meant to and for the forthright swearer; anyway, she deserves a jokey sympathy ($75? 'It did seem a cruel turn of the screw...'). But then it is clear just where Kincaid's sympathies are. Apparently all those who are not naive are now aware that building an accusation of plagiarism is akin to 'building legal castles on what literary theory warns is the quicksand of language'. 'But, no doubt because there's so much uncertainty around, fervent denunciations of plagiarists are popular: out-and-out plagiarists are criminals who safeguard the idea of originality they threaten, giving us conscience-clearing villains to hiss. They copy; we don't.' Fervent denunciations of plagiarists are popular? Not in the higher intellectual world, they aren't; there, every conceivable excuse, and many inconceivable ones, will be made for them. True, plagiarists are not criminals (or very seldom are) – they are dishonest, dishonourable, and sometimes sick, people. Kincaid, relishing the problematics of it all, ducks and weaves: 'Even educators may be learning how not just to punish but to employ plagiarism' – really?...and then at once the dodge: 'how not just to punish but to employ plagiarism, or something very like it'. Ah. 'Copying or imitating, they say, is vital to gaining initial entry into a discourse.' Not even the arrival of our comfy old friend 'discourse' quite sets my mind at rest. Need no attempt be made to distinguish the dishonesty that is plagiarism from responsible kinds of copying or imitating? 'What all of this suggests is that we might try to entertain the idea that plagiarism, and even originality, are relative concepts.' True, anciently true, in one way. Even Edward Young, who is usually blamed these days for having, in his *Conjectures on Original Composition* (1759), set the world on a grievously wrong course, declared himself 'content with what all must allow, that some Compositions are more so [original] than others'.[48] But not true, Kincaid's point, in so far as it insinuates that disapprobation need not constitute any part of the malpractice that has for centuries been called plagiarism. Kincaid has his thumb in the sliding scales. 'Plagiarism is best understood not as a sharply defined operation, like beheading, but as a whole range of activities, more like cooking, which varies from deliberate poisoning to the school cafeteria to mother's own.'[49] Maybe so, but whether 'sharply' defined or not, plagiarism is, and has always been, defined pejoratively.

Amoral jocularity about dishonesty is, in my judgement, immoral. Kincaid tells us not to 'get ourselves in a tizzy'. This demotic moment is the successor to 'but ethics are ethics, I told my student', and it serves the same end as that mock-pomposity: the evacuation of responsibility and of honesty. Demoralization.

In an essay that has been widely cited, 'Two Extravagant Teachings', Neil Hertz subjected to scrutiny and to mockery the Cornell University pamphlet on plagiarism. He wrote of its 'ill-assured moral exhortation',[50] its symptomatic rhetoric. Some of his criticisms strike home – yes, there are lapses of tone, and even gouts of feeling within the admonishments that lend themselves to Hertz's Freudian detections. Even perhaps to his aligning a teacher's anxiety about the young's plagiarism with parental anxiety about the young's masturbation. But there is something wrong with the way in which a concern with the plaintiff's, the teacher's, psyche leaves no room at all for concern with the defendant's, the plagiarist's, conduct. It is the teachers alone who are to be morally judged. What, asks Professor Hertz, of the authorities' motivation?

> We might attribute it to justifiable moral indignation, the righteous contempt of the honest for the dishonest, but that wouldn't quite account for either the intensity of this rhetoric or its peculiar figuration – or for the strong fascination that student plagiarism generally seems to hold for academics.[51]

The phrasing is prejudicial: 'indignation' contaminated by 'righteous', and 'righteous' contaminated by the likelihood of self-righteousness, with 'fascination' contaminated by prurience. Not, as might be supposed at least sometimes to be the case, a principled dislike of dishonesty, and the exercise of an essential professional responsibility when it comes to judging (often with lifelong consequences) a student's writing.

About any such matter, yes, there can be impurity of motive in the moral insistence; but shouldn't educators in the American world of Hertz (and of me), where the selling of term-papers is big business and is a threat to education, be against plagiarism? Not if Hertz's line of talk were to be followed (whatever his own practice as a teacher), for he moves on to deprecate the 'uneasiness' in teachers 'that produces the ritual condemnation of student plagiarists when they are unlucky enough to be caught'. 'Ritual condemnation': this minimizes or even extirpates moral responsibility, as does 'unlucky', and as does the ensuing reference to 'such a scapegoating'. Scapegoats are, by definition, innocent, they bear the burden of imputed unjust guilt; a dishonest student, or colleague, or novelist, is something else. But Hertz's exculpatory term 'scapegoating' has caught on, and is put to use, with due acknowledgement, by a later critic when for his own reasons he needs to put in a good word for Pecksniff, Pecksniff who stole Martin Chuzzlewit's architectural plans.[52] All is forgiven. But not to those who make scapegoats of plagiarists.

And the future? More of the same, I fear; and in the immediate future, next month to be precise, there will be a new book by Robert Scholes, *The Rise and Fall of English* (1998). He, too, knows, in the matter of plagiarism, that it is the plaintiff, not the defendant, who is the real enemy:

> In the academy the introduction to intertextuality received by most students takes the form of a stern warning against plagiarism. In a culture organized around property, patents, and copyrights, plagiar-

ism has become a sin, occasionally a crime. In other cultures, or in certain contexts within our own, this sin does not exist.[53]

Not a sin, agreed, and not a crime, but that might be thought to leave plenty of room for plagiarism to be (and not just to have 'become', in what passes here for history and for anthropology) morally wrong, and for exculpations of it to be morally wrong too. 'A stern warning against plagiarism': how relaxedly we accede to the assurance that education should be made of less stern stuff.

In her weighing of plagiarism, 'The Wasp Credited with the Honey-comb' (*Theophrastus Such*), George Eliot first granted imaginatively the ways in which it is true that creation is re-creation, true that we are all indeed in debt to the world that went before and the world that is around, and then went on indeflectibly:

> I protest against the use of these majestic conceptions to do the dirty work of unscrupulosity and justify the non-payment of debts which cannot be defined or enforced by the law.

> Surely the acknowledgement of a mental debt which will not be immediately detected, and may never be asserted, is a case in which the traditional susceptibility to 'debts of honour' would be suitably transferred.

I think it an honour to teach at a university which has returned, in the courts, to the costly fight against term-paper fraud that it began twenty-five years ago, when a victory was duly secured; on 19 October 1997,

> Boston University filed suit in U.S. District Court against eight online companies that sell term papers to students in Massachusetts. The University charges that accepting orders and distributing fraudulent term papers by phone, wire, and mail are acts of wire and mail fraud and violate the Massachusetts law prohibiting such sales and other laws.

But let me end by proposing one stubborn consideration that has, ever since Martial, ministered to these dishonourable exculpations. This is simply, but crucially, that Martial's inspired figure of speech, *plagiarius*, the thief, has itself had a distortive effect. For it must be conceded, not as bespeaking leniency for the crime of theft but as distinguishing one form of theft from most others, that it is importantly not the case that what the plagiarist does exactly is steal your poem. William Walsh in his *Handy-Book of Literary Curiosities* (1909): 'For although we are pleased to say, in our metaphorical language, that a plagiarist shines in stolen plumes, not a plume is really lost by the fowl who originally grew them.' The *New Yorker* illustration to Kincaid's article showed a rectangle of print (some lines from the article itself), at pocket height, that had been cut away from a man's clothes and is clutched by the pickpocket, no longer the rightful owner's. But the illustration inadvertently brought home that the invocation of the pickpocket (by Coleridge, by Poe, by many others), or of the thief, both is and is not apt. And in being in some respects unapt, it then ministers to special pleading. For it is scarcely ever the case that the rightful owner actually loses possession of, or credit for, his or her creation. Martin Amis did not wrongfully lose credit for his novel; Jacob Epstein wrongfully gained credit for 'his'.

True, every now and then there will be a case which really does constitute theft, and is contrastively helpful for that very reason: a work claimed by X, published by X, not ever credited to its rightful author. Anne Fadiman, in her essay on Bowers' book in *Civilization* (February/ March 1997), tells the touching story of how her mother's work was taken by John Hersey: 'The only time she ever saw her dispatches in print was inside a cover that said BY JOHN HERSEY'. But this is best judged to be piracy. Fadiman says: 'after your words – unlike your VCR – are stolen, you still own them. Or do you?' No, her mother didn't, never had been allowed to. But Glyn Jones still possessed, and still possessed credit for, the passage of prose of which Hugh MacDiarmid possessed himself for his poem 'Perfect'. Neal Bowers tells how a bronze cast that carried a poem of his called 'Art Thief' (mourning the theft of a work of sculpture from the site) was itself then stolen. Stolen. But the plagiarising of a poem is not characteristically its being lost to its originator.

What then, if anything, is stolen? We often say 'the credit', but even here there is almost always something misleading, the definite article. The plagiarist does not take the credit, he takes credit, credit to which he is not entitled. This is often despicable and always reprehensible, but it cannot be reprehended in quite the terms in which theft ordinarily is. To concede this is not to concede anything else, and is not to make any excuse for the wrongful, rather to make clear what the wrong is.

There is no chance of our ever giving up the vivid figure of speech which thought in terms of theft, but we should be aware that the very terms in which we speak (we are all guilty . . . – how delicious) play a part in contributing to the disingenuous discourse through which plagiarism steals.

3
Plagiarism: Hammond versus Ricks

Brean S. Hammond

The University of Wales, Aberystwyth, had its academic procedures audited by the Quality Assurance Agency in 1998, and one of the Agency's gripes was that there was no University-wide statement on plagiarism. I was then Pro Vice-Chancellor in charge of academic affairs, and was at once detailed to produce one. I did what most people would do under such circumstances: took a look at other institutional statements on plagiarism – to find, of course, that they are widely plagiarized one from another. What I finally produced is given as an appendix, in case anyone should want to plagiarize it: it is, as Touchstone says of Audrey, 'an ill-favoured thing, sir, but mine own'. Mine own, except that I have deployed (plagiarized?) the definition of plagiarism that Professor Christopher Ricks gives on p. 3 of his 1998 British Academy lecture on the topic, a definition itself borrowed (with due acknowledgement) from Peter Shaw's essay 'Plagiary'.[1] If I have any authority to write on the subject of plagiarism, one source of it derives from having had to compile this document.

Another derives from Professor Christopher Ricks himself. Professor Ricks was kind enough, in his British Academy Lecture delivered on 10 February 1998, to mention in despatches my book *Professional Imaginative Writing* (that is, before dispatching it), since it had something to say on the topic of plagiarism.[2] In Ricks's version of me, I appear as one of several literary historians who have forwarded an argument to the effect that 'plagiarism is a recent construction in need of demystifying' (p. 155). Such historical relativists take their place in a rogues' gallery of exculpators of plagiarism: they exculpate it because, in the wet-fish grip of a 'weak and wizened' political slant, an anaemic liberal progressivism, they have evacuated the discussion of proper ethical considerations. Professor Ricks's own view is that plagiarism is always and everywhere the same – that the Roman poet Martial, for example, had a perfectly serviceable concept of it. As long as there has been a concept of author-ship, Professor Ricks believes, it has been unethical for anyone to pose as the author of something s/he did not write, thus taking the credit away from whosoever did write it. For how long, then, has there been a concept of authorship? Enter Hammond.

As with other prelapsarian history, as with any telling of the Fall itself, the moment is elusive, contested, often gets pushed further back. Brean Hammond, in *Professional Imaginative Writing in England, 1670–1740* (1997), makes a good case for dating the 'originality' debate earlier than usual, retrieving it from the eighteenth century: 'there is, I would contend, an earlier cultural formation, that of dramatic writing in the 1670s and 1680s, wherein the problematic nature of borrowing from earlier works was already under heated negotiation'. But why stop there, when it comes to negotiating the problematic nature of borrowing? Best, moreover, for Hammond to tread carefully on this 'original composition' ground, since there have been heavy investments in the eighteenth-century allocation. So Hammond prudently claims less than he might and should: 'In this period, therefore, earlier than is sometimes supposed...there was the *beginning* of an *attempt* to define "originality" in writing and the *ur-conception* of proprietary authorship'. (p. 158; italics sup-plied).

This is a fairly honourable mention, though Ricks takes deadly aim at the tentative, even hesitant, expression of some of my claims. And although it may seem as if he accepts my argument – even encourages me to extend it further into the past – in fact he does not. For when he asks 'but why stop there, when it comes to negotiating the problematic nature of borrowing?', he would seem to be asking a rhetorical question, ignoring the fact that 300 pages of my book are devoted to answering it. When he says that I 'claim less than I might and should', he means that I might and should push my dating of the beginning of modern propri-etary authorship back into the timeless past where he would wish it to be. Let us therefore be clear that I do *not* claim 'less than I might and should'. I claim exactly what I think is warranted by a knowledge of literary history.

Professor Ricks uses and endorses Peter Shaw's definition of the term 'plagiarism': it is 'using the work of another with an intent to deceive'. There follow three main arguments in Professor Ricks's lecture:

1. Plagiarism is straightforward to define, even if the supporting evidence for any accusation of it may be 'elusive, insufficient, or uncertain'. Confusion between definitional certainty and probative uncertainty has led people who ought to know better to exculpate rather than to condemn the practice.

2. One form of this slippage has been the historical claim that plagiarism is a recent intellectual construct: the practice would not at all times and in all places be recognized, this relativist argument goes, and therefore would not be regarded as morally reprehensible. Such a position colludes with the arguments of the politically correct, who have their own reasons for cleansing plagiarism of its moral opprobrium.

3. It has been unhelpful that the very word we use, 'plagiarism', that derives from the Latin 'plagiarius' – a child-stealer or slave-stealer or kidnapper – prompts us to regard the practice on an analogy with theft of property when in fact nothing material is stolen.

The first argument is probably the biggest fish Professor Ricks fries, and I am not sure that I can refute it. I do, however, have very grave doubts about it. Before I reveal those, let us remind ourselves of a few basic distinctions. 'Plagiarism' is not a crime, nor can it give rise to a civil action. It is germane to three areas of law: breach of copyright, breach of confidence and defamation of character, the first being the most significant. To prove breach of copyright, however, no conscious intention need be established. If a judge agrees that there is 'substantial' copying of one work by another, where 'substantial' is as much a qualitative as a quantitative judgement, (the singer James Brown has, it seems, a characteristic grunt, and to mix just this into another piece of music could be deemed an infringement) and whether it is intentional or not, then copyright is breached. In copyright law, there is an issue over *access* to allegedly infringed work, because 'independent creation' can be a defence against it. But in contexts where plagiarism is significant as a moral issue, most notably in academic contexts, access needs to be supplemented by what in criminal trials would be called *mens rea*, the degree of mental guilt required by the offence – according to Shaw and Ricks, a conscious intention.[3] There is, I think, a difficulty in importing this concept from criminal law into quasi-legal situations. Academics who have been concerned with plagiarism enquiries involving students or staff members testify to the discomfort that this causes them. They are reluctant to find a *mens rea*, and import a high burden of proof to avoid doing so. Our relationship with students and colleagues is not normally judicial, and perhaps because the situation feels so unnatural, academics who find themselves members of such *ad hoc* judiciaries, rather than condemning, tend to put pressure on every key term in the definition: 'using', 'work', 'intent' and 'deceive'. It is perhaps a psychological phenomenon, but a widely shared one, that investigations of student 'plagiarism' cases seldom meet with the kind of Machiavellian villain, the *intentional* deceiver, that Professor Ricks's definition interpellates. I have met people under various kinds of pressure: whether that is the pressure of their own relative inadequacy in mastering a discipline or the pressure of their desire to succeed, or a thousand others. How valuable is it to be able to provide a watertight *definition* of 'plagiarism' if in fact we can seldom provide a watertight *case* of it? Does not the muddy circumstantial water trickle back to stain the purity of the definition? Should any person who so much as *expresses* such a view of plagiarism be accused of malfeasance?

I will refer briefly to one other area where there seems to me to be a bad fit between infringing copyright and plagiarizing, causing the quasi-judicial treatment of plagiarists to be fraught with difficulty. Ideas are not protected by copyright. Anyone can write a play about two derelicts talking aimlessly while waiting for something to happen, but anyone cannot write a play about two geezers called Vladimir and Estragon which incorporates elements from *Waiting for Godot*. However, when one is investigating plagiarism cases, one very often *is* operating broadly in the realm of ideas because the accused has usually had the wit to change the exact wording of what s/he is using. Very slight changes in wording can dissolve certainties in this area.

Even in breach of copyright cases that reach the law courts, accusatory certainties have a habit of dissolving. One instructive case-history is provided by David Lodge, who, in 1992, was writing a series of likeably middle-brow articles on literary criticism for the *Independent on Sunday*. He illustrated a pointed piece on 'plagiarism' with a series of similarities between a Mills & Boon novella entitled *The Iron Master* (1991) and his own *Nice Work* (1988). Lodge describes the resemblances in the following way:

> The heroine of *Nice Work*, Robyn Penrose, is a lecturer in English literature at the Midlands University of Rummidge, who is reluctantly obliged by her superiors to 'shadow' Vic Wilcox, the managing director of a local foundry, for one day a week. The heroine of *The Iron Master* is Carly Sheppard, teacher at a community college in Yorkshire, who is reluctantly obliged by her superiors to shadow Nick

Bradley, manager of his father's foundry, for two days a week. Both men are hardworking, self-reliant, aggressive, and have not had a university education. Both women are graduates from genteel south-of-England backgrounds. Robyn gets off on the wrong foot with her boss by arriving a week late: Carly by arriving six weeks late.

The first thing both men do is show their shadows round their respective factories. Both women are impressed by the dirt, noise, danger and spectacular cascades of molten metal in the foundry. Images of hell occur to them. In the afternoon, Robyn attends a meeting of Vic with his managerial staff in a smoke-filled room, and endures some coarsely sexist teasing from Vic's sales-director, who is 'flushed' from his lunch. On her first afternoon, Carly accompanies Nick to a meeting in a smoke-filled room, where she endures some coarsely sexist teasing, especially from a 'red-faced' man.[4]

And Lodge continues to point out a number of very close parallels. Subsequent to this publication, Pauline Harris, a retired schoolteacher from Worcestershire who wrote for Mills & Boon variously as Rachel Ford and Rebecca King, having lost her contract as a romance-writer, successfully sued Lodge for substantial damages for defamation. She was able to show that both she and Lodge were indebted to Elizabeth Gaskell's *North and South*, and, one presumes, convinced the judge that she had never read *Nice Work*. *Prima facie*, this appeared to be an exceptionally clear case of unacceptable borrowing. Accusations of copyright infringement are levelled at almost every successful major film release. The novelist Faye Kellerman, for example, a successful thriller writer, alleged infringement of her 1989 novel *The Quality of Mercy*. This is a novel in which one Rebecca Lopez, the beautiful fiery daughter of Roderigo Lopez, Queen Elizabeth's physician, keeps many secrets. She and her family are *conversos*, or Jews who must practise their religion in secret. Despite the danger, Rebecca craves adventure and walks about London in male dress. One day she actually crosses swords with a fledgling dramatist called Will Shakespeare. The latter is having trouble getting his writing together and Rebecca inspires, even instructs, Shakespeare to write *The Merchant of Venice*.[5] If this sounds vaguely familiar, it is probably because it slightly resembles the screenplay written by Marc Norman and Tom Stoppard for *Shakespeare in Love*. I understand that there were at least three other plagiarism accusations pending against the film (including the 1941 Caryl Brahms and S. J. Simon novel *No Bed for Bacon*). All will have difficulty in succeeding once ownership of the infringed copyrights is contested, access to infringed material is refuted and substantial similarity is disproved.

Perhaps these illustrations are not much to the point except that they underline the summative comment I want to make on Ricks's first argument: plagiarism calls for an ethic of understanding rather than an ethic of condemnation. Lodge's newspaper article mobilized a tone of ironic moral outrage tantamount to a set of judgements about someone's conscious intention to profit from literary labours not her own: and then found that his allegations could not be sustained in a court of law. There is in Professor Ricks's moral absolutism an echo of the 'understand less and condemn more' message that makes me a little uneasy. I suspect that it would get universities that adopted it into courts of law far more often than they want to be. That is why I have stressed in my statement on plagiarism written for the University of Wales, Aberystwyth, that there should be a second tier of 'bad' rather than 'unfair' practice, covering the majority of students against whom there can be no clear evidence that they set out to deceive. Such persons may be acting recklessly, using practices that fall below acceptable standards. Rather than *intending* to plagiarize, individuals like this can be said to have taken insufficient care to *avoid* doing so, and can therefore be punished according to a lesser code. This seems to me to be an equitable response to the fact that most university 'unfair practice' codes are very severe in their effects.

In some respects, Ricks's third argument, that we are misled by regarding plagiarism on an analogy with theft, actually conduces towards such an ethic, and I sympathize with it. In industrial law, it is widely recognized that stealing trade secrets, for example, is only metaphorically theft: what one is actually doing is multiplying the number of people who know them. The 'stealing' aspect of it is probably a reference to the clandestine way in which it is popularly imagined that such information is obtained: and if it *is* obtained by such means, there would doubtless be another offence involved. I read this argument first in J. O. Urmson's contribution to the debate that the *TLS* held on April 9, 1982 in the aftermath of the D. M. Thomas *débâcle*: when Thomas was accused of using *verbatim* the testimony of the only survivor of the Babi Yar massacre in *The White Hotel*.[6] I do not for one second suggest that Professor Ricks was plagiarizing Urmson, but I wonder whether the indignation he would feel if anyone were to make such a suggestion would be in any way salutary. I do wish to return, though, to the question of the analogy between plagiarism and theft of property in the context of Ricks's second argument.

I am cited as one of several commentators on plagiarism who are responsible for the historical relativizing of the concept, that has in turn contributed to a generally exculpatory climate. We are the kinds of people who give plagiarism a good name. Ricks argues contrary to those who consider that the representation and significance of plagiarism has altered over time and that our current pejorative attitude towards it is relatively modern, that plagiarism has always been identified, has always attracted moral opprobrium and that the cultural set towards it is constant throughout time. After all, he points out, the Roman poet Martial first used the word 'plagiarius' in one of his Epigrams, and plagiarism occurs as a motif in several (though actually they may all be variants of the same single case). The structure of this argument is troublesome. Professor Ricks's argument here appears to be a late example of the Ancients/Moderns debate that was such a prominent feature of seventeenth-century intellectual life. One is reminded of Sir William Temple in the *Essay upon Ancient and Modern Learning* claiming that Harvey did not discover the circulation of the blood and that the Copernican system is probably not true and changes nothing if it is.[7] There are constellations of concepts that appear to have been with us for a very long time, one might almost say 'eternally', such as patriarchy or sexism; but the forms of social and intellectual organization that they designate may have altered many times in recent history. The *longue durée* does not entail a homogeneity of the forms in which such concepts present themselves. To support his intellectual paradigm, Ricks needs to refute those who have argued for significant epistemic difference in the concept of literary borrowing between earlier times and our own: for instance, the argument made by Harold Ogden White in his 1935 study *Plagiarism and Imitation During the English Renaissance: a Study in Critical Distinctions*. White's thesis is that certainly until, and he would say also during, the English Renaissance, the classical episteme of imitation prevailed. That congeries of attitudes towards literary borrowing is characterized by White as follows:

> The writer should take only what he finds usable in his predecessors, should add to it whatever changes or improvements later ages, including his own, have developed, and should transform and supplement all he has gathered by the operation of his own literary genius.[8]

Writers could and did acknowledge their debts as an act of *pietas* and, we might add, as an attempt to locate themselves within, or seek the protection of, a glorious literary tradition. Reviewing the argument, Ricks considers that the book is 'full of' examples that contradict the thesis, 'indictments of plagiarism, from classical and Renaissance times, that are entirely at one with what he deplores as the modern attitude towards plagiarism' (p. 156). No, not 'full of', in my reading of White. White's weakness is less that he is self-contradictory than that his account of an unchanging classical episteme, even though it is implicitly contrasted to early modernity, is itself insufficiently nuanced: and that he does not consider any material mechanism of conceptual change. For the nub of the issue is *how* concepts change. Imitation of earlier writers was indeed distinguished by sophisticated ancient critics from theft; and several Greek and Roman writers laid a claim to originality, amongst them Pindar, Aristophanes, Lucretius, Virgil, Horace and Propertius.[9] Do the key terms here mean exactly the same thing in radically different institutional contexts? What are the enabling conditions of conceptual change? One can suspect the pinpoint accuracy of Virginia Woolf's claim in her 1919 *TLS* essay 'Modern Novels' that 'On, or about, September 1910, human nature changed', without denying that concepts can function differently at different times in cultural representation. I think human nature changed in the 1670s, at least as far as attitudes towards plagiarism are concerned, and I would like to elaborate a little on that claim.

My argument in *Professional Imaginative Writing* was that although it is usual to argue for the mid-eighteenth century as the point at which attitudes towards the imitative practices of earlier poetry altered, as 'originality' came to be valorized, originality itself precipitates out of earlier processes. During the theatre wars of the 1670s, in the battles between professional playwrights and gentlemen-amateurs, and the internecine contests between professionals such as Dryden and Shad-well, accusations of plagiarism hail down so thickly as to be difficult to ignore. Although the term 'plagiary' and cognates were first introduced into the English language at the turn of the seventeenth century, the collocation of ideas against which it operated was different. During the so-called 'poetomachia', Jonson accused Marston and Dekker, and was accused in turn, of plagiarism. What really outraged Jonson, however, was the charge that he was a slow burner, taking time and trouble over his literary production. This was to suggest that Jonson, the son of a bricklayer, was without the courtly *sprezzatura* required to toss off masterpieces in his leisure, that he was a lumbering journeyman-oaf with vain aspirations for the eight lines per day that he strained from his hard-bound brains. Some decades later, Dryden and Shadwell, especially the latter, felt the opposite anxiety. Shadwell is almost eager at times to plead guilty to charges of plagiarism, and represents it as a last shift to which he must resort in a hard-pressed professional career. If only he had the time and leisure to write enjoyed by aristocratic amateurs like Rochester... For Dryden, Shadwell, Otway, Crowne and other post-Restoration writers there is a new consciousness of making a living, of the equation between money and time, of one's own wit as a species of stock-in-trade, that operates to congeal the notion of literary property. When a conception of literary *property* thickens up, I argue, attitudes towards plagiarism also harden. If you are in direct competition with another theatre company, have a deadline to produce a script for which a fee is due, and in those circumstances find a rival writer stealing your plot, even purloining your source – you are likely to be aggrieved. No more graphic illustration of literary professionalism can be produced than the argument that Dryden offered for abandoning verse drama. This was not an exalted aesthetic defence of blank verse over couplet as a much less constrained and artificial form. It turned on the fact that rhymes took time to find and that therefore you simply couldn't write rhymed verse quickly enough to make money.

Attitudes to literary *meum* and *tuum* did alter under such material determinants, and the practice of classical allusion certainly became more self-conscious as a result. That is the lesson that mock-epic, incident to this historical juncture, has to teach us. There is also vital evidence for an attitude-shift to be found in the fact that, from the 1680s onwards, a distinction began to be drawn between appropriating from ancient sources and appropriating from modern sources. As Paulina Kewes has shown in her magisterial *Authorship and Appropriation: Writing for the Stage in England, 1660–1710*, Gerard Langbaine was a pioneer here: and in Langbaine's 1688 *Momus Triumphans* and 1691 *Account of the English Dramatick Poets*, the formation of characteristically modern attitudes to literary property can be traced in action:

> Langbaine's persistent questioning of the fairness of financial rewards for plays made up of appropriated materials firmly anchors the debates about plagiarism in the commercial context of the theatrical marketplace, and signals a recognition that literary creations may be very profitable property. Such concern about illicit profits from the labour of another is precisely what motivates the restriction of fair use in modern copyright law.[10]

This crucial distinction between appropriating from the ancients and despoiling living authors is taken up by John Dennis in 1711, and directly related to the question of the protection of intellectual property:

For you know, my dear Friend, that a Plagiary in general is but a scandalous Creature, a sort of spiritual Outlaw, and ought to be treated as such by all the Members of the Commonwealth of Learning. But a Plagiary from living Authors is most profligately impudent... As Laws are made for the Security of Property, what pity 'tis that there are not some enacted for the Security of a Man's Thoughts and Inventions, which alone are properly his? [11]

By mid-century, Fielding is able to ironise the entire topic in Book XII.1 of *Tom Jones*, a chapter headed '*Shewing what is to be deemed Plagiarism in a modern Author, and what is to be considered as lawful Prize*'. The Ancients and the Moderns are mapped onto a comic status division, where the ancients are wealthy squires and therefore ripe for plunder, whereas living authors are a confederacy of the poor who should not rob one another:

In like manner are the ancients, such as Homer, Virgil, Horace, Cicero, and the rest, to be esteemed among us writers, as so many wealthy squires, from whom we, the poor of Parnassus, claim an immemorial custom of taking whatever we can come at... All I profess, and all I require of my brethren, is to maintain the same strict honesty among ourselves, which the mob shew to one another. To steal from one another, is indeed highly criminal and indecent; for this may be strictly stiled defrauding the poor (sometimes perhaps those who are poorer than ourselves) or, to see it under the most opprobrious colours, robbing the spittal.[12]

The narrator will 'claim a property' in anything that he transcribes from the ancients into his own writings, but 'shall never fail to put their mark upon' anything he has occasion to borrow from his own brethren. As the reference in the next paragraph to James Moore Smyth's purloining from Pope makes clear (a theft that earned him a place in *The Dunciad*), Fielding's satire here is descended from the *Battle of the Books* modulated in the Scriblerian mode. He would not *wish* to be mistaken for the author of anything he could actually find in the daubings of his brothers in the trade. Nevertheless, the irony depends upon an ability to police the boundaries between alluding to the long dead, and invading the property of the living.

Early modern attitudes to plagiarism are distinctively different from their ancestors, and closer to our own, because they are conditioned by the professionalisation of writing. Anxiety about the protection of property is of course the engine that drives demand for a Copyright Act. Widespread accusations of plagiarism are an important aspect of the discourse surrounding writing for a livelihood that finds one nodal point in the inscription of the category 'author' into a piece of legislation in 1710. 'Originality', one might think, can take off as an aesthetic category only *after* a legal means has been found of preventing unauthorized replication of books. For the point about the presence of the word 'author' in Queen Anne's Act for the Encouragement of Learning is that the creation of copyright laws across eighteenth-century Europe brought into being a framework whereby authors could claim infringement even when there had not been wholesale copying of their work: where a few elements had been lifted rather than a wholesale piracy. Certainly, it was not until much later – until the early nineteenth century – that the first prosecutions for infringement began to be brought; but the enabling legislation was the Copyright Act.

My point is, then, that even if some such concept as the theft of another's work and dissemination of it as one's own is not a new phenomenon in the English Restoration period, the degree of cultural salience and penetration of plagiarism is new. Such rhetorical prominence requires explanation, which I supply in terms of a set of concepts, discourses and material practices that surround writing for money, 'hackney for bread' as my sub-title puts it. Crude formulations are frequently given of the social mechanisms that give rise to conceptual change, and those can make us wary of ever proposing it. Roy Strong says in his recent *The Spirit of Britain: A Narrative History of the Arts* that 'the novel could never have happened without John Locke'.[13] Preposterous – one thinks of Cervantes – but in so far as Locke has a part to play in redefining attitudes to property that, in turn, lie somewhere behind the formation of what historians call the military-fiscal state in the late seventeenth and early eighteenth centuries (the development of a system of paper credit and invisible wealth out of the need to finance European wars, that makes the conception of a purely *intellectual* property more compassable) he certainly is a figure in the landscape of the English novel's development. There is now a fairly extensive literature on the growth of the book market in the latter decades of the seventeenth century, on the spread of literacy, on the post-1688 politico-ecclesiastical consensus that, despite challenges and ruptures, was good for trade, on the non-renewal of the Licensing Act in 1695, on the gradual domestication of the literary agenda that enabled people, female people in particular, from different social provenances to join the categories 'writer' and 'reader': on, in short, the conditions that make it very plausible that Samuel Johnson the arch-professional, when he sometimes deplored and sometimes exculpated plagiarism, was not expressing precisely the same conception of that nefarious activity as was Martial in the first century AD, whose epigrams were a hugely successful attempt to attract the attention of the Flavian Emperors Titus and Domitian. If the understanding of 'property' has altered, as has the understanding of 'public domain', it is reasonable to suppose that the understanding of 'plagiarism' that depends crucially on the relation between those two concepts, is also not the same.

Permit me, at the risk of repetition, to specify further the clear blue water that exists between Christopher Ricks's view and my own. Let me make clear that I am *not* giving any kind of approval whatsoever to the nefarious practices of present-day plagiarists. I think that conceptions of authorship really did change as an aspect of wider Gestalt-shifts resulting from what is sometimes referred to as the 'commodification of culture' in post-Restoration society. Plagiarism begins to be perceived as a species of moral crime against authorship because it threatens literary livelihoods. Assuming another writer's credit, the plagiarist is seen to be robbing that writer of a commodity just as vital, however intangible, as is a tradesman's credit. This view I would present as historically accurate, consonant with the evidence. I do not see that it has any consequences for how one chooses to treat plagiarists in the present time. On that matter, however, I would again dissent from Ricks. Coming at it from the angle of the university administrator, I ask myself whether I would wish his absolutist view to determine institutional policy – and I answer, emphatically, 'no'. An old canard frequently trotted out in plagiarism discussions goes: to borrow from one source is plagiarism, to borrow from several sources is research. This feeble witticism makes its point. It is actually very difficult to specify exactly, for students learning the discipline of English, the line that is drawn in the sand of acceptable and unacceptable degrees of critical stimulation. This perhaps instils anxiety in those who try to do it. If we cannot spell out the rules of our discourse with such precision that neophytes can internalize them without difficulty, what kind of a discipline do we have? Do we have a discipline at all? It may be that the permissive reactions of the 'anything goes' brigade and the authoritarian reactions of those who call for clear definitions, convictions that stick, and harsh punishment, are equal though opposite reactions to this root insecurity.

Drawing to a close, let me say just a few words about the nature of that insecurity. Reviewing a clutch of recent books on the crisis in English studies for the *New York Review of Books* on 4 November 1999, Andrew

Delbanco has provided what is rapidly becoming the accepted wisdom in some quarters on the 'culture wars' in the American academy. The decline of English as the central discipline of the humanities may be due to sociological and demographic factors far wider than the academy itself, but internal weaknesses have made it more vulnerable to those than it needed to be. English had at one time a very coherent story to tell about its own importance. That story was provided by Emerson and the New Critics in the US, and by Arnold and Leavis (whose name is not actually mentioned by Delbanco) in the UK:

> Students who turn with real engagement to English do so almost always because they have had the mysterious and irreducably private experience – or at least some intimation of it – of receiving from a work of literature 'an untranslatable order of impressions' that has led to 'consummate moments' in which thought and feeling are lifted to a new intensity.[14]

Faith in the power of literature to transform the experience of those who come into contact with it, is what its professors now lack. This sense of secular vocation has been replaced by poststructuralist dogma that empties literature of most positive meaning and relativises the little that it cannot altogether deny. 'English', says Delbanco:

> has come to reflect some of the worst aspects of our culture: obsessing about sex, posturing about real social inequities while leaving them unredressed, and participating with gusto in the love/hate cult of celebrities... English today exhibits the contradictory attributes of a religion in its late phase – a certain desperation to attract converts, combined with an evident lack of convinced belief in its own scriptures and traditions.[15]

Delbanco's solution presumably lies in counter-reformation: a weeding out of those heretics, commencing with Paul de Man, whose views on the infinite iterability of the sign have led us to question the scripture according to which there is a sacred original text, and others who would traduce it or claim falsely to be its originators. No doubt the arbitrariness of the signifier has its limits. A colleague described to me the experience of being at a conference in the heyday of French poststructuralism, when a woman delivered a paper that was, as most of the audience recognized, a *verbatim* copy of a published essay by the influential Gaston Bachelard: an example of 'the undecidability of the sign', or old-fashioned plagiarism? Yet if one's credentials to be a student of English literature really depend upon mysterious and irreducably private experiences, every essay becomes a form of spiritual autobiography, an attempt to render the essence of one's conversion experience. That kind of thing is difficult to assess. Quackery would become a more significant problem than plagiarism.

And there I rest my case.[16]

Appendix: University Statement on Plagiarism

Plagiarism is the act of using someone else's work with an intent to deceive. In academic contexts, the point of the deception is normally to obtain higher marks than you think you would get for your own unaided efforts. There are several ways of going about this. You might decorate your essay with some choice expressions from some other source[s], without making it clear that you have done this. You might take substantial chunks. You might copy from notes or essays written by fellow students or even taken from the internet. In more extreme cases, students might actually submit work to which they have contributed nothing at all, something that is entirely the work of another mind.

People who do this do it for various motives. A good and ambitious student might do it because s/he desperately wants a very good degree result, and is doubtful if s/he can achieve that on his/her own; or because there is a course in which s/he is relatively weak. A poor student might do it because s/he has been in the pub when s/he ought to have been working and has no work to submit. Sometimes the motives can be very complex. Whatever they are, plagiarism is intellectual dishonesty.

Plagiarism is straightforward to define, but it is not always easy to establish. This is because no intellectual endeavour is ever absolutely original. Even the most original minds depend on the thoughts and discoveries of their predecessors. And in most intellectual disciplines, students are expected to demonstrate familiarity with the established literature in their field: indeed, this is one of the key competences that you need to demonstrate in most academic fields. Most of the time, you will be citing articles and books that are especially relevant to your enquiry, and making your own contribution to it. That contribution might not be a great one, especially in the early years of a degree programme; but it will, or should, be your own.

Each Department will have its own subject-specific account of the best ways in which to avoid plagiarism. This guidance is frequently to be found in Course Handbooks, and you should familiarise yourself with it.

Sometimes students can be so weak or under-confident in a subject, again especially early on in their studies, that they really find it difficult to tell what is acceptable borrowing from other sources and what is not. Sometimes, unacceptable degrees of borrowing can occur when a student has not actually intended to engage in unfair practice. For this reason, when a member of the academic staff reads work that s/he suspects is not the unaided work of its supposed author, s/he may not at once notify this to the Chairman of the relevant Examining Board. University staff will exercise proper academic judgement.

If and when s/he decides to do so, the Chairman will normally interview the student in the presence of the staff member making the enquiry, to establish whether there was an intention to benefit unfairly. The panel may decide that there was not. This, they may then think, is not unfair, but bad practice. They will probably assign an appropriately low mark to the examined element. If, however, the panel is convinced that there is on the face of it a case of unfair practice, and if the course element constitutes more than 3 per cent of the overall assessment weighting for the year of study, the Chairman will notify the University authorities and what happens next will be governed by the University's Academic Regulation on Unfair Practice. The most significant part of this is reproduced in the Students' Examination Handbook, which you should possess. If a case of plagiarism is established, the penalties can be very severe indeed.

Clearly, however, the most sensible course for a student to pursue, and the course that most students do pursue, is to develop enough academic judgement and self-confidence for them not to be in any danger of such an accusation being made against them. Most students have no wish to gain credit for what they have not themselves contributed, or to gain a qualification that is, even in part, a bogus achievement.

4
Plagiarism and Original Sin

Stephen Orgel

Twenty-five years ago I wrote an essay called 'The Renaissance Artist as Plagiarist'.[1] I was moved to write it by a puzzling crux in my work on Inigo Jones, an instance in which Jones's published statements about the genesis of a particular court masque seemed to contradict all the other evidence about the production. Two modern scholars of great learning and eminence had explained the contradiction by invoking the concept of plagiarism. This explanation, however, struck me as unconvincing on two counts: nobody could reasonably call what Jones had done in the masque plagiarism; and declaring it plagiarism didn't seem to me to explain anything. In the essay I came up with an alternative explanation, which didn't involve plagiarism and solved the puzzle to my own satisfaction; but the solution still left me wondering where the charge of plagiarism had come from, since it was, to my mind at least, so clearly irrelevant to the facts. I shall return to the specifics of this case, but I now summarize the rest of the essay, as the essential background of my remarks here. From the Jones masque I was moved to wonder what kinds of artistic imitation could reasonably have been called plagiarism in Jones's time, and what sorts of changes one could chart, historically, in the acceptable limits of artistic imitation. I wasn't entirely convinced by my historical arguments in this part of the essay, which were based on far too little knowledge, and I have since revised my thinking on the matter a number of times, as I have been enlightened by classicists, medievalists and neo-Latinists. However, I never felt moved to pursue the matter in print again, not least because it seemed to me that the essay had sunk without a trace. Nobody responded to it, I never saw it cited; so far as I was aware, no one took any notice of it at all.

Imagine my surprise, then, when twenty-four years later my old friend Christopher Ricks came to visit and announced that he was about to disagree with me publicly on the subject of plagiarism. And my even greater surprise at learning, when he sent me an offprint of his British Academy lecture, that my essay was 'influential'. Really! It never seemed to me to have influenced anyone, except, of course, Ricks to object to it. I found, moreover, that when I read Ricks's essay I pretty much agreed with it – and certainly agreed that there were problems with my historical account, which I'd already revised for myself long before. So when I was subsequently asked whether I would agree to open the conference on which this volume is based by participating in a debate with Ricks, I firmly declined. First of all, there seemed to me little to debate; second – and perhaps, to be honest, more compelling – Ricks and I have known each other for thirty-five years and spent the first ten or so arguing, and I don't remember ever coming out ahead. I do, I suppose, come off fairly well in the present case: I am allowed to be, on the particular matter in question, muddle-headed and unpersuasive but basically well intentioned, whereas most of the other people Ricks disagrees with are very bad news indeed – 'weakly, wizenedly, political', they 'demean and . . . degrade moral thought'. I'm extremely relieved not to be in that class. I can't, of course, match the intensity of Ricks's indignation – I never could – but I do certainly share his ethical principles.

My primary concern was in the historical and scholarly aspects of the subject, and I shall return to those; but since Ricks is chiefly concerned with the current practice of plagiarism and the decay of moral values in response to it, let me start with practical matters. I begin where most of us who teach begin, with how to deal with students who cheat. Ricks cites, as a kind of moral barometer of the modern condition, James Kincaid's story, in an article on plagiarism published in *The New Yorker*, of a student indignant over having ordered an original paper on the Internet and having been sold a plagiarized one. ' "Shit!" she said. "I paid seventy-five dollars for that." ' Ricks's indignation is directed primarily at Kincaid's cool and cynical reaction, but what interests me is that he also swallows the story whole. Outrageous the story certainly is; original it certainly is not. The same story was making the rounds when I was a graduate student at Harvard in the 1950s, and when I was teaching at Berkeley in the 1960s – long before the Internet there were outfits supplying papers on demand and students buying them (the *Encyclopedia Britannica*'s research service was an egregious supplier, widely used at Harvard). This tale is a piece of American academic mythology, invented, I imagine, a few minutes after the first student bought the first paper. The only thing Kincaid's version adds to the story is the 'Shit!'. I venture no opinion about whether or not such an incident actually happened to Kincaid, and/or to some Harvard or Berkeley colleague; I've just heard a version of it at Stanford, where the price has dropped to $60: perhaps it happens all the time these days – imitation is the essence of life, as of art. How significant is the truth or falsehood of this story – why isn't originality an issue for Ricks here? Because everything depends on the genre: its primary function in this discourse is not factual, but as a classic exemplum, a rich subject for moralization, both Kincaid's and Ricks's.

My own plagiarism story is much less epigrammatic, though it is original. Nobody could have thought it up. Stanford operates on an honour system, which means that students formally subscribe to a code of ethics. I'm not allowed to proctor exams, and students who are aware of other students cheating are required to turn them in. I have never known this to happen, but I also don't put the system under much pressure – for the kinds of exams I give, it doesn't do you any good to look over somebody's shoulder, and my essay topics are usually too specific for anyone except a student in the class to write them. Still, there are opportunities – optional papers, which can be on anything; short papers for section meetings where the student picks the topic. The only culprits I can catch, of course, are the inept ones – students who copy the introduction to the text we're using or crib from essays I've assigned, so that I'm bound to recognize them. If the plagiarist takes a paper from the Internet (or, in the old-fashioned low-tech way, out of the sorority files), I have no way of knowing it. I may decide the paper is too good for this particular student or doesn't match the style of her other work, but the only way for me to be sure that she hasn't been suddenly transformed by my teaching into a first-class critic is to extract a confession.

In my fifteen years at Stanford, I've had only one such case, in 1998. In contrast to the banal predictability of the *New Yorker* story, mine seemed to me positively surreal; but it is directly relevant to Ricks's insistence that we all know and have always known that the crucial element in plagiarism is the intention to deceive. One of my section leaders in a Renaissance survey course asked her students to write a page about any aspect of the Shakespeare sonnets, as a basis for class discussion. A student turned in a page copied verbatim from Hallett Smith's introduction to the sonnets in the Riverside Shakespeare. When confronted, the student freely admitted cribbing the material, but exculpated himself by explaining that his Oxford tutor had taught him to write papers that way. (Mentioning Oxford or Cambridge at Stanford is usually enough to silence any criticism – if you do it with an English accent, you can get away with almost anything.) The Oxford tutor was reported to have told her charges that one could never hope to write something original about great poetry, so one should find excellent critical work and copy that. But surely the tutor hadn't said one should copy it without acknowledgment? Yes, he insisted, she had. I declined his offer to put me in touch with the tutor, and the section leader and I contented ourselves with making sure he understood the local rules he had agreed to about the citation of sources, gave him a stern warning, elicited an apology and considered the matter closed.

A month later the section leader presented me with a paper on *Paradise Lost* by the same student. It was cribbed verbatim from a book which happened to be by another former student of mine. The section leader, who had been suspicious of the prose, had found the original instantly because the paper had the same title as the book – this was not, you can see, a very sophisticated plagiarist. This time, however, the Oxford tutor was not invoked; the student flatly denied any knowledge of the original, though eventually, confronted with the absolute identity of the two texts in question, agreed that he must have, at some point, looked at the book and forgotten about it. But here the exculpatory explanation was in his method of taking notes: he copies good things from critical works into the margin of his text; since these are simply reading notes he doesn't indicate their source, and doubtless he simply mistook these passages for ideas of his own. His copy of *Paradise Lost*, which he was asked to produce, didn't, in fact, include such marginalia – he thought perhaps the text he had used was home in Maryland, or had even, unfortunately, been disposed of – but he did show me his copy of *The Tempest*, the margins of which were indeed full of good bits, copied directly from my own critical prose. I pointed out that this method of taking notes practically guaranteed that his papers would be plagiarized, but he replied coolly that the crucial element in plagiarism was intention, and he had no intention of deceiving anyone.

The whole matter meanwhile had been referred to the university's judicial board, which, after an extended investigation and a very long hearing, declared him guilty. It then went through several appeals, all of which he lost. Throughout the many months that all this took he maintained his innocence and seemed baffled that nobody believed his explanations. He was especially aggrieved at me for refusing to pass him in the course – this was a real blow, since it meant he had to register for an extra term, which at Stanford is an expensive business. This was the only point at which he seemed to take the matter seriously, the point at which it turned out that it was going to cost him money. I never succeeded in getting him to admit that he had done anything unethical; he remained throughout courteous, patient, slightly pained, but unflappable. His metaphor for what had happened was that, entirely unexpectedly, a brick wall had fallen on him. He had never, he assured me, been accused of lying in his life. You will perhaps not be surprised to hear that he intends to go to law school, though I am told that with an ethics violation on his undergraduate record he will have difficulty being accepted. (I must say I'm surprised to learn this.) He'd probably do quite well running for president.

However inept this student was, he perfectly understood that intention here was everything; originality nothing. I turn now, for an oddly parallel case, to two of my most prized possessions, a pair of Dürer engravings. The first, the famous and mysterious *Melancholia I*, I bought in 1968 during a year when I was working at the Warburg Institute. It was in a box of Northern Renaissance prints at the late, lamented Craddock and Barnard on Museum Street, and I was thrilled to find it. It is a beautiful, crisp impression, signed in the plate with the monogram AD and the date 1514; but even my minimal expertise was sufficient to tell me that there was something not right about it. The something was that it was priced at £12, and even in 1968 Craddock and Barnard didn't sell Dürers for £12. It is, in fact, not by Dürer, but by an expert copyist working in the latter half of the sixteenth century named Jan Wierix. With a magnifying glass and the original print, it is possible to see slight differences – in hatching and such – and there is one real giveaway, though it's difficult to spot unless you know what to look for; but the copy is a very expert one. My second Dürer, of the Holy Family, I found a couple of years later, also at Craddock and Barnard, and paid £8 for it. I was on to Wierix by this time, but this time also there was no question about it: Wierix had signed the print with his monogram and the date, IHW 1566 – though he had also included Dürer's original monogram. It is a very accurate copy, but it does declare itself a copy.

Wierix made his living, not to put too fine a point on it, both as a copyist and as a forger; and I take it that the first of my Dürers is a forgery, intended for sale as an authentic Dürer, the second a copy, intended for sale to those who wanted the Dürer print but couldn't afford it. (In fact, both pictures were produced in both signed and unsigned versions.) These two prints, then, inhabit quite different ethical worlds. Does this affect my feeling about them? Not at all: I am delighted with both. Would I have bought them if Dürer hadn't been an issue – if I knew nothing of Dürer but simply liked the pictures? I believe I would; I'm a sucker for nice Renaissance pictures, and usually buy them first and find out about them afterward. But then if I merely like the picture, would any copy do? What about a perfect digitalized repro-duction, which would be an even closer approximation to the original than my Wierixes? Well, no, that wouldn't give me the same kind of pleasure. Part of what I like is the simple age of the objects, the fact that they're real survivals from the sixteenth century, but a significant part too is the genuine craftsmanship involved, the excellence not merely of the copy but of the copyist.

So the fact of the forgery doesn't bother me at all? No: the print was misrepresented by the artist, but not by the dealer, who wasn't selling it as a Dürer. *I* wasn't cheated; the fraud – and there certainly was one – was back in the sixteenth century; it's history. But what if I had been cheated, either by a dealer who hadn't done his homework on the *Melancholia I* or who had lied about it? It's the same picture in either case; wouldn't I like it just as much? Well, perhaps not *just* as much: the fact of the fraud would matter. I'd be very angry, and not only because if it had been sold as an authentic Dürer I'd have paid a heap more money for it. Ah, but what about the difference in cost? The extra money would then have been paid not for Dürer's inimitable expertise, since the engravings looked to me virtually identical, but merely for his name. Yes: it's the intangible that would matter here, and not even because it affects the resale value of the print: I'm not a dealer, and have never sold a print of mine; I buy them exclusively to look at. My outrage would be purely moral; there would be nothing at all practical about it. And I would grind my teeth and do my best to extract some satisfaction from the ignorant or fraudulent dealer; but I suspect that I'd keep the picture on the wall and continue to look at it with undiminished wonder.

These, however, are the *simple* cases. The most successful forgeries have been those with no original, those that do not copy the work of art but impersonate the artist, such as Van Meegheren's notorious Verm-eers. Forgeries like these are especially subversive because they call into question the whole system of artistic value. This is not to say that questioning the system, or indeed subverting it, would necessarily be a bad thing; and it may be that, given the way the art market works, such forgeries constitute the only way to question it. To observe that in this case, and any number of similar ones, the experts were mistaken or deceived, or even defrauded, is also to concede that the usefulness of expertise in such cases is extremely limited. Picasso himself was con-stantly being asked by dealers to authenticate his own work, and was often found declaring the same picture to be both real and fake at different times. The later Picassos especially are very easy to imitate;

one often feels, in those thousands of quick sketches, Picasso imitating himself. In an art that depends on imitation in this way, what constitutes authenticity? It is not that there is no answer to this question, but that the basis of the answer, indeed the possibility of an answer, keeps changing. The most basic answer would certainly invoke the concept of misrepresentation – a common-sense answer – and there are clearly many such cases everyone could agree on. But even these bear so heavily on the question of what constitutes value that even the most obvious of them need a harder look: the problem is precisely the Picasso problem – that there is an unclear and uncertain relation between authenticity and authentication, and it is not always possible to know whether something is being misrepresented. An unknown painting by Vermeer is worth a great deal more than an unknown painting in the style of Vermeer, even when it is the same painting. This suggests that the issue is not the quality of the painting, but the construction of the artist. Rubens was quite open about this, selling both paintings by his own hand and paintings from his workshop at very different prices. We might say that there is no problem as long as nothing is misrepresented; but there will inevitably come a point at which the documentation is lost and you can tell only by looking, and the question then will have to do not with the craft of painting or the ethics of the artist or the dealer, but with the art (and ethics) of attribution. In the most recent sensational international art forgery case, the crucial forgeries were not the paintings, which were fakes, but precisely the documentation – it was the paper trail that constituted authenticity.[2] Had the paintings been authentic, the dealer might have found it no less desirable to fake their provenance.

I return now to history – and to Ricks. I was certainly wrong to suggest that plagiarism wasn't taken seriously before the late seventeenth century. It is true that there is very little discussion of the subject in the Middle Ages, and what there is tends to be concerned with fears about the dissemination of corrupt texts rather than with authorial usurpation: Petrarch worries about plagiarism precisely because he assumes that the purloined and corrupted works will continue to be marketed as his – assumes, that is, that his authorship constitutes the crucial element in the text's value. Medieval poets employed a variety of methods of asserting and maintaining their authority over their writing. Dante not only made himself the hero of the *Commedià*, he numbered the lines of the poem and alludes to the numbering within the text to preclude revisions and interpolations. Chaucer didn't merely compose his tales, he represented himself as narrating them. There are even cases of poets embedding their names in their poems, so that the author would remain an integral element of the work – these are rare, but the fact of their existence at all is to the point. I doubt that any of these can be seen primarily, or even significantly, as strategies designed to prevent plagiarism, but they all involve notions of intellectual property and authorial control, and these in themselves imply a concept of plagiarism.

The Renaissance revival of the classics, however, was also a revival of the classical sense of plagiarism, which was clear and explicit; and the smoking gun in Ricks's account, the proof that, far from being a post-Renaissance phenomenon, plagiarism has been a serious moral crime since ancient times, is Martial. Here the account, I think, needs some fine-tuning. Ricks points out that it is to Martial that we owe the application of the term *plagiarius*, the abductor of somebody else's slave, to literary theft, and he cites epigram, i.66, in a rather clumsy translation by William Cartwright. Here it is in one that's easier to follow, by Henry Killigrew, 1695:

> Thou sordid felon of my verse and fame,
> So cheap dost hope to get a poet's name,
> As by the purchase barely of my book
> For ten vile pence eternal glory rook?
> Find out some virgin poem ne'er saw day,
> Which wary writers in their desks do lay
> Lock'd up, and known unto themselves alone;
> Not one with using torn, and sordid grown.
> A publish'd work can ne'er the author change,
> Like one ne'er pass'd the press, that ne'er did range
> The world trimly bound up: and such I'll sell,
> Give me my price, nor will the secret tell.
> He that another's wit and fame will own,
> Must silence buy, and not a book that's known.[3]

This certainly condemns plagiarism, at least in the opening lines; but is it about plagiarism in general or in particular – is it, that is, really about a case of somebody stealing Martial's poems and taking credit for them? If so, why isn't the culprit named and what poems did he steal? What's the point of attacking someone who is appropriating your work if you don't reveal his identity and say which purloined poems are yours? And if it is an actual case of plagiarism, how outraged really is Martial about it? He certainly starts out sounding indignant – the plagiarist is 'fur avare', a greedy thief of Martial's work. But by the end of the poem Martial is actually offering himself as a ghost writer: the passage literally says, 'a book already known (i.e. one that has been published) cannot change its author; but find an unpublished one and buy that – I have some, and no one will know: anybody who wants to become famous by reciting somebody else's poems must buy not a book but the author's silence'. Martial ends by declaring himself quite willing to participate in the deception as long as he is paid; it's not the deception that bothers him, but the fact that he's been left out of it. This is nicely ironic, but it's also quite cynical, and doesn't look like a smoking gun to me. It should be added that all of it depends on a totally constructed persona: Martial, as a gentleman poet, does not in fact write for money – he doesn't even sell his books, he gives them away.

In i.72, Martial does name names, attacking a plagiarist named Fidentinus. Once again, the crime seems more generic than particular: it appears that this is not the name of someone real, but a symbolic name – according to Peter Howell's commentary on Martial, it is 'intended to hint at the bearer's shamelessness'.[4] *Fidens* means audacious or fearless, and *fidentinus* is a diminutive of it – something like calling him Rambino instead of Rambo. The *-tinus* ending, moreover, was a frequent marker of the names of ex-slaves; so the name also implies that the *plagiarius*, the slave-stealer, is a former slave himself. Here is the poem, again in Henry Killigrew's translation:

> For verses, Fidentine, thou stealst from me,
> A poet fain thou wouldst reputed be;
> Old Aegle so, well-tooth'd would yet be thought,
> When she a set of ivory teeth hath bought;
> Painted Lycoris to her self seems fair,
> Who only with a gypsie can compare,
> On like account, a poet thou art nam'd,
> And may'st, tho' bald, for youthful locks be fam'd.[5]

How bad, in this poem, is the false poet's theft? As bad, says Martial, as old women wearing dentures, or unattractive women wearing makeup, or bald men wearing wigs. As bad as that! Not, at least to a modern eye, in the same league with kidnapping, or even with theft. Both these poems certainly address a danger faced by anyone pursuing a poetic career, but the danger is represented as being built into the system, and Martial sees himself in every sense as part of the system – just as this most social of poets remains part of the society in which women use cosmetics and want nice-looking teeth, men wear wigs . . . and rich phonies pay ghost writers. (There is actually no 'theft' word in the epigram; the opening lines say literally 'Do you believe you'll be thought a poet with my verses?' – Martial has a lighter touch than Killigrew.) There are several other Martial epigrams on the subject, in all of which the tone strikes me more as ironic and cynical than as ethically fervid; the indignation is there, but it turns immediately to wit. It should be noted that the word *plagiarius*, from which all future uses of the term to apply to literary appropriation derive, appears in only one of them, i.52, where the purloined poems are conceived as Martial's slaves, whom he has freed by publishing them and whom the plagiarist is attempting to re-enslave. This is where the metaphor comes from, and it is represented as something being done to the poems, not to Martial.

The plagiarism in all this strikes me as curiously disembodied – curiously, when I consider how outraged I feel when a student does it, to say nothing of when it's done to my own work (as it once was, in an MLA paper, to my face – I emphatically did not feel like writing an amusing epigram). Consider this even more disembodied example in an epigram by Sir Thomas More entitled *Ad Gallum Sublegentem Veterum Carmina*, to a Frenchman stealing the poetry of the Ancients – the word used for the plagiarism here, *sublego*, is a straight theft word, carry off secretly (so there's no question about whether what More is objecting to constitutes criminal behaviour). Here's what it says:

> Frenchman, surely you in our time have the same wit and inspiration that ancient poets had, for you write the same poems, and frequently word for word.[6]

This is quite witty: is it really an attack on some anonymous Frenchman? Is the saintly More really contenting himself here with condemning the fault and not the actor of it? Or is this epigram perhaps a way of distinguishing himself as a poet from all the poetasters who shall remain nameless – perhaps even from that whole nation of poetasters across the Channel – the defining feature of poetasters being precisely that they have no wit of their own? The trouble is, however, that the defining feature of humanist poetry is precisely how closely and accurately it replicates the ancients; maybe this is not really a francophobic barb, but a sly joke about humanism itself, the thieving Frenchman as the *reductio ad absurdum* of the humanist ideal. Many of More's own epigrams are direct translations from the Greek Anthology; often this is made clear, but sometimes it is not. More surely would say that any properly educated humanist would recognize the poems as homage, not theft – but so, doubtless, would the Frenchman. Whatever plagiarism is here, it is not a danger – nobody's stealing from More, and the condemnation, despite the charge of theft, produces irony and wit, but not outrage.

None of this, I think, gets us anywhere near accounting for Sir Thomas Browne's extraordinary effusion on plagiarism, which I cited in the influential essay but didn't spend much time over, and which has continued to fascinate me. Something did change in the seventeenth century. In Chapter 6 of the *Pseudodoxia Epidemica*, Browne deplores 'a peremptory adhesion unto Authority, and more especially the establishing of our belief upon the dictates of Antiquity', which he calls 'the mortallest enemy unto knowledge, and that which hath done the greatest execution upon truth'. What is pernicious about this is not simply that it impedes the possibility of any sceptical empiricism of our own, but even more that there is nothing about classical writers that *entitles* them to be considered authoritative: their 'volumes are meer collections, drawn from the mouthes or leaves of other Authors', and here we come to the real point:

> Not a few transcriptively; subscribing their names unto other mens endeavours, and meerly transcribing almost all they have written. The Latines transcribing the Greeks, the Greeks and Latines each other.[7]

He then gives a compendious list of classical offenders, including many of the monuments of ancient literature, history and science: Pliny, Lucian, Apuleius, Aristotle, Aelian, Athenaeus 'and many more', he says. And then, hitting his stride,

> the wittiest piece of Ovid [the *Metamorphoses*] is beholding unto Parthenius Chius; even the magnified Virgil hath borrowed almost all his works: his Eclogues from Theocritus, his Georgicks from Hesiod and Aratus, his Aeneads from Homer; the second Book whereof containing the exploit of Sinon and the Trojan horse (as Macrobius observeth) he hath *verbatim* [note that *verbatim*] derived from Pisander. (p. 125)

Browne then moves on to the classics of his own profession, with ancient medical writers cribbing from Galen and from each other. Here is the moralization he draws from this catalogue of thievery:

Thus may we perceive the Ancients were but men, even like ourselves. The practice of transcription in our daies was no monster in theirs: Plagiarie had not its nativity with printing . . .

And lest we say that none of this is *really* plagiarism, since none of it involves the crucial intention to deceive, Browne blocks that exit too:

> Nor did they only make large use of other Authors, but often without mention of their names. *Aristotle*, who seems to have borrowed many things from *Hippocrates*, in the most favourable construction, makes mention but once of him, and that by the by, and without reference unto his present Doctrine. *Virgil*, so much beholding unto *Homer*, hath not his name in all his Works; and *Plinie*, who seems to borrow many Authors out of *Dioscorides*, hath taken no notice of him. I wish men were not still content to plume themselves with others feathers.

Browne does not even allow the distinction between plagiarism and allusion, or acknowledged borrowing, to be a real one:

> Fear of discovery, not single ingenuity [simple honesty] affords Quotations rather than Transcriptions . . . (p. 126)

The only reason people put things in quotes is not that they're honest, but that they're afraid of being found out. 'The ancients were but men, even like ourselves': everybody is guilty here – and one of Browne's modern editors remarks tartly, predictably, about this passage, 'his comments were not very original'.[8] Plagiarism is the original sin, the sin we're all guilty of. The only reason Homer isn't indicted is that Browne doesn't know whom he copied from. What Browne says is that the price of literature, the price of a written tradition, is plagiarism; without plagiarism there is no Homer, no Virgil, no Ovid, no Aristotle . . . This is not, obviously, being offered as an argument in favour of plagiarism, but it also isn't a claim, as it well might be, that plagiarism is a necessary evil, that the sin that makes us mortal also makes us human. Plagiarism is the symptom, not the disease: the attack on plagiarism becomes almost at once an attack on Virgil, Ovid, Aristotle. That is the disease: literature, culture, the classics, are precisely the problem. They are the stronghold of the pernicious adherence to authority, the enemy of experience and empirical science. Virgil imitated Homer because Homer was a classic, the poetry he cared most about, the centre of the canon; and that is what has to go – the canon, the tradition, the desire to preserve and renew the greatness of the past. I really don't think Ricks wants Sir Thomas Browne as an ally.

What I find fascinating here are the totalizing aspects of this passage, especially coming from someone as genuinely literary as Browne, whose writing is so deeply and obviously imbued with a rich and detailed sense of – love of – the literary tradition, and is the product of great learning and long and wide reading. The argument is undeniably perverse, and is not without its nonsensical side (how can Virgil's Latin be cribbed *verbatim* from Pisander's Greek?); but I find it nevertheless curiously compelling and moving. It indicates how much strain the scientific revolution – or more precisely, construing Baconian science as a revolution – put on the whole concept of culture. There is no way of arguing that Browne doesn't really mean what he says here, but his convictions run counter to his deepest beliefs, what he cares most about. The implied dialectic between science and culture is a striking expression of a particular moment of intellectual history, comparable to Milton's dialectic between his praise of, indeed identification with, Galileo, 'the Tuscan artist' – this is the only use of the word artist in Milton's poetry – and Raphael's rebuke to Adam for asking questions about astronomy.

I return now to Inigo Jones. Here is the story, rehearsed for the benefit of those who haven't read my influential article. In 1638 Jones and Sir William Davenant produced two masques for the court. The first, *Britannia Triumphans*, danced by the king in January, celebrated the imminent success of the royal scheme of Ship Money – the famous trial was about to reach its conclusion in the Star Chamber, with a narrow victory for the Crown. Three weeks later, at Shrovetide, the queen danced in *Luminalia*, Jones's most elaborate scenic spectacle up to that time. The complexity of the engineering was all the more impressive, Jones tells us in the published text of the masque, because it had to be devised very quickly:

> The King's majesty's masque being performed, the Queen commanded Inigo Jones . . . to make a new subject of a masque for herself, that with high and hearty invention might give occasion for variety of scenes, strange apparitions, songs, music, and dancing. . . . This being suddenly done and showed her majesty, and she approving it, the work was set in hand, and in all celerity performed in shorter time than anything here hath been done in this kind.

Modern scholarly opinion has been very hard on *Luminalia*, and Enid Welsford believed she had found the source of its poetic and dramatic deficiencies: 'in no other masque,' she writes, 'is the plagiarism so blatant and so extensive. *Luminalia* is in fact nothing else but a clumsy adaptation of Francesco Cini's *Notte d'Amore'* (this being a Florentine production of 1608).

Leaving aside the question of whether an adaptation from a foreign language, much less a clumsy one, can be considered an example of blatant plagiarism, clumsiness is not the only problem faced by the critic of *Luminalia*, because Jones's account of its sudden inception and hasty preparation, if it means what it seems to mean, cannot be true. Court correspondence in November and December 1637 reported that the queen was preparing a Shrovetide masque, so the project had been under way for many months. G. E. Bentley believed that this contradiction, like the production's structural flaws, could also be explained by invoking the concept of plagiarism:

> No doubt Jones was in a great fret, first getting his masquing hall finished, then cleaning it all away before he could set his men to work on the elaborate constructions for *Luminalia*, but he did not need to wait all this time to begin on the designs.... Perhaps his uneasiness about the plagiarism led him to magnify and advertise the pressure of time.

Bentley's explanation for the apparent conflict between Jones's account and the other evidence seems to run this way: Jones was sufficiently uncomfortable about the plagiarism to want to cover himself by pleading extenuating circumstances; and he did so by producing a lie which everybody who had been at court since November would have known to be a lie.

This strikes me as very implausible. We have no way of determining what really happened, but with the same information I can devise a more credible hypothesis. All that the court correspondence tells us is that in the autumn, the queen was planning a Shrovetide masque. It says nothing about what the subject was to be, how elaborate the spectacle was, how complex the engineering. But we know that the king's masque in January, *Britannia Triumphans*, was an exceedingly elaborate one, with multiple scene-changes and lots of machinery; it included visions of hell, the Palace of Fame, a sea-triumph of Galatea, the fleet in full sail. And Jones tells us that after the queen saw this masque, she commanded him 'to make a new subject of a masque for herself, that with high and hearty invention might give occasion for variety of scenes, strange apparitions', and so forth. This account suggests to me that the queen wanted just what Jones says she wanted: 'a new subject of a masque' – not the masque they had been planning, but a new and much more elaborate one that would compete in splendour with the masque Jones had devised for the king.

In this hypothesis, it will be seen that the question of plagiarism has become a red herring. In fact, I was and continue to be puzzled about where it came from, because what Welsford discovered behind *Luminalia* was not a smoking gun; it was simply a source. There are few Stuart masques, and indeed few Stuart plays, that are not similarly based on earlier examples of the genre. If *Luminalia* constitutes plagiarism, so does Shakespeare's use of old plays like *Hamlet*, old romances like *Romeus and Juliet*, old novels like *Rosalynde*. There is nothing in Welsford or Bentley attacking Shakespeare on such grounds, and I speculated that the charge of plagiarism was here doing service for something else – for all those other qualities of Jones's that displease the modern critic but somehow don't seem sufficiently actionable: preferring spectacle to poetry, disliking Ben Jonson enough to get him fired. (Bentley actually doesn't like Jonson's interest in the masque much either, and finds the form on the whole trivial and immoral. Declaring a masque plagiarized is a good way of removing it from serious consideration.)

Ricks doesn't contest my analysis of this material, and I imagine he doesn't disagree with it. My interests in the subject, however, are really the opposite of his. Ricks finds a general tendency nowadays to excuse or overlook or argue away plagiarism; I am concerned with a general tendency in modern scholarship to invoke it as a universal explanation. Here are a couple of other examples, which are also cited in my original article. Don Cameron Allen discovered a particularly flagrant example of plagiarism in that indispensable classic of Elizabethan literary criticism, Meres' *Palladis Tamia*. Allen demonstrated that the book was a pure pastiche and that its material derived, moreover, not even from classic or obscure sources, but from absolutely standard Renaissance compilations of the sort that were used as school texts. This established, for Allen, the meretricious worthlessness of the book, and became the basis of an attack not only on the ignorance of modern critics, who take Meres seriously, but on the whole Renaissance educational system which, grounded as it was exclusively in the practice of imitation, fitted a student like Meres (and, it presumably follows, like Jonson or Shakespeare) precisely for nothing better than plagiarism.

Here, the facts seemed to me incontrovertible, but the conclusions did not follow. What did the Renaissance reader see in this blatant rehash? If Meres' material was cribbed from standard schoolbooks, wer-

en't contemporary readers aware that they'd heard it all before? Why
was the book popular? It went through three editions, the last as late as
1636, and it was only one of a great many such compilations in the
period. Were Renaissance readers simply being deceived? Or did they
find in the book precisely the force of the *commonplace*, a term that
suggests to us a thing not worth saying, but implied to the Renaissance
a universal truth? The volume's full title is *Palladis Tamia, or Wit's
Treasury*. Did anyone buying a book called *Wit's Treasury* think he was
paying for originality?

The commonplace book, indeed, was a commonplace undertaking in
Renaissance culture, and everyone understood its conventions. Jonson's
Timber, or Discoveries was his commonplace book, duly published in the
second volume of the 1640 folio among his works. There are original
thoughts in this miscellaneous compilation, but Jonson mingles his
own ideas with a good deal of continental wisdom, to which his only
contribution is a translation into English. There is rarely any indication
of the source of the quotations, and therefore no way of knowing,
without a good deal of detective work, what is original with Jonson
and what comes from the great *copia* outside his head. I doubt that the
question of deception is relevant here, any more than it is with Meres; it
is clear that this is a commonplace book. What is striking and significant
for us is surely that Jonson apparently did not want, or require, a record
of where his wisdom came from.

I observed in the essay that modern critics are usually willing to allow
Renaissance authors their sources provided they are sufficiently classical. If *Luminalia* had been based on Ovid, rather than on Francesco
Cini, Welsford and Bentley probably wouldn't have felt they had a case.
Even with classical sources, however, the idea of intermediate texts
disturbs us. Allen has it in for *Palladis Tamia* not because it's a pastiche
of classical passages, but because Meres didn't go to original texts. He
used contemporary handbooks and anthologies, and Allen therefore
believed that his intention was to deceive the reader into thinking he
was a scholar. E. W. Talbert used the same line of argument to level a
charge of plagiarism against Ben Jonson. Talbert discovered that Jonson's learned citations are often copied from Renaissance dictionaries
and encyclopedias; Jonson's learning, Talbert felt, was thereby
impugned. On this basis he accused the poet of lying when he claims,
in the dedicatory epistle to *The Masque of Queens*, that he wrote the work
'out of the fullness and memory of my former readings'. But (I am
quoting myself; the point still seems to me valid) every age has its
reference books, and a more scrupulous generation than ours may

criticize us for failing to acknowledge our use of bibliographies and periodical indexes – to say nothing of the Internet – as if we were thereby pretending to carry all the relevant scholarship in our heads. I find these examples more offensive than amusing, and what offends me in them is the way invoking plagiarism enables these scholars to condescend to their material – indeed, D. C. Allen's characteristic attitude towards much of the work he spent his life editing and elucidating was one of amused condescension. Talbert's charges seem to me particularly offensive, impugning not only Jonson's ethics, but his learning. Literally hundreds of volumes of the classics survive from Jonson's library, many with copious marginalia in his hand. It is simply preposterous to claim that Jonson wasn't familiar with the texts he cites because he sometimes cites them from secondary sources. As a poet who habitually lived beyond his income, he was always selling off books and buying new ones as he could afford them, and he used whatever texts were conveniently available. The fact that Talbert was eventually forced by Percy Simpson to back down seems to me only to reveal how clear the case is. Invoking plagiarism was the first, automatic response, the one that came without thinking.

Talbert's charge against Jonson was in fact, as I pointed out, anticipated 250 years earlier by Aphra Behn. For Behn, it formed part of an invidious comparison between Jonson and Shakespeare, the invidious point being that since the uneducated Shakespeare wrote better plays than the learned Jonson, and since the only intellectual advantage men have over women derives from their education, there was no reason why women should not be as good playwrights as Shakespeare, and better than Jonson. But the trouble with Jonson goes deeper than his erudition: Behn goes on to argue – a little self-contradictorily – that Jonson wasn't even all that learned,

> for I am informed his learning was but grammar high (sufficient indeed to rob poor Sallust of his best orations)...

Jonson clearly has to be disposed of, not simply demoted; but as a way of disposing of him, this is a very odd example. The Sallust quotations are used by Jonson in *Catiline*. They are Catiline's speeches and Jonson includes them because, according to Sallust, they are what Catiline actually said. To accuse Jonson of plagiarizing from Sallust makes about as much sense as accusing Sallust of plagiarizing from Catiline.

Idiotic as Aphra Behn's plagiarism claim certainly is, it isn't merely idiotic: there is an agenda behind it. The agenda is largely self-serving, concerned with establishing her own credentials, and thereby those of any woman, as a playwright, but Behn is completely open about that; moreover, she is clearly having a good time. There is also an agenda behind Welsford, Bentley, Allen, and Talbert, but it is unacknowledged. It has to do with the kind of control modern scholarship has wanted to exercise, the kind of moral superiority we have wanted to assert, over the material we work on; with our general attitude toward the past; and ultimately with the kind of attitude toward literature and culture that we have wanted to inculcate in our students. It treats the past as a childish or recalcitrant or incomplete version of ourselves; it fails to acknowledge the ways in which Renaissance societies were genuinely different from ours and their terms significantly untranslatable – requiring us, that is, not to 'modernize', but to learn their language. In this agenda, charges of lying and bad faith become simply a routine way of disposing of whatever we do not like or understand. Most of all, it ignores or suppresses any cultural differences that might call our own standards into question, and resists any contemplation of the standards and assumptions from which we regard the past. It is an agenda that I would call 'weakly, wizenedly, political'. As to whether current academic moral standards really represent a decline from this ethical eminence I hesitate to say. But certainly if the history of our response to plagiarism constitutes an ethical barometer, it is several centuries since we had anything to be proud of.

5
Forgery, Plagiarism, Imitation, Pegleggery

Nick Groom

> As Apothecaries we make new mixtures every day, pour out of one vessel into another.
>
> Robert Burton, *The Anatomy of Melancholy*

> Shall we for ever make new books, as apothecaries make new mixtures, by pouring only out of one vessel into another?
>
> Laurence Sterne, *Tristram Shandy*

I

Plagiarism is a metaphor, and not a particularly good metaphor at that. A plagiary, from the Latin *plagiarius* (first used by the poet Martial), is one who forcefully possesses another.[1] Plagiaries abduct slaves and steal children, disfiguring them to pass them off as their own; plagiaries are man-stealers and press gangsters; plagiaries are kidnappers, seducers and, of course, literary thieves – stealing bodies and brains. So they are like writers who have fatally misunderstood the nature of inspiration and become possessed not wisely but too well. Plagiarists can be uncanny creatures, then: in 1711, John Dennis called a plagiary 'a sort of spiritual Outlaw' and in 1751 Richard Hurd described them as 'those base and abject spirits, who have not the courage or ability to attempt any thing of themselves, and can barely make a shift, as a great poet of our own expresses it, *to creep servilely after the sense of some other*'.[2] This moves us on from Martial. *Plagiarius* derives from *plagium*, a net to entangle game, and so plagiarism could conversely be imagined as a snare, a trap for an unwary writer, rather than as theft and kidnapping.

74

The word has other ramifications too – some of which will be discussed below – but these are little considered today: plagiarism excites because on the one hand, it can be historicized in arguments about the construction of authorship and literary property, and yet on the other, needs to be policed with zero tolerance – establishing stringent controls against student cheating. The most germane example here is of course Christopher Ricks, who in his 1998 British Academy lecture (reprinted pp. 21–40 in this volume) vehemently responds to what he perceives to be the dangerous trend of historicizing plagiarism, thereby making it a relative rather than an absolute transgression. For Ricks, the definition of plagiarism is clear-cut: it is fundamentally dishonest and therefore immoral, and condemnation applies equally and universally from antique writers to contemporary students. It is the difficulty of establishing the certainty of particular examples of plagiarism that has (illogically, Ricks thinks) created the grounds for culturally relativist positions proposing that plagiarism is an historically contingent practice, rather than simply, universally wrong. These new, fallacious positions then allow the possibility that in some instances plagiarism might be in some way excused.

Ricks recognizes that the expectations of the word plagiarism distort its meaning, yet he refuses to entertain any more nuanced understanding, and is a bit too handy with Ockham's Razor. He highlights 'wrongful' from the *OED* definition, and 'intent to deceive' from Peter Shaw's article 'Plagiary', and this gives him an essentially certain, unambiguous and ethically rooted meaning of the word. For Ricks, 'The morality of the matter, which asks of us that we be against deceit and dishonesty, is clear, and is clearly defined.'[3] Surely in literature, things are never so clear. But Ricks's confidence in the clarity of the question comes here from the first – but by no means the last – appearance in his text of the word 'dishonesty'. Dishonesty is never far away – in one short paragraph, for example, ticcing three times in three lines. And as such, this crotchet persistently distracts Ricks from making more sense of plagiarism: 'plagiarism being dishonest', 'Plagiarism is a dishonesty', 'plagiarists ... are dishonest', and so on.[4] It is no analysis at all.

This sort of morality is also unhelpful because it places the word in a straitjacket in an inflexible and somewhat elementary fashion; it presupposes too much, too quickly. It is like Plato exiling the poets because 'poetry has no serious value or claim to truth' – although at least he does that only after a couple of hundred pages of *The Republic*.[5] One could in any case argue, with an impressive battery of illustration, that literature is already a form of dishonesty – if only to provoke a clarification of

what is really meant by fictions and lies. But Ricks declines the opportunity to think about what constitutes poetry and fiction, and would
rather condemn plagiarism first on moral, and then on legal grounds: 'It
is a natural move to infringement of copyright when thinking of plagiarism.' Actually, this is an easy rather than a natural move, because it
takes us away from the aesthetic towards those very legal codes of law
and order and the regulation of literature – structures of power – of
which Ricks is elsewhere rightly suspicious. The law, despite condoning
the moral condemnation of plagiarism, is a mare's nest here. How many
writers have been hanged, or whipped, or imprisoned, or fined, or
sentenced to hours of community service for plagiarism? Not enough,
presumably.

Plagiarism is not even a civil offence – such suits tend to be settled out
of court or pursued under breach of confidence or defamation of character laws, moreover, plaintiffs are discouraged from instigating even
these. Copyright legislation, when it came in the eighteenth century,
defined the relationship between an author, his or her work, and a
bookseller (publisher); it was used to settle author–bookseller and bookseller–bookseller disputes, mainly against pirate printers.[6] In any case, as
Brean Hammond indicates, 'To prove breach of copyright ... no conscious intention need be established.'[7] So even the commonplace assumption that wrongful copying is a consciously criminal act is not fully
endorsed at law. Copyright infringement, intellectual property rights,
libel, book piracy – proper crimes lurk in the wings when plagiarism is
on stage because they are replete with legal authority. Plagiarism has no
such status: it is a literary term, and so it is always being supplanted by
the certainties of these other, bullish and inappropriate words. In a
sense, plagiarism is itself always being stolen away – plagiarized – from
the very world in which it usefully exists.

Nevertheless, it has been around for a long time. It is tempting to
argue with 'constructivist' critics like Martha Woodmansee and Peter
Jaszi that plagiarism rose as printing technologies became more widespread, as an ideological consequence of the mass availability of texts
and the relative ease of theft.[8] Indeed, its first English usages are at the
end of the sixteenth century, but as a concept it is much older and more
fraught than that.[9] Sir Thomas Browne remarked darkly that plagiarism
has a long criminal record: the charge was so frequently made by
authors in ancient Greece that the investigation of plagiarism was a
prominent feature of Alexandrine scholarship. The *OCD* notes that
Aristophanes, Isocrates, and Democritus, for example, accused others
of ὑφηρῆσθαι ('filching'), that Plato took the concept of the *Republic*

from Protagoras, and that to avoid accusations of plagiarism, dramatists like Plautus and Terence acknowledged their sources in prologues. Anthony Grafton describes Porphyry's account of a dinner party that degenerates into gossip about plagiarism.[10] But the most influential ancient use of the concept is, of course, Horace's version of Aesop's fable of borrowed plumage: the crow who disguises himself with peacock's feathers. The image was deployed repeatedly in English literary criticism: by Robert Greene against Shakespeare, by Browne, and by William Wordsworth against Thomas Gray.

The severity of the accusation indicates an anxiety of originality becoming an obsession, with the concomitant fears that the sacred well of individual genius can be poisoned or simply drawn dry by intruders. Plagiarism is therefore a fear, a panic, a plague – and a lethal threat to an order of knowledge. And like other aspects of social abnormality, such as illness, madness and death, it is imagined as a despotic signifier – contagious, sickening, unnatural and terminal; to be guarded against only by the utmost vigilant surveillance. William Hazlitt declared that plagiarism was a terminal condition: 'If an author is once detected in borrowing, he will be suspected of plagiarism ever after', and Ricks himself at one point calls plagiarists 'sick'.[11]

But Samuel Johnson's definition of plagiarism is surprisingly mild: 'Theft; literary *adoption* of the thoughts or works of another' (my emphasis). It was, perhaps, a trap he was in frequent danger of falling into himself: first with his *Dictionary of the English Language* (1755–56), and second, with his compendious variorum edition of Shakespeare (1765), which reprinted the commentaries of previous editors. Lexicographers (and editors too) are indeed plagiarists of a certain kidney: neither definitions nor illustrative quotations are invented for the occasion, but are meticulously gleaned from earlier scholars and writers.[12] It is a form of collaboration with the dead, a genealogical project. Hence Johnson's charitable assessment of plagiarism in *Rambler* 143, in which he decides that a preponderance of parallel images is the only proof of the charge, and that chance is always a sure defence.[13]

Yet notwithstanding all this, in 1766 Johnson was accused by John Bowle of precisely the offence. 'Dictionary' Johnson, author of the homiletic *Rambler* papers and now editor of Shakespeare,

> seems to have made it his study to cull out others['] sentiments, and to place them in his works as from his own mint. This surely is an odd species of improvement from reading, and savours very little of Invention or Genius; It borders nearly upon, if it is not really plagiarism.[14]

The suggestion that even one's sentiments can be commodified as a form of artistic property or unminted aesthetic feeling is a typical example of the ridiculous and over-interpretative zeal that often accompanies rallies against plagiarism, real or imagined.

There are better ways to tackle the problem. Laurence Sterne, for example, was rather more subtle in his vivaciously crack-brained novel *Tristram Shandy* (1760–8), an anti-Johnsonian gallimaufry of whimsy and self-begetting curiosity. Sterne too was attacked for plagiarism, in particular from Robert Burton's *Anatomy of Melancholy* (1621–51): plagiarizing, it transpires, Burton's own remarks on plagiarism – and so Sterne succeeds in squaring the circle of plagiarism and inverting the whole problem into a delightful paradox.

Sterne uses plagiarism creatively (literary honesty and dishonesty being irrelevant principles here), and for most of the eighteenth century the different modes of copying – from mimesis and imitation to parody and satirical pastiche – were the prevalent modes of composition, particularly in poetry. There were certainly attempts to distinguish mimesis from plagiarism, and indeed both are discussed by Longinus in *On the Sublime* – a late classical and often half-mystical treatise which, through Pope, Addison and Burke, had a considerable influence on eighteenth-century and Romantic literary composition and criticism. Longinus argues that mimesis (the imitation of other writers) is one of the characteristics of noesis, or the instinctive intellectual conception of the artist, and is therefore a way of approaching the sublime. It is a conscious – and inspirational – participation in a recognized tradition of expression: 'Nor is such Proceeding to be look'd upon as Plagiarism, but in Methods consistent with the nicest Honour, an Imitation of the finest pieces, or copying out those bright Originals.'[15] In effect, the artist's genius is announced in the ability to copy well.

Under the influence of Longinus and also Horace, literary theories of the eighteenth century tended to seek authority rather than originality, and Johnson defines imitation as 'a method of translating looser than paraphrase'. Imitation was an idealistic activity, whereas creative fabrication was somehow dangerous, and for a poet like Alexander Pope, imitation was the very key to poetic composition. He imitated everyone and everything: Horace, Homer and Virgil; Chaucer, Spenser and Shakespeare; and Waller, Cowley and dozens of others in passing. One way of understanding this is to argue that Pope was engaged in continual and enriching dialogues with earlier poets. But the very range of 'allusion' has proved troubling to Pope's readers, and if plagiarism and piracy could land a writer in the pillories of *The Dunciad* and a bookseller in court, where does the clear distinction with allusion or imitation lie?[16] What qualifies as an echo, an allusion, a borrowing, a copy, a steal, a plagiarism...? Can we account for Pope's recycling of the works of others without reconsidering the idea of plagiarism (or perhaps proposing Pope as a pioneering eco-poet, recycling rubbish writing)? Do we excuse Pope's sophisticated mischief by claiming that the cultural context of Augustan satire differs from (by which we really mean 'is inferior to') later Romantic confession? Shakespeare, of course, lifted plots and passages from Chapman's *Homer*, North's *Plutarch*, Golding's *Ovid*, Holinshed's *Chronicles* and a host of other sources. John Wilmot, Earl of Rochester composed a cynical carnal love song virtually entirely from lines taken from three of Francis Quarles's devotional 'Emblemes'. In music, J. S. Bach's *Goldberg Variations* conclude with a *quodlibet* of two popular songs of the time, 'Long Have I Been Away from Thee' and 'Cabbage and Turnips'. Is this plagiarism, or is there a cultural law operating here that permits some transformative use of pre-existent elements? Samuel Taylor Coleridge was a notorious 'borrower' in his lectures on Shakespeare, in his *Biographia Literaria* and in many places elsewhere, but it was only after his death that Thomas De Quincey 'exposed' him as a plagiarist and inaugurated a minor school of misreading, but it can be argued in defence of the Sage of Highgate that (in line with Pope and Sterne) he was perhaps imitating, decanting, twisting and parodying the language of German metaphysicians: recasting their old words in new, heretical ways.

One way of categorizing the terms was to consider the economic implications of appropriation. Henry Fielding, for instance, distinguishes between Ancient and Modern borrowing in just this way when he defends himself against plagiarism in *Tom Jones*. He describes the Ancients as common ground where all may graze, but to steal from a living author is 'highly criminal and indecent; for this may be strictly stiled defrauding the poor (sometimes perhaps those who are poorer than ourselves)'.[17] The work of the Ancients was common property – gold ore ready to be freshly minted – and therefore in contrast to the rights of Modern authors and publishers. Brean Hammond notes that by the end of the seventeenth century, 'Plagiarism begins to be perceived as a species of moral crime against authorship because it threatens literary livelihoods.'[18]

Hence it was in 1751 that Richard Hurd attempted a comprehensive and contemporary defence of indebtedness in a 'Discourse concerning Poetical Imitation', appended to his edition of Horace. Hurd proposed that the critical term 'invention' be defined precisely as the philosophical term 'imitation', and that 'The *objects* of imitation, like the *materials* of human knowledge, are a common stock'.[19] Six years later he had another go, giving examples of rules for the discovery of imitation – and in doing so finding many more instances of borrowing than he appears comfortable with. Roger Lonsdale suggests that Hurd is 'baffled' by the extent of his discoveries, and consequently somewhat crestfallen at the poverty of the English tradition.[20] Like Gerard Langbaine, who also endeavoured to distinguish between classical imitation and modern literary theft, he is compelled to propose a category of 'learned *Allusion*' – in which thankfully 'even *Shakespear* himself abounds'.[21]

Yet despite Hurd's forlorn rearguard, it was only two years before Edward Young famously routed imitation by defining it as mere duplication. The rise of commodity culture was encouraging the 'imitation' to be contrasted to the genuine or authentic, as in the composition of manufacture of luxury goods, and indeed in the composition of fiction: 'Simulative, fictitious, counterfeit', as the *OED* has it. Young decried imitations as 'a sort of *Manufacture* wrought up by those *Mechanics*, *Art*, and *Labour*, out of pre-existent materials not their own',[22] and William Cowper complained that 'Imitation even of the best models, is my aversion; it is servile and mechanical'.[23] By 1768, Gray was sufficiently concerned to acknowledge his sources, yet he was still subsequently accused of plagiarism.

From this point, definitions of 'imitation' gradually collapse, moving from 'after the manner of', to 'copy', and thence to 'mimic', 'counterfeit', and 'ape' (*OED*). The word was eventually overtaken by meanings of falsehood rather than of truth. According to Bernard Dupriez's *Dictionary of Literary Devices*, 'Pressed too far, imitation turns into *plagiarism*' (again, plagiarism is determined to be a trap), although he provides a disingenuous escape through literary theory. Some so-called examples of plagiarism surpass their sources: 'In such a case,' Dupriez blithely declares, 'one speaks of intertextuality to avoid the pejorative connotations that would be out of place.'[24] Intertextuality does not, however, merit its own entry in his dictionary, and so we shall return to the eighteenth century and unpick another thread.

II

In 1747, William Lauder (a Jacobite who had managed to lose a leg on a golf course) began publishing articles in the *Gentleman's Magazine*, articles that were collected in 1750 as *An Essay on Milton's Use and Imitation of the Moderns, in his Paradise Lost*. Lauder argued that Milton had plagiarized from modern poets when writing *Paradise Lost*, the case being made by lengthy quotation of passages from mid-seventeenth-century Latin poems by the likes of Jacobus Masenius and Hugo Grotius. But these proofs were doctored. Lauder in fact took lines from a 1690 Latin translation of *Paradise Lost* and then interpolated them into the extracts of Masenius and Grotius he reproduced.[25]

Although the forged plagiarisms – and Lauder with them – were soon exposed, the case is appealing because it is a cat's cradle of forgery and plagiarism, imitation and translation: Lauder forges Latin poems by plagiarizing lines from the later Latin *Paradise Lost* and attributing them to earlier poets, in order to prove that Milton was, in translation, imitating to the extent of plagiarism. But it is Lauder himself who is then declared to be a forger – a word with heinous criminal undertones. Lady Anson, for instance, wrote an intemperate letter against him, in which she declared:

> I want to devise some grievous punishment for Lauder, for surely it is hard that the Laws should not reach so atrocious a crime. Caligula's decree about bad Authors is this minute come into my head, & I think the making him lick out all his lies and Forgeries would be no severe, & a proper kind of penalty for him.[26]

Of course, there is no way of dealing with him: plagiarism, forgery – these may be, as Susan Stewart suggests, 'crimes of writing', but they are not indictable offences. No one is going to prison, no one will die, but Lady Anson wants Lauder to pay some sort of grotesque forfeit for telling scandalous lies about Milton and therefore for being a bad writer – meaning bad as in wicked, rather than bad as in weak.

Not everyone agreed, however. On 23 December 1749, William Warburton wrote to Richard Hurd:

> I have just read the most silly and knavish book I ever saw; one *Lauder*, on Milton's Imitations.... I think he has produced about half a dozen particular thoughts that look like imitations – but the matter of *Imitation* is a thing very little understood. However, in one view the book does not displease me. It is likely enough to mortify all the silly adorers of Milton, who deserve to be laughed at.[27]

Warburton favours the word imitation over that of plagiarism – imitation being an accepted literary technique. But Milton was considered a poet of particular and characteristic originality, whose declared achievement was to realize 'Things unattempted yet in prose or rhyme', and even slender evidence that he imitated, let alone any imputation he plagiarized, could do terrible harm to his reputation (although perhaps the most calamitous possibility was that *Paradise Lost* might be revealed to have been written by *'Germans* and *Dutchmen'*).[28] Samuel Johnson, in his eventual and begrudging 'Life of Milton' (1779), noted that

> Invention is almost the only literary labour which blindness cannot obstruct, and therefore he naturally solaced his solitude by the indulgence of his fancy and the melody of his numbers.... He would have wanted little help from books, had he retained the power of perusing them.[29]

One single writer of such originality was, however, more than enough, and Johnson concluded that Milton is 'to be admired rather than imitated'.[30]

Thirty years earlier, the same Samuel Johnson had written the Preface to Lauder's *Essay on Milton's Use and Imitation of the Moderns*. This was a partisan attack, which presented Milton's alleged imitation as plagiarism. Johnson praised Lauder's book for demonstrating 'from what stores materials were collected, whether its founder dug them from the quarries of nature, or demolished other buildings to embellish his own'.[31] Lauder rather disingenuously claimed in his early articles, in a sentence that pinpoints where imitation slips into plagiarism, that this was not really an attack on Milton: 'I no way intend to derogate from the glory or merit of that noble poet, who certainly is intitled to the highest praise, for raising so beautiful a structure, even granting all the materials were borrowed...'.[32] Instead, he declared he was tracing the 'original' of *Paradise Lost* (first published in 1667). Lauder, for example, claims he had found the following lines in a piece written by Masenius in 1650:

> Principium culpæ, stygiæque tyrannidis ortum,
> Et quæ sera pramunt miserandos fata nepotes,
> Servitio turpi scelerum, poenaque malorum
> Pandimus.

Milton had merely to translate them into:

> Of man's first disobedience, and the fruit
> Of that forbidden tree, whose mortal taste
> Brought death into the world, and all our woe.

But such 'proofs' provoked an indignant and sceptical correspondence in the *Gentleman's Magazine*. 'Miltonicus', for example, inquired: 'what does this gentleman mean by *imitation*?' (answer: plagiarism). He went on to argue that Lauder's examples 'I should call *transcribing*, or, if in a different language, *translating*, but hardly *imitating*'[33] – and if not imitating, certainly not plagiarizing. 'Miltonicus' gamely retranslated the passage supposedly from Masenius to read:

> The rise of evil, source of hellish pow'r,
> The fatal woes, which all the wretched race
> Of men oppress with slavery base to sin,
> And punishment of crimes...[34]

Clearly it is not just imitation but also translation that is here being compounded by plagiarism. Moreover, Lauder himself was also, albeit fraudulently, mimicking the rigorous historicism and source-hunting of a scholar like Richard Bentley, the arch-modernist, in the intellectual debate over classical learning between the Ancients and the Moderns. Bentley's relentless empirical logic had been extraordinarily effective in exposing as forgeries canonical classical texts such as the *Epistles of Phalaris*, but his approach was considerably less effective on Modern writers, and unfortunately generated a fantastically misguided edition of *Paradise Lost* (1732) with the thesis that Milton's amanuensis and printer had miscast the poet's lines, made unsubstantiated revisions and even interpolated their own work into the poem: it was up to Richard Bentley to mend the verse.

Lauder's new genealogy for *Paradise Lost* is then, like Bentley's and various 'parallelist' editions, a template to trace the paternity of every poetic allusion in a vast family tree of the genesis of Miltonic genius. Lauder, however, proposes that plagiarism is fatal to the myth of Milton's originality. Yet once the accusation of plagiarism is shown to be false, Lauder's work runs counter to itself, effectively arguing that Milton is now super-original, utterly without precedents.

This is partly because of the self-defeating logic in mixing forgery with plagiarism: they are mutually exclusive 'crimes of writing'.[35] Forgeries are profoundly contextual and carry with them stories of provenance, secrecy, discovery and transmission – all of which endorse the significance of a source. Plagiarism, on the other hand, proposes a forged narrative of originality, which replaces a tale of discovery and transmission with an independent narrative of creation: a moment of originality that assumes the reader's ignorance of the specific source, which is the thing being plagiarized. In other words, Lauder was projecting a readership of Miltonists erudite enough to know certain arcane things about seventeenth-century Latin verse, but to be entirely ignorant of others; to accept the existence of sources pre-dating the poem, but not to continue the source-hunting and discover that these same sources actually postdated the poem.

Despite this contradiction, forgeries are often constructed out of plagiarized fragments – effectively deploying a tactic, plagiarism, that deconstructs their narratives of verification. Why is this? Well, it could be argued that both plagiarism and forgery are a reminder that art is part of the cultural practice of capitalism, and they could both be described as strategies for the negation of art as a commodity – plagiarism, for instance, subverts the work ethic that value is defined by the expenditure of labour and capital in production.

Such a conclusion would incline towards the historical materialism of 'constructivist' critics. The plagiarized text is clearly designed to function under the same cultural laws of authenticity and composition as non-plagiarized texts – which is precisely why it is potentially so subversive. Plagiarism is in this account a perversion of Romantic notions of origin: it is a narrative of discovery that seeks to disguise its origins and present itself without precedent; in fact, it seeks to obliterate its origins entirely by moving them forward to the here and now. Once it takes hold, it is treated like a virus that debilitates culture, a crash that can bankrupt cultural value, and it thrives in the mechanisms of cultural dissemination and reproduction: paper and pen, or printed book.

Plagiarism, once perceived as this sort of demolition job on serious culture, becomes enticing for Lauder's cultural heirs: 'art terrorists' intent on overthrowing the 'society of the spectacle'. Stewart Home, for example, claims that:

> Plagiarism is the negative point of a culture that finds its ideological justification in the 'unique'. Indeed, it is only through the creation of unique identities that commodification can take place.... The plagiarist ... recognises the role the media plays [*sic*] in masking the mechanisms of Power, and actively seeks to disrupt this function.[36]

Indeed, in the notes to the Festival of Plagiarism which ran in London, Glasgow, Berlin and San Francisco in 1988, Home and others proposed an aesthetics of crime, arguing that plagiarists should plagiarize blatantly, without attempting to conceal their 'art', and in doing so would re-evaluate social change as an antidote to postmodernism. As

Hillel Schwartz puts it, 'plagiarism must be a thoughtful assault upon privilege, retaking that which should belong to everyone'.[37]

As implied by his use – and acknowledgement – of Lautréamont's aphorism 'Plagiarism is necessary. Progress implies it', and also by arguing that plagiarism can disrupt the operations of the media, Home is clearly reviving plagiarism as a Situationist stratagem. But he also has to admit that plagiarism relies on the very ideas of originality and the ensuing commodification of the art object that came under attack during the Festival of Plagiarism. 'While we refute the concept of "originality",' he declares in a non-answer to the most pressing implication of his work, 'we do not find it problematic that the idea of plagiarism implies an original'.[38] He does not find this a problem because he does not think that plagiarism need remain in disguise – yet surely plagiarism is first (and by definition) a covert activity. If a plagiarist cheerfully admits to plagiarizing, the act stops being plagiarism and becomes something else entirely, like Home's eventual brand of Situationism, or 'postmodernist' patching, or, more specifically, the 'Appropriation Art' of Sherri Levine in the visual arts and Kathy Acker in literature, and in contemporary music the 'plunderphonics' of collectives like Negativland.

Such assumptions and admissions of borrowing were already woven deep into the literary discourse long before T. S. Eliot exhorted mature poets to 'steal'. In the eighteenth century, the relationship between literary activities such as imitation, quotation, academic citation, allusion and plagiarism was, as we have seen, both delicate and precarious. Every approach to this aesthetic complex is riddled with pitfalls, but Lauder's antics are clearly worth attending to because they posed questions of pressing relevance to his contemporaries, and are still compelling today. Certainly, the case highlights the confusion in the eighteenth century between forgery and plagiarism, and also the slightly more rarefied muddle into which literary techniques such as imitation and allusion eventually disappeared, but importantly the case continues to arrest attention today because of a Pavlovian (that is, a learnt) aversion to plagiarism. In particular, it focuses on the old canard of artistic intention – which in this case would become identified as the 'malice aforethought' of the plagiarist. But theories of intention travel with far too much legal baggage to be able to come very close to a helpful analysis of plagiarism, and literature is not a courtroom in which to prosecute, cross-examine and sentence.

Still, without being either morally absolutist or historically relativist, the Lauder affair can help us to think more obliquely (and more soberly) about contemporary literary issues. For example, his attack on Milton could be seen as a sort of future-retrospection of origin, a making of history, or to put it another way (Jacques Derrida's way in *Monolingualism of the Other*), Lauder attempted to produce the truth of what never happened simply by avowing it:

> to translate the memory of what, precisely, did not take place, of what, having been (the) forbidden, ought, nevertheless, to have left a trace, a specter, the phantomatic body, the phantom-member – palpable, painful, but hardly legible – of traces, marks, and scars.[39]

It is Derrida's passing reference here to 'the phantom-member' that suggests the 'pegleggery' of Lauder's work.

William Lauder contributed significantly to the typology of the eighteenth-century literary forger, and he was eventually canonized in the doggerel verse, 'Four forgers in one prolific age', in which Lauder, James Macpherson, Thomas Chatterton and William Henry Ireland constitute a sort of forgers' dynasty. It is worth recognizing that such pedigrees of tricksters can be traced back to the earliest stories, and that from Hermes to Loki, from Afro-American myth to Keyser Soze in the film *The Usual Suspects*, the practical joker or liar or forger limps between different worlds: they negotiate through trickery and marginality, in the twilight of dogma. There is an uncanny ghostliness in plagiarism: from the metaphor of phantom-limb syndrome to Joseph Addison's notion that the biographer is haunted (that the dead revisit the living). Lauder was a sort of hopalong biographer, kidnapping – plagiarizing – the life of Milton in order to disfigure it.

Plagiarism can be considered, then, as a textual prosthesis, a false limb that both conceals and reveals a lack; a false, phallic pegleg that is there, haunted by the ghost of the body part that is not there. Indeed, Lauder's imprint on Milton is not unlike that of the single, inexplicable footprint on the beach in the epic of prostheses, *Robinson Crusoe*: a devastatingly uncanny impression that both affirms and denies the Crusoe-centric world. But Lauder was not only adding to and taking away from Milton's life and work, he was also stealing Milton's own tactics. He later argued that Charles I's plagiarism of Sir Philip Sidney in *Eikon Basilike* had been forged by Milton in an attempt to discredit the king. Lauder himself described this as 'a master-piece of fraud and forgery', and three decades later Johnson irresponsibly repeated the libel in his 'Life of Milton'.[40] So, in other words, Lauder was merely replicating Milton's own first disobedience, and he implies that Miltonists don't have a leg to stand on if they accuse him of knobbling *Paradise Lost* by adding false feet to the poet.

III

The Lauder case is mesmeric, extremely suggestive in indicating a poetics of plagiarism, and rather than reduce this complexity to a black-and-white legal morality, I have set hares running – not to evade a definition, but to trace its contours. Indeed, this happy difficulty in defining plagiarism in part accounts for William Warburton's satisfied remark about the trouble Lauder was stirring up, quoted above and worth requoting: 'in one view the book does not displease me. It is likely enough to mortify all the silly adorers of Milton, who deserve to be laughed at.' Warburton recognizes that a 'silly' book about plagiarism can, for 'silly' readers, have a necrotizing effect on a writer's work, because it encourages all sorts of non-literary forms of criticism to be exercised upon a text. In this respect, Christopher Ricks's denunciation of plagiarism as a moral disgrace is entirely typical of such condemnations. His attempts to clarify plagiarism in ultra-dogmatic flourishes are made possible because he sets up the word to carry too much, and then relishes its inevitable collapse.

This is the problem with writing quasi-legal statements on undergraduate plagiarism – an area that could be entirely dismissed from the discussion if it did not have such grievous consequences in the endless claims and counter-claims bandied about regarding the reception of all sorts of literary texts. What we are really talking about in university cases is students cheating, and we should call it precisely that, *cheating*, not plagiarism – with all its rich and subtle variations and insinuations. A student submitting fraudulent term papers is not at all like a writer plagiarizing phrases or sentences, poems or stories. The student is being asked to perform a series of intellectual exercises to particular standards of critical and scholarly rigour, policed by published codes of academic conduct, in which plagiarism (so called) is a specifically named, defined and condemned offence. It is clear within this context what is right and what is wrong. And a workable university policy on cheating is certainly essential to the academic teaching of literature (or indeed any discipline), and also to the cultivation of good habits of reading and comprehension, note-taking and prose composition.

But literature itself is very different, and the same rules do not apply: writers are not governed as members of a formal institution, and though they might feel an outrageous, or devastating, or even a handily violent sense of indignation and violation at being plagiarized, writers do not have a professional body able to assess cases of plagiarism. Plagiarists cannot be struck off the canon, or barred from ever writing again, or have their poetic licences revoked, or pens impounded (although breaking their fingers would be satisfying to some). And if critics might turn against a plagiarist, or it might become impossible for such a one to find a publisher, these are secondary effects, more subtle things. Writers need to be considered as an entirely different kettle of fish than cheating students, who are so many more red herrings.

Certainly the merciless academic condemnation of plagiarism succeeded in creating an ugly and oppressive critical atmosphere when Graham Swift's *Last Orders* was unfairly drubbed for being plagiarized from (rather than imitative of) William Faulkner's *As I Lay Dying*. And most recently, there have been tediously righteous attacks on Susan Sontag, who clearly adopted lines and images from, among others, Willa Cather's *My Mortal Enemy* for her last novel *In America*, and Linda Grant, who did likewise for her Orange Prize winner *When I Lived in Modern Times*, utilizing Joshua Sherman's *Mandate Days*. But readers will still read their books – and some will doubtless enjoy them (and even write essays about them) – and so public 'shaming' seems the only recourse against such pseudo-plagiarism. But both Sontag and Grant, like Swift, are unabashed and unrepentant, and this is telling. The current enthusiasts, excitable things who get overexcited in redefining plagiarism after legal or moral or historicist fashions, are revealingly incapable of coming to terms with this attitude – mainly, I think, because they tend to be academics with professional allergies to undergraduate plagiarism. Somewhere, they lost sight of literature.

Plagiarism is, in other words, a purely textual transaction, and accusations of plagiarism are themselves textual (rather than, say, physical – and if other forms of transaction take place, like the financial, the activity is called something else, like theft or fraud). In part because of this textual purity, and also because of its apparently direct opposition to ideas of originality, plagiarism appears to be the definingly unethical position of the scholar and critic – indeed of the profession of the humanities as a whole. But although plagiarism is governed by the academic discourse, there is little power exercised by the academy against it: the occasional student may be docked marks or even expelled for plagiarism, but in confronting plagiarizing writers themselves, all the plagiarized can do is write more.

And yet at the same time, literary values should not be eclipsed by institutional morality; rather, it is the academic discourse itself that should be questioned. In every plagiarism case, plagiarism is presented as a form of knowledge from outside a given text that puts a reader under strain and will, in varying degrees, rewrite the meaning of that text (which is also, of course, how allusion, for instance, works). The current tendency in English studies is to allow the immediacy and proximity of the *literary* context to recede further and further into the background as more and more other, miscellaneous contexts are introduced, whether historical, material, ideological, blah-blah, moral, legal, academic, so on: in such hands, any debate about plagiarism is going to be less about literature and more about retrenching favourite positions.

Far from the madding crowd, there is a simple, unfashionable alternative: revive the appreciation of the craft and construction and technique of writing – not least in discovering how to criticize most shrewdly the creative skills of imitation, allusion and overt or covert copying, hopping from text to text, and how they all play a part in contributing to the disingenuous discourse through which plagiarism steals.

Part II
Contexts of Plagiarism

6
Plagiarising the Word of God: Tyndale between More and Joye

Andrew Hope

Who was the author of the Bible? Gregory the Great, discussing the authorship of the book of Job at the end of the sixth century, had no doubt:

> It is very superfluous to enquire who wrote the work, since by faith its author is believed to have been the Holy Spirit.

The human author was a mere instrument:

> If we were reading the words of some great man with his epistle in our hand, yet were to enquire by what pen they were written, doubtless it would be an absurdity.... [I]n raising a question about the writer what else are we doing but making enquiry about the pen as we read the epistle.[1]

In the Middle Ages, whilst no one in Christendom doubted that God was the author of the Bible, the application of Aristotelian notions of causality opened a way for human authors to be accorded some agency in the production of the biblical text. The efficient cause, the *causa efficiens*, was God, but there could be intermediate efficient causes – human authors, compilers, collectors and scribes.[2]

Thus the divine *auctor* and human *auctores* combined to produce texts. These texts were then viewed as composites of *auctoritates*, sayings or statements which should be believed. They should be believed because they participated in *auctoritas*, and God was the ultimate source of all *auctoritas*. Human *auctores* were not restricted to the authors and compilers of scripture. Church Fathers, popes, the wise pagans of Antiquity, accepted theologians, all could speak with authority, albeit with lesser measures.

Auctoritates, as statements of truth which should be believed, were common property. They could be used and re-used at will. Principally Christian, but also classical in origin, there was a sense in which they were the boundaries within which writers were expected to operate.[3] Thus the temptation which beckoned to writers was not so much to pass off the work of another as one's own, but to pass off one's own as having an *auctoritas* it did not possess. Hence the number of writers of late Antiquity or the Middle Ages known in retrospect as pseudo – Pseudo-Dionysius, Pseudo-Augustine, Pseudo-Bede, and so forth.

With two exceptions, translators did not receive much attention in all this. The first exception was in the generation of the Septuagint, the Greek translation of the Hebrew Scriptures made supposedly at Alexandria in the third century BC. Here God had miraculously guaranteed the *auctoritas* of the translation by ensuring that although each of the seventy-two translators worked alone, they all produced the same translation. The miracle was accorded its own chapter in Augustine's *City of God*.[4] The second major act of translation was that of the Greek scriptures into the Latin Vulgate in the late fourth century. Here the *auctoritas* was guaranteed by the name of St Jerome, one of the four great pillars of the patristic Church. Jerome's version became the single authoritative version of the Middle Ages. Erasmus' older contemporary, Jacques Lefèvre d'Etaples, could bring himself to correct parts of the Vulgate only after he had persuaded himself that they did not represent Jerome's work.[5]

The conditions of manuscript transmission invariably meant that various kinds of textual corruption crept in. However, the Chinese box theories of causation in which God was the ultimate efficient cause made it very difficult to accommodate error: God could not be the cause of error. A consequence was that even apparent flaws in the text had to have meaning. When Luke in 10:42 describes Jesus being entertained by Mary and Martha, Mary is said to have chosen the best part. As every schoolboy knows the superlative implies at least three. There were therefore three 'parts' from which she had chosen, and not, as one might have expected, two. From this it was believed that Christ had said that there was a hierarchy of three modes of the Christian life – secular, monastic and contemplative. This interpretation was built into the foundations of mystical theology and had to bear the weight of several chapters of no less a work than *The Cloud of Unknowing*.[6] Even the author of one of the Lollard sermons found it necessary to find an explanation for three ways.[7]

Of course, common sense forced the admission that there might be human error in individual copies of manuscript bibles. Copyists could be fallible, even when engaged upon such a sacred task. Medieval scholars periodically set about purging the text of corruptions, and some could be outspoken in their estimate of the extent of the corruption and others have insights into the ways in which change to the text might have occurred and how the original text might be restored.[8]

Erasmus

Towards the end of the fifteenth century, disparities in manuscript bibles, alternative texts of the Latin Bible and texts in alternative languages had become a pressing intellectual concern. What status was to be accorded them?

In Spain the team of scholars assembled by Cardinal Francisco Ximénez took from 1502 to about 1522 to publish what became known as the Complutensian Polyglot, a Bible containing the Old Testament in the Hebrew, Latin Vulgate and Greek Septuagint versions, along with a Chaldee paraphrase; and the New Testament in the Latin Vulgate and the Greek. Although edited with care,[9] the Complutensian Polyglot was a profoundly conservative work which tended to adopt the Vulgate text as its standard and to edit the Greek against it.[10]

For the Spanish scholars the Greek texts did not present a purer but a debased form of the text. The scholars who worked on it had no doubt about the relative status of the texts with which they were dealing: their Old Testament pages presented the reader with three main columns. In the centre was the text of the Latin Vulgate, on either side of the Vulgate was the text in Hebrew and Greek. It was being presented, they said, as Christ between two thieves, and they meant every word. Christ was God's Word and God's Word was the Vulgate. The Greek and the Hebrew versions were thieves. They had appropriated a text that was not their own, and in this sense Christ was crucified between two plagiarists. But what these versions were really appropriating was authority: the authority that properly belonged to the Vulgate text.

Ad fontes: Erasmus believed the authoritative text was the primary text. The original, true text of the Bible could be recovered only with painstaking scholarship into the ancient original languages. The world of biblical *auctoritates* was to be policed not by theologians conversant with revelation or philosophers conversant with reason, but by philologists conversant with languages. Erasmus could be cautious; many enthusiastic Erasmians were less so. A knowledge of Greek was soon being trailed as the unique badge of Christian authority.

Erasmus's Greek New Testament appeared in 1516 and a second edition with a revised Latin translation in 1519. The *Novum Testamentum* was to be the asteroid which altered the course of sixteenth-century theological evolution. It opened up a multitude of ecological niches in which many new and strange theological forms could flourish. Swathes of *auctoritates* were wiped out. In the example we have looked at, Mary now simply chose a good (not even the better) part.[11] In other emendations, people were no longer to 'do penance' but to 'be penitent'. Luther took note of that revision. Significantly, from a Humanist viewpoint, the Word at the beginning in St John's gospel was 'sermo' not 'verbo': 'Sermo' was dynamic: the word preached, proclaimed, creative. 'Verbo' was static: the word as logical counter to be assigned its correct place in the scholastic scheme of things.[12]

William Tyndale

It was in this context that William Tyndale translated the Greek New Testament of Erasmus into English. After an aborted attempt at Cologne in 1525, it was printed at Worms in the spring of 1526. It was an immediate success. Nicholas Love's *Mirror of the Life of Christ* which had been officially promoted as a rival to the manuscript Lollard English New Testament was knocked out of the market. It was in its eighth printed edition when Tyndale's New Testament appeared. There was a ninth edition in 1530, but that was the last of the century.[13] Tyndale's New Testament was such a success indeed that even before 1526 was out, Antwerp printers, always well informed about English markets, were shipping over further editions.

Tyndale, however, was conscious of the provisional nature of his translation. He wrote in the 1525 prologue that he beseeched

> those that are better sene in the tonges then y and that have hyer gyftes of grace to interpret the sence of the scripture and meanynge of the spyrite then y to consydre and pondre my laboure . . . And yf they perceyve in eny places that y have not attayned the very sence of the tonge or meanynge of the scripture or haue not geven the right englysshe worde that they put to there handes to amende it, remembrynge that so is there duetie to doo.[14]

Tyndale himself promised a revised version, but he became so taken up with theological polemic, with learning Hebrew and with producing

an English Old Testament – which indeed was to remain unfinished at
his death – that year after year went by and no revised edition appeared.

George Joye

The English market meanwhile continued to be supplied by editions
printed in Antwerp. Errors in the text, however, began to accumulate:
the printers were, after all, working in a foreign language. It was thus
decided to recruit an Englishman to oversee the cleaning up of the text.
The man employed was George Joye. Joye was in many ways an ideal
candidate. He had been educated at Cambridge and was there when
Erasmus was teaching Greek, although he did not avail himself of the
opportunity to learn it.[15] Ten years later, in the early 1520s, he was one
of a group of Cambridge scholars animated by the new theologies
coming out of Germany. In late 1527, with a heresy prosecution imminent, he went into exile on the continent.[16]

Joye had an interest in liturgical and devotional works which Tyndale
did not share, but he does seem to have nurtured the ambition to follow
in Tyndale's footsteps. If Tyndale had given England its New Testament,
Joye could give it the Old. However, Tyndale was able to translate from
the original Greek: Joye, who had no Hebrew, had to make do with
translating the new Latin translations of the Hebrew text which were
just appearing.

Joye's translation of the Psalms from the edition and notes of Martin
Bucer was published by Martin de Keyser in Antwerp in January 1530.[17]
The following day de Keyser published Tyndale's English Pentateuch.[18]
It is not clear what the relationship was between the two men at this
time. There is no evidence that they had agreed any division of the Old
Testament between them, though this may have been the case. A year
and a half later in May 1531 de Keyser published Joye's translation of
Isaiah from the Latin of Zwingli and Tyndale's translation of Jonah
within a fortnight of each other.

Joye's next two biblical translations were again Old Testament books
from the Latin of Zwingli. First, Jeremiah appeared in May 1534 from
the van Endhoven press, the press which was responsible for the Tyndale
New Testaments. Second, a new translation of the Psalms came from the
de Keyser press in August.

Joye embraced the Erasmian values of textual revision. In his preface
to his 1530 Psalms he told the reader that 'ye may not mesure and luge
after the comen texte'; in other words, it should not be judged by

reference to the Latin Vulgate, since 'Dauid with the other syngers of ye Psalmes firste sunge them' in Hebrew.[19] Joye went on:

> Let ye gostly lerned in ye holy tonge be juges. It is ye spirituall man (saith Paule) which hath the spirit of god yt muste decerne & juge all thynges. And ye men quietly sittynge (if the truth be shewed them) muste juge and stand up and speke (the firste interpreter holdynge his pease) god geve ye true spirituall & quiete sittynge juges.

Joye's implication here is that the 'gostly lerned' and the 'spirituall man' are one and the same. The equation of knowledge of ancient tongues with spiritual authority was implied in the Erasmian programme of reform. The 'quiet sitting judges' come from Paul's first letter to the Corinthians:

> Let the prophets speak two at once, or thre at once, and let other judge. Yfeny revelacion be made to another that sitteth by, let the fyrst holde his peace.[20]

In the event, the passage was remarkably prescient. Joye was to take upon himself the role of the 'spirituall man' to whom the truth had been shown. He set about revising Tyndale's 1526 New Testament on the basis of his own theological understandings. The problem was that Tyndale – 'the firste interpreter'? – most certainly would not hold his peace.

In August 1534 Joye published not only (as we have seen) a new translation of the Psalms from the de Keyser press, but also from the rival van Endhoven press his revision of Tyndale's 1526 Worms New Testament. The result was a spectacular breach in relations between the two pioneering English biblical translators.

Whether Joye knew it or not, and Tyndale plausibly claimed that he did, Tyndale's own long-awaited revision was also just then in the de Keyser press. In his preface to this edition, Tyndale repeated his offer of 1525–26 to accept corrections and revisions:

> If anye man fynde fautes ether with the translacion or ought besy-de . . . to the same it shalbe law full to translate it themselves and to put what they lust thereto. If I shall perceave ether by my selfe or by the informacion of other, that ought be escaped me, or myght be more playnlye expressed, I will shortlye after, cause it to be mended.[21]

But Tyndale was opening the stable door after the horse had bolted: George Joye's revised version was already through the rival van End-hoven press. Tyndale recalled:

> But when the pryntynge of myne was almost fynesshed, one brought me a copie and shewed me so manye places, insoche wise altered that I was astonyed and wondered not a lytle what furye had dryven him to make soche chaunge and to call it a diligent correction.[22]

Most of Joye's corrections were minor and of no great moment. The one that outraged Tyndale was that wherever Tyndale had the word 'resurrection' Joye had substituted the phrase 'life after this life' or something similar. What lay behind this was a dispute about the fate of the soul after death. Conventional Christian belief was that on death the soul went to be with Christ. Only at the Day of Judgement, would the soul then finally be reunited with its resurrected earthly body. Luther rejected this view and held that after the death of the body the soul sleeps until the general day of resurrection when it is reunited with its body and suffers judgement. Tyndale followed Luther in this respect.[23] Joye did not. Joye believed the soul continued living after the death of the body. It was this view which his translation of 'life after this life' was intended to preserve. In fact, among Protestant reformers, only a few Anabaptists followed Luther and Tyndale in believing in 'soul-sleep': the mainstream magisterial reformers remained wedded to the traditional view. However, this was not sufficient to assure Joye's 'life after this life' translation any future: there was little philological warrant for it, it gave rise to unwieldy and unrhythmic English phrases, and it was far from clear that the term 'resurrection' necessarily entailed Luther and Tyndale's ideosyncratic view of the fate of the soul.

Tyndale immediately added a second preface to his edition attacking Joye's revision. There was little room for philological argument of the point that divided them. Both assumed that the Bible must present a coherent view of the fate of the soul after death and that theirs was it. Instead, Tyndale's principal attack was on Joye's motives. Twice in two sentences he accused Joye of covetousness and vainglory.[24] If Joye was right, then not only Tyndale's translation must be wrong, but 'Saynt Jeromes and all the translatours that ever I heard of in what tonge soever it be'.[25]

Tyndale may at this point have been mindful that the argument he was using against Joye was uncomfortably close to the one which, as we shall see, had been brought against him by Thomas More. Tyndale shifted his ground to discuss the question of authorship:

> But of this I chalenge George Joye, that he dyd not put his awne name therto and call it rather his awne translacion: and that he playeth boo pepe, and in some of his books putteth in his name and tytle, and in some kepeth it oute. It is lawfull for who will to translate and shew his mynde, though a thousand had translated before him. But it is not lawfull (thynketh me) nor yet expedyent for the edifieinge of the unitie of the fayth of Christ, that whosoever will, shall by his awne autorite, take another mannes translacion and put oute and in and chaunge at pleasure, and call it a correccion.[26]

It was a point Tyndale kept returning to:

> But though it were the verie meaninge of the scripture: yet if it were lawfull after his ensample to every man to playe boo pepe with the translacions that are before him, and to put oute the wordes of the text at his pleasure and to put in every where his meaninge, or what he thought the meaninge were, that were the next waye to stablyshe all heresyes and to destroye the grounde wherewith we shuld improve them.[27]

And again:

> Wherfore I beseche George Joye, yea and all other to, for to translate the scripture for them selves, whether oute of Greke, Latyn or Hebrue. Or (if they wyll nedes) as the foxe when he hath pyssed in the grayes[28] hole chalengeth it for his awne, so let them take my translacions and laboures, and chaunge and alter, and correcte and corrupte at their pleasures, and call it their awne translacions, and put to their awne names, and not to play boo pepe after George Joyes maner.[29]

Tyndale was adamant he would not be compromised as an author:

> But I nether can ner will soffre of anye man, that he shall goo to take my translacion and correct it without name, and make soche chaungynge as I my selfe durst not do, as I hope to have my parte in Christ, though the hole worlde shuld be geven me for my laboure.[30]

The integrity of the original text was paramount:

If the text be lefte uncorrupt, it will purge hir selfe of all maner false gloses, how sotle soever they be fayned, as a sethinge pot casteth up hir scum. But yf the false glose be made the text, diligentlye oversene and correct, wherewith then shall we correcte false doctrine and defende Christes flocke from false opinions, and from the wycked heresyes of raveninge of wolves?[31]

Tyndale's edition, including the new preface, was issued in November 1534. Joye took offence at being so publicly attacked by Tyndale, and the following February defended himself in *An Apology made by George Joy, to satisfy, if it may be, W. Tindale*.[32] Joye draws attention to Tyndale's words offering to accept correction, and then says,

[Tyndale] confesseth even there that hys first translacion was a thinge borne before the tyme, rude and imperfit, rather begun then fynisshed, not yet having her right shape. This I saye hys owne desyer and confession and my conscience so compelled me and caused me where I sawe siche notable fautes to mende them, lest so many false bokis thruste into mennis handis might ether staye the reader or els seduce him into any errour.[33]

Joye denies the charges of covetousness and vainglory. He was paid very little for his work, and that he did not put his name to it is one of Tyndale's major complaints:

[H]e that doth a thing secretly and putteth out hys name, how seketh he vaynglory?[34]

If Joye had put his name to it, Tyndale

had had a juste cause to have writen agenst me for lying and stealing awaye the glorie of his name for first translating the testament.[35]

Nor should the disputed question be consigned to a gloss in the translation:

... as for me, I had as lief put the trwthe in the text as in the margent ... so that the reder might once swimme without a corke.[36]

Such a picturesque aspiration could do nothing to allay Tyndale's fears that this manipulation of the text represented a corruption which it was the chief duty of the translator to avoid. Just as alarming for Tyndale was Joye's use of the Latin text. Joye described coming across in Tyndale

> some derke sentencis that no reason coude be gathered of them whether it was by the ignorance of the first translatour or of the prynter; I had the latyne text by me and made yt playn: and where any sentence was unperfite or clene left oute I restored it agene: and gave many wordis their pure and native significacion in their places which thei had not before.[37]

Although Joye is here partly cleaning up the text set by Dutch type-setters, he is also, by his own admission, correcting Tyndale's translation from the Greek by reference to a Latin text, which was itself a transla-tion from the Greek – a major offence against the tenets of Humanist scholarship.

Towards the end of the *Apology* Joye finds it irresistible to bring a charge of plagiarism against Tyndale. Tyndale had drawn heavily on Luther's sermons for his *Exposition upon the Fifth, Sixth and Seventh Chapters of Matthew*. Joye comments that

> herd I never sombre and wyse man so prayse his owne workis as I herde him praise his exposicion of the v. vj. and vij. ca. Mat. in so myche that myne eares glowed for shame to here him and yet was it Luther that made it, T[yndale] onely but translating and powldering yt here and there with his own fantasies.[38]

This was a very unedifying dispute. 'Some good men,' observed Joye 'wysshe vs bothe neuer to haue ben borne, and saye we be bothe full of poyson'.[39]

Thomas More

Someone who did not fall into Joye's category of 'good men', but who did indeed both wish they had never been born and believe they were both full of poison, was Thomas More. More had been one of the most enthusiastic defenders of Erasmus' Greek New Testament against those who believed that an assault on the Vulgate was an assault on a central citadel of the Christian faith. In Germany and the Low Countries many Erasmian humanists sided with Luther.[40] In England, on the other hand, there was some general assumption that the humanist enterprise of biblical textual amendment favoured the papal rather than Lutheran cause.[41] In his first polemical work, the *Responsio ad Lutherum* of 1523, More observes that many of Paul's epistles may be lost 'and of those which are extant, some are translated incorrectly, some are translated ambiguously, the copies in the two languages do not agree at all points, and there is incessant controversy about their meaning'. More concludes against Luther that scripture cannot therefore be the sole or final arbiter in matters of Christian belief. Truth is to be found in the common and public faith of Christendom.[42] Thus whilst More leaves question marks hanging over the precise meaning of the accessible biblical text, the textual inheritance from the fathers and medieval theologians is fully endorsed: 'the writings of our predecessors represent to us the faith of their own times' and this is 'the public faith of the whole church' which is 'true and unable to err'.[43] It was a brilliant polemical shift which paradoxically enabled More to use Erasmian assumptions about the nature of the biblical text to defend highly traditional assumptions about ecclesiastical authority. Where Joye incorporated his gloss into the text to keep the reader afloat, More's Christian was safely aboard the barque of St Peter and needed to do no more than trust a pervasive tradition.

More brought these ideas into play against Tyndale whom he saw as the greatest of threats to Catholic Christianity as he conceived it. The 'public faith' of Christendom was ultimately grounded not just in scripture but in a tradition reaching back to truths entrusted by Christ to the apostles, but not then put in writing. The life and traditions of the Church and the lives and teachings of the post-apostolic saints then become testimony to and guarantors of

> those wordes unwryten which ye chyrch beleveth, [which] were and be his wordes, as well and as veryly as those that be wryten in any parte of scrypture.[44]

More, as a Humanist scholar having given ground on the divine *auctor* of the Vulgate text, is obliged as a defender of the Church against Luther and Tyndale to stand firm on the *auctoritas* of Catholic humanity. In so far as Luther and Tyndale place themselves in the line of Erasmian biblical scholarship, the arguments which More can use against them are far more limited than the arguments available to the conservative theologians of Cologne, Louvain or Paris, who had long warned of where Erasmus' texual criticism was heading.

Thus, even when More launches into his sustained attack on Tyndale's famously contentious translations – using 'congregation' for 'church', 'senior' or 'elder' for priest, 'love' for 'charity' – he does so usually from the territory of 'the public faith of the whole church' not from the territory of philological scholarship.[45] At the same time that 'public faith' includes scripture as it has been commonly understood. The new translations by their innovations have placed themselves outside of this circle. More is insistent that to call one of them 'the newe testament calleth it by a wronge name, except they wyll call it Tyndals testament or Luthers testament'.[46] Just as Tyndale wanted Joye's name attached to Joye's revision, so More wanted Tyndale's version to be labelled with Tyndale's name. For the texts *not* to be so identified was for them to lay claim to an authority they did not possess. But conversely, More was manoeuvred into arguing that the authority the Bible did possess derived from the community of those who used it, and not those biblical authors the recovery of whose words had been the principal goal of Erasmian humanism.

Conclusion

Erasmus's new Greek and Latin versions, Luther and Tyndale's translations, Joye's amendments, More's unwritten verities: in a few years an extraordinary fragmentation had taken place. The injection of philological scholarship and theological tenets into a world of communal texts had generated disputes such as those between Tyndale and Joye. Could the old *auctoritas* ever be restored? When Thomas Cromwell's agent Stephen Vaughan paid Tyndale a secret visit in May 1531 hoping to enlist his support for the annulment of the king's marriage, Tyndale told him that if the king would 'grant only a bare text of the scripture to be out forth among his people . . . be it of the translation of what person soever shall please his majesty, I shall immediately make faithful promise never to write more'. Was this a rash promise, like his similar concessions in his prologues saying he would welcome corrections? Perhaps not, since for Tyndale kings were part of the divinely created order. They stood in the stead of God, and God was to rule the world through them – not through the Church.[47] The way was open for Henry VIII, dynast and part-time theologian, to become the supreme head of the Church in England. It would be he who held sway over *auctoritas*.

Henry's sister's grandson, James, was to have his name attached to a biblical version.[48] On the road to the King James Version were a succession of bibles, among them Coverdale's Bible, the 'Matthew' Bible, Taverner's Bible, the Great Bible, the Geneva Bible and the Bishops' Bible. Recognizing the inevitable, the Catholic authorities issued their own English versions, Rheims and Douai. The sixteenth century had witnessed its own postmodern shift from the Bible – the Vulgate – to bibles. Coverdale for one welcomed it. 'It was never better with the congregation of God,' he wrote, 'than when every church almost had the Bible of a sundry translation.' Coverdale felt no need for a Septuagint-like miracle to validate philological scholarship. He believed diversity dated from patristic times and attributed the 'darkness of men's traditions', which had subsequently clouded the church, to the monopoly of the Vulgate.[49]

The vernacular bibles used by the English Church up to and including the Authorized Version of King James were all, in some substantial measure, based silently upon Tyndale's version. It was not merely Joye but all translators from the Greek who appropriated Tyndale, perhaps the greatest single act of plagiarism of the sixteenth century. The Authorised King James Version, was, on the latest estimate, indebted to Tyndale for some 84 per cent of its readings.[50] Ironically, if the Tyndale–Joye controversy is anything to go by, it was precisely because Tyndale's name was omitted that this was acceptable. Leaving aside Joye's self-serving yoking of his name with Tyndale's, he had been proved correct:

> But I doubt not but that aftir T[yndale] and me bothe there be or shal come which shall mende bothe our translacions and paradventure cal them theirs, which I pray god sende us, and I, for my parte, shal geve place vnto siche one withe grete and many thankis.[51]

If God was the author, anonymity was not to be despised.[52]

7

Plagiarism and Imitation in Renaissance Historiography[1]

Lisa Richardson

I

At the turn of the seventeenth century John Hayward's history of the usurpation of Richard II, *The First Part of the Life and Raigne of King Henrie the IIII*, was attracting official attention because of its dedication to the recently disgraced Robert Devereux, second Earl of Essex. One of Essex's prosecutors, Francis Bacon, 'asked' by Queen Elizabeth 'if I could not find any places in it that might be drawne within case of treason', 'answered; for treason surely I found none, but for fellonie very many. And when her Majestie asked me hastily wherein; I told her, the Author had committed very apparant theft, for he had taken most of the sentences of Cornelius Tacitus, and translated them into English, and put them into his text'.[2]

Hayward had overlaid a painstakingly constructed, authentic, historical narrative with characteristics, political and military descriptions, stylistic details and critical commentary borrowed from first-century Roman historiography, transcribing without acknowledgement and usually without significant alteration almost five hundred passages from Sir Henry Savile's 1591 translation (and expansion) of Tacitus, *The Ende of Nero and Beginning of Galba. Fower Bookes of the Histories of Cornelius Tacitus. The Life of Agricola*. Varying from ornamental set-pieces to functional three- or four-word phrases, and including material embedded deep in the historical narrative as well as more obvious meta-historical commentary, they amount to almost a fifth of his history.[3] Equally impressive are the sensitivity and methodical persistence with which Hayward selected appropriate Tacitean material for his English characters and situations, over-writing the personalities and events described by his historical sources so convincingly that his intervention

has gone unnoticed by most readers and his work remains an historically faithful, as well as a stylistically enhanced and implicitly allusive,
account of late fourteenth-century events.

   In his acquiescence in the activities of corrupt favourites and vacilla-
tion and surrender in the face of rebellion Hayward's Richard II borrowed
attributes directly from the Roman Emperors Nero, Galba, Otho and
Vitellius. His jealousy and tyranny were transcribed from Domitian.
Hayward's apparently authorial commentary upon his character and
style of government actually combined the reflections of Tacitus and
Savile upon their imperial subjects.[4] Thus Hayward's Richard was resistant to good counsel and 'accompted all sharpe that was sounde, and liked
onely that, which was presently pleasant, and afterwards hurtfull'. Vitellius had 'accounted all sharpe that was wholesome, & liked of nothing
but that which was presently pleasant, and afterwards hurtfull'.[5] Richard
was 'a Prince weake in action, and not of valure sufficient to beare out his
vices by might'. Nero had been 'a Prince weake in action, not of vertue
sufficient to upholde his vices by might'.[6] Richard's rival Henry's character and insurrection were borrowed with similar directness from the
leaders of provincial rebellions against Rome; from the Emperors Galba,
Otho and Vespasian in their early integrity and resistance to tyranny; and
from Tacitus's heroic father-in-law, Agricola.[7] For his history's epigrammatic minor characters Hayward simply transcribed Tacitean types, some
inspired by similarity of reported character or situation, others imposed
more randomly for largely ornamental purposes.[8] He dissected his Tacitean model into hundreds of pieces and reassembled it as a mosaic upon
his own historical framework, redistributing Roman commentary, characteristics and fragments of narrative description (usually almost *verbatim*) across a range of his own figures and episodes.[9] Almost everything he
could appropriate and reapply he did, and little such material remained
by the time he had finished with it.[10]

   This was only one of Hayward's unhistorical and unacknowledged
sources for the *First Part* of his history of Henry IV. He borrowed equally
deliberately and directly, although on a considerably smaller scale, from
Sir Thomas More's *History of King Richard III*; and transcribed arguments
and precedents from Jean Bodin's *De Republica libri sex*. The ancient
Roman and Renaissance French historians Livy, Suetonius and Philippe
de Commynes were also useful.[11] In his later historical writing Hayward
continued to transcribe liberally from Savile and de Commynes, and
added Richard Grenewey's 1598 translation of Tacitus's *Annals*, Thomas
Nicholls's translation of Thucydides and even Sir Philip Sidney's *Arcadia*
to his portfolio of models.[12]

This historiographical technique was not unique to Hayward, although the directness and persistence of his Tacitean over-writing is unusual, and his preference for Savile's translation and tendency to close transcription make it more easily identifiable. Tacitus himself had repeatedly taken characteristics and descriptions of situations and incidents from Sallust. He has been described as 'merely a "scissors-and-paste" historian', 'at times willing to depend on a literary predecessor in a way that is unacceptable by modern standards'.[13] Earlier in the sixteenth century, More's *Richard III* had borrowed silently from Sallust and Tacitus; and Polydore Vergil's *Anglica historia* from Sallust, Tacitus and Suetonius.[14] Bacon himself later employed a technique similar to Hayward's, including unacknowledged transcription from Savile's translation, albeit on a more modest scale. Even the supposedly reliable Elizabethan archival historian William Camden borrowed descriptions of characters and situations, commentary and political analysis from Tacitus, and occasionally alluded implicitly to More and de Commynes.[15]

Closer to Hayward in the directness and persistence of their transcription were two other early Stuart historians, John Clapham and Peter Heylyn. Clapham's Tudor history was a tribute to his former patron William Cecil, Lord Burghley, to immortalize whom he drew a close, deliberate and sustained analogy with Tacitus's commemoration of Agricola. Clapham also accumulated stylistically satisfactory or typically appropriate characteristics for Cecil from a range of other Roman figures, distributed Tacitean material among his minor characters, and transcribed from More's *Richard III*.[16] Heylyn's *Augustus, or an Essay of those Meanes and Counsels whereby the Commonwealth of Rome was altered, and reduced unto a Monarchy* (London, 1632) also transcribed liberally and without acknowledgement from Tacitus (who barely touched on this historical subject). Thus, for instance, Heylyn's version of Augustus's oration to his fleet before the battle of Actium borrowed Agricola's speech to his army in Caledonia; and Maecenas' advice to Augustus to retain control of the Roman Empire reproduced Mucianus's argument that Vespasian should attempt to attain it.[17] Heylyn's Augustus also acquired imperial characteristics from Tacitus' Nerva and Tiberius, and admirable personal qualities from Agricola.[18] Like Hayward, Heylyn did not confine himself to broad analogies, but pasted Tacitean fragments opportunistically into his narrative.[19] Unacknowledged imitation and allusion were important and uncontroversial strategies of ancient and early modern historical writing; and unobtrusively close, deliberate and sustained imitation and allusion appear to have been distinctive characteristics of late sixteenth- and early seventeenth-century English formal literary historiography.

II

Was such unacknowledged imitation 'fellonie' and 'apparant theft'? John Hooper considered 'the diminution of any man's fame, as when for vain glory any man attribute unto himself the wit or learning that another brain hath brought forth', a breach of the eighth commandment, 'Thou shalt not steal'.[20] *The Arte of English Poesie* was indignant that John Southern, who had claimed the honour of the first English translation of Pindar, 'finding certaine of the hymnes of Pyndarus and of Anacreons odes and other Lirickes among the Greekes very well translated out of Rounsard... translates the same out of French' and 'doth... impudently robbe the French Poet both of his prayse and also of his French termes'. It declared that 'This man deserves to be endited of pety *larceny* for pilfering other mens devises from them & converting them to his own use'.[21] However, accusations were rarely made so categorically. Definitions of plagiarism depended upon a distinction between acceptable and unacceptable imitation that was drawn in widely different places by both classical and Renaissance literary theorists.

At one end of the spectrum Vida permitted the pillage of ancient literature by right of conquest, recommending that imitators 'address themselves one and all to thefts, and from every place... carry off the booty' (although it might be prudent to 'proceed cautiously when attempting thefts from famous poets' and to 'hide the theft by inverting the order of the words, so that a different impression and appearance will be given').[22] At the other, Ludovico Castelvetro denounced all classical imitation as theft and its most illustrious proponents as thieves. Thomas Churchyard also considered it intrinsically dishonest and claimed that he alone had 'never robd no writer'.[23] Opinion also varied widely between those who advocated the concealment of sources and process of imitation, and those who recommended their open avowal. Seneca had advised that 'our mind... should hide away all the materials by which it has been aided, and bring to light only what it has made of them'. Yet for Cicero, avowal distinguished whether the imitator had 'borrowed' or 'pilfered'; and Pliny thought it 'the mark of a perverted mind... to prefer being caught in a theft to returning [by acknowledgement] what we have borrowed'.[24] The fact that it was possible to cite respectable authorities for such diverse interpretations of imitation gave the concept an ambiguity that was explored by Sir John Harington in epigrams 'Of Honest Theft' and upon 'honourable theeves'. Admitting that 'I the Romanes rob, by wit, and Art' and 'I rob some I do read with praise for guardon', Harington emphasized the inconsistency with which charges of literary theft were applied to unacknowledged close imitations; and the way in which responses to the recognition of such borrowing ranged arbitrarily from admiration of those who gain 'praise and reputation by it' to condemnation of those who merely 'steall'.[25]

Further complicating the definition of the concept, many critics of plagiarism or unacceptably close imitation themselves practised what they condemned in others. Thomas Dekker's pamphlet *The Bellman of London* (London, 1608) censured the hack-writer who, 'having scraped together certaine small paringes of witte...first cuttes them handsomely in pretty peeces, and of those peeces does he patch upp a booke', denouncing the profession as 'Theeves of wit, Cheators of Arte, traitors of schooles of Learning, [and] murderers of Schollers', who 'rob Schollers of their Fame, which is deerer then life'. Yet *The Bellman of London* itself 'word for word copies or paraphrases from six earlier works'. Dekker's pamphleteering rival Samuel Rid promptly accused him of plagiarism in *Martin Mark-All, Beadle of Bridewell: His Defence and Answer to the Bellman of London* (London, 1608), but himself went on to transcribe *The Art of Juggling* (London, 1612) almost *verbatim* from Reginald Scot's *The Discoverie of Witchcraft* (London, 1584).[26] Timothy Kendall included translations of Martial's criticism of the original 'plagiarist' Fidentinus alongside his own virtually *verbatim* reproduction of Tottel's *Miscellany* and George Turberville's epigrams.[27] Even Bacon's charge of 'fellonie' could be turned upon himself with an adjustment of degree.

Formally defining acceptable historiographical imitation was even more difficult. Classical and Renaissance discussions of imitation were almost exclusively concerned with more creative literary activities. They tended to exclude historiography from the discussion by defining 'the deeds of the past [as]...an inheritance common to us all', available to any writer without acknowledgement.[28] Nor was early modern historiographical theory a reliable guide to practice. Clapham had declared that he 'would rather expose [Truth] in the meanest and worst habit Time hath left her, then by disguising her...abuse the world, and make her seem a counterfet'. He claimed to have been 'forced, of many things to make only a bare and briefe relation...unwilling, by adding or diminishing, to alter in substance, what Antiquitie hath left us'.[29] Yet his historiography is peppered with appropriated ornamental Tacitean char-

acters, descriptions and analysis.[30] Hayward condemned those historians 'who affecting to write rather pleasingly then truly, doe enterlace
many jeasts, conceits, tales and other pleasing passages; either omitting
or defacing the solide truth', and transforming 'the truth of many things
into fabulous inventions of their owne'. He virtuously edited a late
colleague's work to prevent it being 'set forth by others as their own: a
thing too much practised'.[31] Theory and practice diverged in part because apparently authorial declarations of historiographical purpose
and method were themselves actually borrowed directly from the classical *ars historia*.[32] However, Clapham and Hayward seem to have been
genuinely unconcerned that their transcriptive technique might 'alter
in substance' 'the solide truth' of the historical record, 'abuse the world',
or usurp the labours of their predecessors.

In practice, the idea of intellectual property had little place in ancient
or early modern historiography. Most historians would have found
denial of Sidney's caricature of them as 'authorising [themselves]...
upon other histories' impossible but irrelevant.[33] Preservation of the
historical record was preferable to authorial originality. John Speed's
historiographical method included literal 'scissors-and-paste' compilation of the works of his predecessors.[34] Most of his contemporaries
also directly transcribed and combined existing historical narratives
without acknowledgement, in an uncontroversial technique that went
back to classical historiography. According to the classical consensus,
history served a didactic and exemplary function, advocating admirable
models of behaviour or illustrating continuously recurring causal relationships. Formal literary historians tended to think in types of character, situation and causality and were often relatively unconcerned with
reconstructing the precise and individual details of the past. As Samuel
Daniel put it, by permitting so many of the records of the past to be lost,

> God in his providence... boundes our searches within the compasse
> of a few ages, as if the same were sufficient, both for example, and
> instruction, to the government of men. For had we the particular
> occurents of all ages, and all Nations, it might more stuffe, but not
> better our understanding. Wee shall find still the same Correspon-
> dencies to hold in the actions of men... the causes of the ruines, and
> mutations of states to be alike.[35]

Historians who conscientiously accumulated and combined all available
historical data were often less interested in recovering and preserving
unique than typical aspects of the past. Hayward's historiography dealt

in types of character, situation and causality: having constructed an exemplary version of each, he transcribed it into history after history, over-writing the individually unique events his sources described.[36] If the purpose of history was to educate by example, the imitation of an exemplary model, with or without formal acknowledgement, may have been considered preferable to the investigation and documentation of a possibly unrepresentative individual character or incident.

III

Hayward was not 'plagiarizing' his sources any more than his classical predecessors had 'plagiarized' theirs. As Seneca had applauded Ovid's use of Virgil, he 'borrowed...not desiring to deceive people, but to have it openly recognised as borrowed'.[37] His failure explicitly to acknowledge his sources was due to the stylistic constraints of his genre and the political circumstances in which his history was read rather than deliberate literary deception.[38] Historiographical convention discouraged explicit attribution. Classical and early modern historians combined their sources into smooth narratives that subsumed identity as well as diversity, rarely citing authorities. Stylistic consistency also demanded subtle and unobtrusive rather than self-advertising allusion and imitation. However, Hayward made no attempt to disguise the directness of his borrowing from Tacitus or other unhistorical sources. He certainly ignored Vida's advice to 'hide the theft by inverting the order of the words, so that a different impression and appearance will be given'. If the reader is familiar with Savile's translation, many of Hayward's transcriptions are, as Bacon described them, 'very apparant'. Although formally unacknowledged, this was not plagiarism seeking to conceal itself, but imitation and implicit allusion intended to be recognized, admired and interpreted by the attentive reader.

Readers familiar with Savile's Tacitus would have appreciated Hayward's careful selection and deliberate application of Roman analogues to his English characters and situations. For example, throughout the first half of his history's description of Richard II's misgovernment, the king enjoyed a monopoly of Tacitean characteristics borrowed from the tyrannical emperor Domitian, while Henry was his heroic, injured victim Agricola.[39] Thus Hayward recounted how Richard, banishing Henry, 'offred himselfe to be...thanked, for so odious a benefit', in imitation of Domitian who, prematurely ending Agricola's career, had 'suffred himselfe to be solemnely thanked, and was not ashamed of so odious a benefite'. However, from the moment when Henry rose in rebellion against his cousin, Hayward pointedly reversed their analogues. At Henry's acceptance of Richard's abdication he too 'suffered himselfe to be solemnly thanked, & thought it not much to have it accounted a great benefit'.[40] Henceforth, Henry ceased to borrow positive characteristics from Agricola and was constructed instead from much more critical Tacitean analogues including Domitian.[41] Meanwhile Richard grew progressively more sympathetic, eventually receiving an idealized description transcribed from Agricola.[42] Later in Henry's reign Hayward associated him primarily with the treacherous Emperor Tiberius, while casting Richard as his exemplary victim Germanicus.[43] Readers who recognized the origin of this material would have appreciated the irony of their carefully graduated and neatly symmetrical reversal of conduct and fortunes. They might have also detected that Hayward often subtly adapted his Tacitean transcriptions to extenuate imperial criticism applied to Richard and undermine the positive depiction of Henry's motives and supporters; and they were surely intended to note that aspects of Henry's rebellion rested upon particularly ambiguous or ironic foundations.[44] Thus, for instance, Hayward depicted Henry's decision to rebel as inspired by rhetoric borrowed directly and at length from the devious Tacitean arch-plotter Mucianus' persuasion of Vespasian to insurgency; and the transparently artificial oration composed by Sir Thomas More for a complicit Duke of Buckingham to address to a villainously mock-unwilling Richard III.[45] Knowing readers were being warned against taking Henry's account of himself and his rebellion at face value.

Hayward's subtly sophisticated Tacitean allusions may have found few fully appreciative readers.[46] However, even unconscious admirers seem to have valued his historiographical imitation.[47] His painstaking Tacitean over-writing was also a deliberate injection of classical narrative models, style and terms of analysis into English historical writing, an idiosyncratic vernacular version of the methods of imitation recommended by the early humanists. When Petrarch 'encouraged his contemporaries to take the classical Latin writers for a model, he meant them to catch the sound of classical Latin' in order to 'find more effective means of expression'. Direct use of the model was advocated: 'The material collected in the course of reading is to be written down in a notebook and when the student writes or speaks he must take great care not to use any word which he has not previously recorded.'[48] Hayward too seems to have made exhaustive use of the notebook system, and diligently incorporated every Tacitean fragment applicable to his own work.

He judged his efforts to reproduce 'the rich compositions of Auncient times', which did 'not only satisfie, but astonish' him, only partially successful, wistfully concluding that 'the farthest reach of our age cannot neerely approach them': 'Of my owne productions, never any did fully content mee....They may happily be somewhat sprinkled over [with classical learning], but throughly died, I conceive they are not.' His rather mechanical transcriptive technique represented a methodical stylistic makeover rather than a radically new approach to historiographical composition.[49] Yet his sensitive, subtle and persistent Tacitean over-writing pervaded and transformed the fabric of his entire narrative without significantly compromising its historical content. His history is not a *certo* of undigested fragments incorporated only by inclusion, and does not easily reveal its complex composite nature. Like Quintilian's description of the highest form of imitation, it 'seems to come into being as the very child of nature', not demonstrating 'an artificial manufacture'.[50]

Although some classical commentators had scorned those who transcribed 'word for word, from former works' or thought that they were imitating their model 'if [they] just use his actual words', Hayward's technique would have found favour with others.[51] For Macrobius, imitation did not have to avoid verbal repetition, it merely had to set material in a new context; and Isocrates considered it sufficiently original 'to recount the things of old in a new manner or set forth events of recent date in old fashion'.[52] This Hayward's Tacitean English historiography certainly did, and in this sense it was both innovative and creative. As a translation in the broadest sense of the word, the introduction of a new genre into native writing, it would have been regarded as a form of original invention.[53] One classicist judged it 'an excellent example of the classical theory of imitation': 'The lifting of whole sentences would be excused from plagiarism ... by the ancients, on the basis of bettering the original by skilful adaptation to the new context, and as complimentary quotation not needing acknowledgement to the initiated.'[54] And for the 'initiated', Hayward was doing much more than 'just' using Tacitus's 'actual words'; he was using them to create elegant and occasionally ironic allusions based upon the reader's recognition and appreciation of their congruity or ambiguity.

IV

Formally unacknowledged historiographical allusion and imitation flourished while historians continued to believe in the constancy of human nature and historical causation, and where the next priorities to narrative content were stylistic elegance and consistency: in effect, for most of the history of the discipline. However, in a polemic context it could be a liability. Writing controversial history was intrinsically different from producing stylish literary narratives about the consensual past, and after 1640 politically engaged historians required a different methodology. They adopted one resembling the most prominent polemic historical genre of the previous century, ecclesiastical history. Literary-political and ecclesiastical-polemic historiography had been distinct disciplines since ancient times, with separate pedigrees, philosophies and methodologies. While the former was 'a rhetorical work with a maximum of invented [or borrowed] speeches [and other narrative details] and a minimum of authentic documents', the latter was 'founded upon authority and not the free judgement of which the pagan historians were proud', and aimed 'to produce factual evidence about the past'.[55]

Like their ecclesiastical predecessors, the more ambitious partisan historians of the Civil War and its aftermath, from the parliamentarian Thomas May to the royalist Edward Hyde, Earl of Clarendon, invoked authority for their arguments and interpretations by explicitly quoting and citing supportive documents. With apparently transparent veracity and conspicuously attributed authority now powerful polemic weapons, 'the imaginary [or borrowed] speeches, elaborate battle scenes, and other rhetorical distortions which had marked the histories of the ancients and the early Renaissance humanists began to disappear'.[56] They were replaced by (at least allegedly) *verbatim* speeches and authentic historical evidence; and explicitly identified and acknowledged classical and literary quotations and allusions, on a significantly smaller scale and clearly differentiated from the historical narrative. Thus Clarendon's *History of the Rebellion and Civil Wars in England* explicitly quoted its classical literary material in Latin; and May's *History of the Parliament of England* identified all but the most well known of its classical allusions, translated most of them for the benefit of English readers, and conscientiously italicized even translated classical fragments absorbed within the narrative.[57] Although some unacknowledged classical and literary allusion and imitation continued, it wholly lacked the directness and persistence favoured by Hayward and his contemporaries. Compared to the even textured, stylistically consistent ancient and early modern histories described above, where implicit allusion and subtle imitation formed an unobtrusive but integral part of the historical narrative, the new controversial historiography, with its explicitly documentary content, typographical differentiation and conspicuous marginal apparatus, looked more like polemic argument, ecclesiastical history or antiquarian historical research.

This shift towards attributed quotation was determined by an established controversial mode in which it had always been a principal device; and necessitated by a self-conscious polemic context in which accusations of plagiarism, however unfounded, had been a popular means of discrediting opponents since ancient times.[58] In a competitive controversial context, conspicuously differentiated and attributed classical quotation and allusion were also ostentatiously effective means of demonstrating erudition and asserting intellectual authority. Thus, material that would previously have been incorporated as unacknowledged allusion or transcription now appeared predominantly as directly signalled and attributed quotation; and a historiographical technique superficially resembling 'plagiarism' to the 'uninitiated' eye was succeeded by one distinguished by more selective explicit allusion or indirect imitation. This was due not to sudden moral or intellectual revulsion at the concept of unacknowledged direct transcription so much as the urgent necessity of convincing a wider readership 'uninitiated' in the established academic conventions of historiographical imitation and allusion, but accustomed to, or at least conscious of, the conspicuous documentary authority of polemic argument. However, although polemic preoccupations inspired apparently progressive stylistic developments in quotation and attribution, the new methodology was not necessarily more scrupulous or transparent than that it succeeded.

A century later, Edward Gibbon used conspicuous attribution to protect his controversial *History of the Decline and Fall of the Roman Empire*. Clerical opponents of his polemic description of the role of Christianity in the collapse of Rome found few chinks in the 'factual bulwark' of his prominent citations.[59] Those who attempted the traditional defamatory accusation of plagiarism 'spectacularly came to grief' when confronted by his substantial and circumstantial critical apparatus and his ridicule of 'the opinion which [they] ... conceived of literary property, [that] to *agree* is to *follow*, and to *follow*, is to *steal*'.[60] However, whilst elements of his argument so obviously open to polemic attack had to be self-consciously watertight, Gibbon was not always so scrupulous in using or acknowledging his sources. Some of his citations, and the relationship between his narrative and the authorities they allege, are more transparent than others. David Womersley discovered 'a more than Tiberian degree of dissimulation' in Gibbon's apparently openly acknowledged use of Tacitus's *Germania*: sustained misrepresentation, mistranslation, conflation, misleading quotation out of context, and absolute fabrication of material apparently transparently cited: a 'deliberate slanting' of the historical evidence to support his argument that Rome declined through internal collapse (caused partly by the rise of Christianity), rather than external assault. For the same reason Gibbon treated Ammianus Marcellinus' history of the later Roman Empire equally unscrupulously, silently conflating disparate contexts, aggressively 'translating' and 'sensationally' exaggerating the sense of his explicitly acknowledged original.[61] Similar discrepancies between his cited sources and Gibbon's implicitly polemic narrative have been identified by other critics.[62] Although he prided himself upon the ubiquity and specificity of his citations, Gibbon's methodology was not always as accountable as they suggested; and his misrepresentation of his sources was a much more serious historiographical transgression than unacceptably close imitation or deficient acknowledgement.[63]

Outside the polemic arena, imitation and implicit allusion remained significant elements of formal historical writing. Gibbon still believed that 'the artist [may not] hope to equal or surpass, till he has learned to imitate, the works of his predecessors'; and that 'the knowledge of human nature' they revealed 'might, on some occasions, supply the want of historical materials'.[64] He implemented both principles in his history, borrowing classical, literary and critical material without acknowledgement, and transcribing it into historically distant analogous contexts.[65] As Tacitus and Hayward might have done, if it had occurred to them that their methodology might require explanation or defence, he argued that, 'If my readers are satisfied with the form, the colours, the argument which I have given to the labours of my predecessors, they may perhaps consider me not as a contemptible Thief, but as an honest and industrious manufacturer, who has fairly procured the raw materials, and worked them up with a laudable degree of skill and success.'[66] As their predecessors had done, Gibbon's readers tended to agree: Walpole was impressed that he could 'make an *original* picture with some bits of mosaic'; and other critics still expected to find 'allusions to the…literary historians…and of course to the literary classics both ancient and modern'.[67]

The polemic transformation of historical purpose and methodology had significant consequences for the particularly close and persistent form of unacknowledged imitation and allusion characteristic of early seventeenth-century English formal literary historiography and most comprehensively and consistently expressed in Hayward's *First Part of the Life and Raigne of King Henrie IIII*. More urgent historiographical priorities may have made subtle and self-effacing classical imitation as an end in itself seem inconsequential or irrelevant; and the new generic conventions that differentiated and emphasized explicitly asserted authority and apparently transparent narrative veracity rendered it increasingly incongruous and unintelligible. Hayward's previously popular history dropped out of print; its unrecognized conventions and allusions have been eluding the appreciation of 'uninitiated' readers ever since;[68] and no subsequent historian appears to have attempted anything of comparable emphasis or persistence. Unacknowledged close imitation was never quite the same again.

8
'The Fripperie of Wit': Jonson and Plagiarism

Ian Donaldson

I

Discussions on the subject of plagiarism seem often to involve extensive repetition, sometimes acknowledged and sometimes not, of the thoughts of earlier scholars. Renaissance accounts in particular of the hazards and proprieties of literary imitation tend to be largely recycled from influential classical sources, especially from the writings of Seneca, whose eighty-fourth epistle, about bees and flowers and honey and the human digestive system and choral performances, is routinely recalled by successive generations of writers.[1] Ben Jonson's thoughts on imitation as set out in his commonplace book, *Discoveries*, stem ultimately from Seneca's epistle, as mediated through Joannes Buchler's *Reformata Poeseos Institutio* (1633), which itself derives from Pontanus's *Poeticae Institutiones* (1594): one scholar following another following another following another in a protracted and self-conscious process of repetition which in some sense confirms, but in another sense curiously complicates, the doctrine that is successively recalled.[2] On the subject of imitation, such repetitions seem to imply, there is nothing much new to be said: all we can do is reiterate what has been said before.

Similar repetitions are sometimes to be found, even more curiously, in texts that appear to proclaim their own originality. The title-page of Jonson's 1600 quarto edition of *Every Man Out of his Humour*, for example, bears the motto: *Non aliena meo pressi pede* ('I walked where others had not trodden'). Jonson's apparent boast of literary independence is actually taken from a famous passage in one of Horace's epistles beginning *Libera per vacuum posui vestigia princeps*. In Niall Rudd's translation, 'Beholden to no one I blazed a trail over virgin country; nobody had trodden that ground'. Jonson announces himself as a literary trailblazer in words that are borrowed from another author, who (as it turns out) had borrowed them in turn from other authors before him: for the boast that one trod in nobody's footsteps had been a familiar classical trope since at least the time of Callimachus. The allusion invites us to recall the context of Horace's epistle: his distinction between thoughtless copying and informed knowledge of a literary tradition, his contempt for slavish imitators, his insistence on the need to make free use of the best artistic models.[3] Yet to the modern eye, perhaps, this practice is not entirely free, for Jonson may seem to be trudging along a familiar track at the very moment that he claims to be striking out across virgin territory; invoking tradition in order to break with tradition. The motto seems to present something of a conundrum, like the well-known saying by the person from Crete that all persons from Crete are liars.

That kind of conundrum, that general predicament, were familiar enough to Renaissance writers, whose acute awareness of their predecessors' footsteps generated an anxiety that borders at times on the comic.

> Yea but you will infer that this is *actum agere*, an unnecessary worke, *cramben bis coctam apponere*, the same againe and againe in other words. To what purpose?

asks Democritus in grave despair at the outset of Robert Burton's huge work anatomizing the categories and causes of melancholy: a disease much intensified by the realization that there is nothing new to be said about melancholy, that each writer must necessarily borrow from another, and that even this melancholy truism has itself been repeated to the point of exhaustion by those who have gone before.

> As Apothecaries we make new mixtures every day, poure out of one Vessell into another; and as those old *Romans* rob'd all the cities of the world, to set out their bad sited *Rome*, wee skim off the Creame of other mens Wits, pick the choyce Flowers of their tild Gardens to set out our owne sterill plots. *Castrant alios ut libros suos per se graciles alieno adipe suffarciant* (so *Jovius* inveighs). They lard their leane bookes with the fat of others' Workes. *Ineruditi fures, &c.* A fault that everie Writer findes, as I doe now, and yet faultie themselves, *Trium literarum homines*, all Theeves, they pilfer out of old Writers to stuffe up their new Comments, scrape *Ennius* Dung-hils, and out of *Democritus* Pit, as I have done. By which means it comes to passe, *that not only Libraries & Shops are full of our putid Papers, but every Close-stoole*

and Jakes, Scribunt carmina quae legunt cacantes; they serve to put under Pies, to lap Spice in, and keepe Rost-meat from burning.[4]

Every opinion and sentiment registered in Burton's brilliantly cascading lamentation is followed, in almost liturgical fashion, by an immediate antiphonal acknowledgement of its earlier expression by writers in Antiquity: if all writing is a matter of theft, this at least is honest theft, no sooner committed but confessed. Yet the comic instability of the author's position is as evident here as in the work which he helped to inspire, Sterne's *Tristram Shandy*, where prodigious writerly effort is constantly checked by the consciousness that writing, an overrated business, is seemingly getting us nowhere. 'The same againe and againe in other words. To what purpose?' Persistently deploring his own apparent inability to invent, Burton-as-Democritus presses despondently, inventively, on.

Sir Thomas Browne takes a somewhat similar view of the nature of literary composition in *Pseudodoxia Epidemica*, as he surveys the successive and seemingly inescapable process of authorial plunder, 'The Latines transcribing the Greekes, the Greekes and Latines each other'.

> Clemens Alexandrinus hath observed many examples hereof among the Greekes, and Plinie speaketh very plainely in his Preface, that conferring his Authors, and comparing their workes together, hee generally found those that went before *verbatim* transcribed, by those that followed after, and their originalls never so much as mentioned. To omit how much the wittiest piece of Ovid* [side-note: *His Metamorphoses] is beholding unto Parthenius Chius; even the magnified Virgil hath borrowed almost in all his works: his Eclogues from Theocritus, his Georgicks from Hesiod and Aratus, his Aeneads from Homer, the second Booke whereof containing the exploit of Sinon and the Trojan horse, (as Macrobius observeth) he hath *verbatim* derived from Pisander.... Thus may we perceive the Ancients were but men, even like our selves. The practise of transcription in our dayes was no monster in theirs: Plagiarie had not its nativitie with printing, but began in times when thefts were difficult, and the paucity of bookes scarce wanted that invention.

There is some irony in the fact that whole sections of this lament are lifted without acknowledgement (as Robin Robbins' notes reveal) from the writings of Salmasius, who borrows extensively in turn from Marcian of Heraclea. Despite Browne's air of scrupulous scholarship, he curiously fails to mention his major source of information about the practice of plagiarism in the ancient world. Both as borrower and lender, Browne was deeply implicated in the process of plagiarism he describes. In a cancelled passage to this section he writes tetchily: 'Mr philips in his villare Cantianum transcribes half aside of my hydrotaphia or vrn buriall without mention of the author.'[5]

'Without mention of the author': this, we might think, is the distinguishing feature of plagiarism, the act (or omission) that constitutes the crime. To borrow openly from another author, to acknowledge that all one can say has been said by others before, seems fair and open dealing; but to borrow furtively – *fur*, a thief; *furtum*, theft – is surely a species of crime.[6] Yet in the classical world, as in early modern times, the issue was not so simple. Seneca himself in his eighty-fourth epistle declares that concealment of one's sources is vital to the art of literary imitation: 'This is what our mind should do: it should hide away all the materials by which it has been aided, and bring to light only what it has made of them.'[7] Macrobius, mentioned by Browne in the passage just quoted as a sharp-eyed detector of plagiarism in others, was so impressed by this advice that he appropriated large sections of this very epistle for re-use without acknowledgement in his *Saturnalia*, hiding away the materials by which he had himself been aided.[8] This classical doctrine of aesthetic dissimulation, of hiding away, was admired and endorsed by many Renaissance writers. 'Did not Cicero himself teach that the chief point of art is to disguise art?' asked Erasmus; 'Therefore if we wish to imitate Cicero successfully, we must above all disguise our imitation of Cicero.' There is (once again) an element of witty paradox about a statement of this kind, whose logic, if taken to the limit, would naturally suppress the very name of Cicero.[9]

Plagiarism, as Christopher Ricks has argued, is not simply a legal issue to be discussed in relation to developing concepts of intellectual property, or a writerly habit to be indulgently viewed in relation to postmodern theories of playful textual exchange. The basic problems that plagiarism presents in all historical periods, he maintains, are unavoidably ethical in nature, and the charge of plagiarism necessarily involves an implication of moral turpitude.[10] The case is powerfully and persuasively made. Yet quite how this turpitude is construed – what exactly constitutes plagiarism, and why it is condemned – is a more puzzling and variable matter than one might at first suppose, as these last examples may suggest. For all the repetitions and recyclings of imitation theory just described, significant differences of doctrine – whether one should acknowledge, whether one should conceal one's borrowings –

are plainly evident; as are certain ironies (more will follow) in the position of those who, down the ages, have complained most loudly about the offence. None of these variations or instabilities drains the offence of moral consequence: yet they do materially affect the manner in which we try to describe plagiarism and say what we think is wrong with it.

II

Ben Jonson is for two reasons a central figure in the history of plagiarism in England. During his lifetime he contended vigorously against various forms of literary theft, introducing to the language a number of words, still in common currency, to describe the practice. After his death he was ironically regarded in many quarters as something of a thief himself. The story of his developing reputation reveals some of the historical shifts in the way in which plagiarism was viewed in England, and some of the contradictions which still beset our understanding of the term.

In the fourth act of Jonson's satirical comedy *Poetaster* (1601), the poet Tibullus indignantly seizes a copy of some verses that have just been sung by Crispinus, a pretender to poetry. 'Why! The ditty's all borrowed!', Tibullus exclaims; "tis Horaces; hang him, *plagiary*' (4.3.95–6) This is the *OED*'s first recorded instance of a term that Jonson remembers from its use by Martial (I. lii. 9), and was to use again a few years later in an epigram addressed 'To Prowl the Plagiary':

> Forbeare to tempt me, Proule, I will not show
> A line unto thee, till the world it know;
> Or that I'have by, two good sufficient men,
> To be the wealthy witnesse of my pen:
> For all thou hear'st, thou swear'st thy selfe didst doo.
> Thy wit lives by it, Proule, and belly too.
> Which, if thou leave not soone (though I am loth)
> I must a libell make, and cosen both.
>
> *Epigrams*, 81

To 'prowl' was to pilfer. Prowl the Plagiary is keen to take a look at the writing of others so he can note down their work and pass it off later as his own. Jonson threatens to have two witnesses present next time Prowl visits, to observe and testify to the act of theft. Though this all sounds very legalistic, authors in this period (as is well known) had in fact no legal rights to protect, and Jonson would have had no luck with

Prowl the Plagiary supposing he had ever got him to a court of law.[11] The poem's final threat is that if Prowl does not improve his behaviour, Jonson will write a 'libel' about him. This was the common term in civil law for the document in which a plaintiff formally set out his complaint in order to initiate legal proceedings (*OED*, 'libel', sb., 2). But the word 'libel' (from *libellus*, a pamphlet or little book) could also refer to any kind of published statement damaging to the reputation of another (*OED*, 'libel', sb., 5): a satirical epigram, for example, such as this very poem, or the further, more explicit, poem, which Jonson now threatens to write. Though the retaliation may sound legal, it proves in the end to be merely literary. In *Poetaster*, likewise, though Tibullus' exclamation – ''tis Horaces; hang him, *plagiary*' – suggests a legal offence, a kidnapping that merits capital punishment, the humiliation that Crispinus endures in the end is simply that of literary ridicule. And what exactly has Crispinus done in any case to warrant hanging? One of the curiosities about the passage in *Poetaster* is that, despite Tibullus's indignant insistence, Crispinus's song, 'Love is blinde, and a wanton', bears no resemblance to any known work by Horace. 'Canidia', the poetic name by which Crispinus chooses to address Chloe, the subject of his poem, happens indeed to be the name of a witch who is mentioned in several of Horace's epodes; it is a comical blunder for Crispinus to have selected this name, but hardly an act of plagiarism, as we would understand that term today.

It is a further curiosity that in the opening scene of *Poetaster* the character of Ovid reads aloud in its entirety a poem he has just composed, *Amores* I. xv, in an English version that had been published in a collection of Christopher Marlowe's Ovidian translations in 1595. Two very similar versions of *Amores* I. xv appear in this volume. The first, beginning 'Envie why carpest thou my time is spent so ill / And termst my workes fruites of an idle quill' is generally agreed to be the work of Marlowe. The second, beginning 'Envie, why twitst thou me, my Time's spent ill? / And call'st my verse fruites of an idle quill?', looks like a slightly improved version of the first translation. It may be by Marlowe himself, and is commonly printed in modern editions of his poems. But in the 1595 volume the poem is actually headed 'The same by B. I.', and has often been thought to be a light revision by Ben Jonson of Marlowe's original translation. This is the version that Jonson uses in the first scene of *Poetaster*. In giving us this version of Ovid's elegy in its entirety in the opening scene of his play, Jonson is boldly paying open tribute to the recently dead Marlowe, whose Ovidian translations just two years earlier had been banned and publicly burnt in the notorious bishops' bonfire of

1599.[12] *Poetaster* begins with Ovid reciting the elegy's concluding couplet: '*Then, when this bodie falls in funerall fire, / My name shall live, and my
best part aspire.*' These lines, asserting the survival of poetry and the
survival of the poet, in spite all that death and fire and angry bishops
can do, were technically forbidden in 1601, and should not have been
spoken openly in a London theatre. They are as clear and affectionate a
tribute to Marlowe as the lines that Shakespeare gives to Rosalind in *As
You Like It*: 'Dead shepherd, now I find thy saw of might: / "Who ever
lov'd, that lov'd not at first sight?"' (3.5.80–1). But in the eighteenth
century Jonson's allusion was seen in a very different light, as an act of
questionable appropriation. Edmond Malone wrote indignantly in the
margins of his copy of the quarto edition of *Poetaster*, now in the
Bodleian Library: 'Jonson's impudence in printing this translation as
his *own*, is perhaps unparalleled. It was done by Marlowe; and he has
merely altered a word here & there, generally for the worse.'[13] Thus the
very work that had introduced the word *plagiary* to the English language
was itself ironically accused of incorporating an act of plagiarism.

In the third act of *Every Man In His Humour* the would-be poet Mattheo
is detected trying to pass off some lines from Marlowe's *Hero and Leander*
as his own:

> *Rare creature let me speake without offence,*
> *Would God my rude woords had the influence*
> *To rule thy thoughts, as thy fayre lookes do mine,*
> *Then shouldst thou be his prisoner, who is thine . . .*
> 3.4.61–3 (Q)[14]

The act of theft is seemingly aggravated by the fact that Marlowe is no
longer alive to protect his work: 'A pox on him, hang him filching
rogue,' exclaims Lorenzo, 'steale from the deade? its worse than sacriledge' (3.4.77–8). When in the final scene of the play Mattheo is found
with further verses in his pocket stolen from the (still-living) Samuel
Daniel, his reworking of Daniel's lines is hailed (in the revised version
folio version of the play) as 'A *Parodie*! a *parody*! with a kind of miracu-
lous gift, to make it absurder then it was', 5.5.26–7 (F). This is the *OED*'s
first example of the word 'parody' in English, but the sense of this word
also differs slightly from its modern meaning, which normally implies
intentional, rather than unwitting, artistic ridicule. Jonson is searching
for a term to describe the surreptitious and ham-fisted appropriation of
another's work, and evidently remembered the Greek term *parodia*,
which his friend John Florio had defined as 'a turning of a verse by

altering some words'.[15] Mattheo's parodic or plagiaristic verses, turning the words of Samuel Daniel, are ceremoniously burnt on stage by Justice Clement in an act which itself seems to parody – to imitate, with minor variation – the official book-burnings of the day, which often took place in the Stationers' Hall.[16]

In *Epigrams*, 100, Jonson coined another contemptuous term, *play-wright*, to describe the kind of shameless artisan who would cobble together pieces of other people's work to create a play that he might then claim as his own.[17] What 'Play-wright' reproduces are not printed texts, but jests he has heard publicly recited:

> Play-wright, by chance, hearing some toyes I'had writ,
>   Cry'd to my face, they were th' *elixir* of wit:
> And I must now beleeve him: for, to day,
>   Five of my jests, then stolne, past him a play.

Though much of Jonson's early dramatic work involved close collaboration with fellow-writers, and hence (presumably) a regular trading of dramatic ideas, he remained remarkably sensitive – especially throughout the earliest phase of his career – to the possibilities of literary theft, and remarkably anxious to assert a title to his own literary property.[18] In the Induction to *Cynthia's Revels*, the boy who acts as Jonson's spokesman wishes that

> your *Poets* would leave to bee promoters of other mens jests, and to way-lay all the stale *apothegmes*, or olde bookes, they can heare of (in print, or otherwise) to farce their *Scenes* withall. That they would not so penuriously gleane wit, from everie laundresse, or hackney-man, or derive their best grace (with servile imitation) from common stages, or observation of the companie they converse with; as if their invention liv'd wholy upon another mans trencher.
>
> Induction, 176–84

This is plagiarism not merely of literary work that is 'in print or otherwise', but – more remarkably – of the casual witticisms of laundresses and hackney-men; a form of 'servile imitation' which Jonson regards with special contempt.[19] His own work, he insists in a familiar figure in the prologue to *Cynthia's Revels*, 'shunnes the print of any beaten path, / And proves new wayes to come to learned eares' (10–11).

Epigrams, 56, introduces another shameless pilferer and promoter of other men's jests, 'Poet-Ape':

> Poor Poet-Ape, that would be thought our chiefe,
>   Whose workes are eene the fripperie of wit,
> From brocage is become so bold a thiefe,
>   As we, the rob'd, leave rage, and pittie it.

The word 'fripperie' meant second-hand clothing, or a place where second-hand clothing was sold; 'brocage' or brokerage is trading in second-hand goods. Jonson is describing a literary world in which dramatic texts circulate like used clothes: a commodity upon which, as Peter Stallybrass and Ann Rosalind Jones have argued in persuasive detail, the Jacobean theatre indeed significantly depended.[20] Who first might have purchased and worn these clothes, who first might have made these plays, are matters of little consequence: all that counts is their present possession. Poet-Ape is like the character of Sir Fretful Plagiary in Sheridan's *The Critic*, who is said to have not a single original idea or phrase of his own, working instead from a commonplace book, 'where stray jokes, and pilfered witticisms are kept with as much method as the Ledger of the Lost-and-Stolen Office'. During the rehearsal of Plagiary's tragedy of the Spanish Armada, a Beefeater enters to utter the words, 'Perdition catch my soul but I do love thee'. Someone asks if there isn't a line rather like that in *Othello*. 'Gad! now you put me in mind on't, I believe there is – but that's of no consequence – all that can be said is, that two people happened to hit on the same thought – And Shakespeare made use of it first, that's all.'[21] This is the very style of Poet-Ape: 'He marks not whose 'twas first; and after-times / May judge it to be his as well as ours.' More of this frippery anon.

  That Jonson himself should have come in time to be viewed as a dealer in the literary rag-trade is one of the deeper ironies of literary history: 'he was not only a professed imitator of Horace,' declared one of the speakers in Dryden's *Essay of Dramatic Poesy* (1668), 'but a learned plagiary of all the others; you track him every where in their snow'. The statement is modified by another speaker in the same debate, who remarks that Jonson 'has done his robberies so openly that one may see he fears not to be taxed by any law. He invades authors like a monarch, and what would be theft in other poets is only victory in him'.[22] Yet the idea of Jonson, scourge of plagiarism, being himself exposed as a notable plagiarist – a scenario all too like that of a Jonsonian comedy – was too good to resist, and throughout the following century took a tenacious hold on the imagination of scholars. It is a further irony that throughout his long career Dryden himself also repeatedly faced accusations of plagiarism.

> Thou plunder'st all, t'advance thy mighty Name,
> Look'st big, and triumph'st with thy borrrow'd fame.
> But art (while swelling thus thou think'st th'art Chief)
> *A servile Imitator and a Thief.*

So wrote Thomas Shadwell, thumpingly, in *The Medal of John Bayes*; but then Shadwell had himself been accused of plagiarism by Dryden in *Mac Flecknoe*, where his methods are contrasted (oddly enough) with those of Jonson, who, it is implied, never indulged in such a practice.[23] In his preface to *An Evening's Love*, written three years after the *Essay of Dramatic Poesy*, Dryden attempted to defend himself against charges of plagiarism by appealing to the practice of borrowing among the Ancients, and in more recent times by Shakespeare; and, finally, by Ben Jonson, who 'indeed, has designed his plots himself; but no man has borrowed so much from the Ancients as he has done: and he did well in it, for he has thereby beautified our language'.[24] Dryden's arguments failed to satisfy all his critics. Gerard Langbaine – a more serious commentator, as Paulina Kewes has shown, than once was thought – expressed his shock at Dryden's apparently double standards:

> I cannot but blame him for taxing others with stealing Characters from him (as he does *Settle* in his *Notes on Morocco*) when he does *the same*, almost in all the Plays he writes; and for arraigning his Predecessours for stealing from the *Ancients*, as he does *Johnson*; which 'tis evident that he himself is guilty of the same.[25]

The growing interest in the subject of plagiarism during the last decades of the seventeenth century and throughout the eighteenth century is intimately connected, as Paulina Kewes has demonstrated, with changing ideas about the status of dramatic authorship and the nature of intellectual property: changes which, as she argues, preceded and were assisted by the Copyright Act of 1710, but were not (as once was imagined) created by it. Concern about plagiarism was also stimulated by the emergence within the same long period of new theories concerning the nature of originality and natural genius. Edward Young's *Conjectures on Original Composition* (1759) shows how Jonson and Shakespeare were drawn into these debates, being used as contrastive examples of literary composition. Shakespeare is adduced by Young as the prototypical genius whose writings sprang directly from his observations of nature and humankind and the inner recesses of the heart; who exemplified a higher order of creativity than one who turned for inspiration to the books of others. Ben Jonson is instanced as an artist of this secondary order, having relied (as it was thought) entirely upon books, by which he was in the end destroyed. Shakespeare is viewed by Young as a kind of primitive and preliterate figure, who flourished in a world that was miraculously devoid of books.

> Perhaps he was as learned as his dramatic province required; for whatever other learning he wanted, he was master of two books, unknown to many of the profoundly read, though books, which the last conflagration alone can destroy; the book of nature and that of man. These he had by heart, and transcribed many admirable pages from them, into his immortal works.[26]

The contrast which Young went on to develop between the untutored Shakespeare and the book-dependent Jonson has been shown by modern scholars to be wholly unfounded. T. W. Baldwin half a century ago demonstrated in massive detail the extent of Shakespeare's classical and Renaissance learning, the impact of which on his creative imagination has been sensitively traced by Emrys Jones and others.[27] If originality of the kind Young imagines is a criterion of any consequence, then it would have to be acknowledged that Jonson as dramatist was arguably somewhat less dependent on books than Shakespeare, few of his plays having specific sources in the way that Shakespeare's do. This was not however the light in which mid-eighteenth-century commentators chose to view him. For Edward Capell in 1766, Jonson was one who seemed

> to have made it his study to cull out others sentiments and to place them in his works as from his own mint. This is surely an odd species of improvement from reading, and savours very little of Invention or Genius: It borders nearly upon, if it is not really plagiarism.[28]

This suspicion about Jonson's methodologies and status as a writer deepened in 1788 when the dramatist Richard Cumberland, grandson of the famous classical scholar Richard Bentley, stumbled upon what he took to be an incriminating fact about Jonson's celebrated 'Song: To Celia':

> Drinke to me, onely, with thine eyes,
> And I will pledge with mine;
> Or leave a kisse but in the cup,
> And Ile not looke for wine.

Cumberland was shocked to discover that Jonson's lyric was not original. In composing it, Jonson had remembered and pieced together several quite separate passages from the epistles of Philostratus. Jonson had also, as it happened, dipped into the Greek Anthology, though Cumberland was not aware of this fact; but what he had so far uncovered seemed to him serious enough.

> I was surprised the other day to find our learned poet Ben Jonson had been poaching in an obscure collection of love-letters, written by the sophist Philostratus in a very rhapsodical stile merely for the purpose of stringing together a parcel of unnatural, far-fetched conceits, more calculated to disgust a man of Jonson's classical taste, than to put upon him the humble task of copying them, and then fathering the translation.[29]

'Poaching', 'copying', 'fathering', 'stringing together': Cumberland's terminology glides him quickly past any complicating issues of literary genetics and imitation theory. Perhaps this was just as well: for Cumberland at this time was himself notorious for the very practices of which he now accused Ben Jonson, being indeed the real-life prototype of Sheridan's dramatic character in *The Critic*, Sir Fretful Plagiary.[30]

But the notion of Jonson's plagiarism was by this time firmly established, and the writer who had once boasted of walking along untrodden ways was now everywhere tracked in the snow of the Ancients. Richard Hurd used Horace's own precepts on imitation to criticize Jonson for 'following too servilely the plain beaten round of the Chronicle' in his Roman tragedy *Catiline*.[31] The broader suspicion that Jonson had stolen most of his best effects from classical authors survived well into the Romantic period. For Hazlitt, in one of the more extraordinary redactions of this idea, Jonson was 'a great borrower from the works of others, and a plagiarist even from nature', while Shakespeare, 'even when he takes whole passages from books, does it with a spirit, felicity, and mastery over his subject, that instantly makes them his own'.[32] Henry Crabb Robinson, enjoying a reading of *The Gypsies Metamorphosed* in his room at night, was bothered by the memory of Wordsworth telling him that 'Ben Jonson was a great plagiarist from the ancients'. Perhaps Crabb Robinson was further bothered by the memory of Landor telling him a couple of years earlier that Wordsworth himself was a great plagiarist from living authors, having stolen the famous passage in the fourth book of *The Excursion* about the seashell on the beach from Landor's own poem *Gebir*: an alleged offence that Landor was never to forgive or forget.[33]

III

Two features in particular are apparent in many of the charges just discussed. These charges are (to begin with) generally imprecise. The word 'plagiarism' is often used to denote a kind of writing, based on imitative practice, towards which the complainant happens to feel discomfort or dislike. Hazlitt's charge that Ben Jonson was 'a plagiarist even from nature', for example, is never explained or elaborated, while Crabb Robinson's sense that Jonson 'was a great plagiarist even from the Ancients' is acquired largely through hearsay. The very absence of close definition and analysis allows the accusation to ricochet perilously back and forth, sometimes injuring the party who has initiated the attack.

Second, the accusations are often animated by a sense of high moral outrage. The indignation which Jonson's classical borrowings provoked in eighteenth- and nineteenth-century readers curiously resembles the indignation that Jonson himself had expressed in his various dramatic exposures of poetic malfeasance: 'steale from the deade? its worse than sacriledge'. Plagiarism is regarded as a social transgression of a peculiarly exasperating and uncategorizable kind: as a crime, and something more than a crime. The idea is succinctly conveyed in a comment by the neo-Platonic writer, Bishop Synesius of Cyrene, that is recalled by Gerard Langbaine in *Momus Triumphans*. 'I am not a sufficient Casuist,' writes Langbaine,

> to determine whether that severe Sentance of Synesius be true, *Magis impium Mortuorum Lucubrationes quam vestes furori*; that 'tis a worse sin to steal dead mens Writings, then their Clothes: but I know that I cannot do a better service to their memory, than by taking notice of the Plagiaries, who have been so free to borrow, and to endeavour to vindicate the Fame of those ancient Authors from whom they took their Spoiles.[34]

To steal dead men's clothes – so Synesius suggests – may be a simple act of larceny, but to steal their writings is a graver sort of offence. This traditional notion may lie in the background of Jonson's epigram on Poet-Ape, whose writings are seen in terms of a constantly recirculating wardrobe, a 'fripperie of wit', entirely made up of garments belonging to others. But clothes are not, as it happens, quite like most other chattels, nor is their theft always an act of simple larceny. For clothes are also indicative of personal identity, as the action of Jonson's own comedies repeatedly reminds us.[35] To steal the garments of another person is thus to invade and appropriate a part of their very selfhood, and to masquerade under an alien identity; a violation that runs deeper than most common crimes, and is consequently punishable – as it is characteristically in Jonson's comedies – in other, meta-legal or 'poetic' ways. It is in this fraudulent spirit that the mischievous servant Musco in *Every Man in His Humour* surreptitiously obtains the clothing of Doctor Clement's clerk; that Volpone acquires the suit of a Venetian commendatore in order to gain covert entry into the courtroom at a time when he is generally believed to be dead; that the young Pug in *The Devil is an Ass* steals from the dead in a quite literal sense, filching the clothes and the body of a cutpurse who has been hanged that very morning at Tyburn. These are all, as Jonson presents them, exhilarating moves, comic up to a point, but menacing too in their implications, and disastrous for the most part in their consequences. Like plagiarism, they are criminal but more than criminal acts, and are similarly disruptive to conventional notions of the stable individual self.

Behind Jonson's phrase 'the fripperie of wit' lies an even older figure which he often elsewhere remembers, that of language as the garment of thought.[36] Such a garment must be appropriate to the personality of the wearer, and to the social context in which it is found. 'Would you not laugh, to meet a great Counsellor of state in a flat cap, with his trunck hose, and a hobby-horse Cloake, his Gloves under his girdle, and yond Haberdasher in a velvet Gowne, furr'd with sables?' Jonson writes in *Discoveries*, 2056–60, pondering questions of stylistic decorum. But how is a writer to use words (to wear clothes) that are socially acceptable and also expressive of individual style; how are one's words and clothes to be truly and finally made one's own? As in all forms of imitation, Jonson concludes, the solution lies in boldness: 'to use (as Ladies doe in their attyre) a diligent kind of negligence, and their sportive freedome' (*Discoveries*, 2263–5).

In his suggestive essay on the education of children ('De L'Institution des enfans') Michel de Montaigne had wrestled with this very question, and proposed a curiously similar solution.

> I have sometimes pleased my selfe in imitating that licenciousnesse or wanton humour of our youths, in wearing of their garments; as carelesly to let their cloakes hang downe over one shoulder; to weare their cloakes scarfe or bawdrickewise, and their stockings loose hanging about their legs. It represents a kind of disdainfull fiercenesse of these forraine embellishings, and neglect carelessnesse of art: But I commend it more being imployed in the course and forme of speech.[36]

Is it possible that Jonson had read Montaigne, and that this passage, so compatible with his own thinking, had lingered in his mind? Despite his friendship with Montaigne's English translator John Florio, Jonson might well have been cautious of echoing too literally Montaigne's ideas, which, as he allows Lady Would-be disdainfully to remark in *Volpone* (III.iv.89–90), were too often stolen by English writers, who attempted to present them as their own. And it is curious to realize that Jonson appears to have regarded Montaigne as something of a plagiarist himself. In *Discoveries* (719–44) he places Montaigne at the head of a group of writers who merely transcribe what they find in the books of others, and never disclose their sources, thereby thinking 'to divert the *sagacity* of their Readers from themselves, and coole the sent of their owne *fox-like* thefts'.

In the history of plagiarism Ben Jonson himself may be viewed, by turns, as huntsman and as fox: as a sharp-eyed detector of theft in others, and suspected raider of hen-coops himself; a double role like others he was accustomed to playing within his own lifetime.[37]

9
The Medium of Plagiarism: Rogue Choreographers in Early Modern London

Barbara Ravelhofer

Originality has been in crisis since Antiquity. As early as 1500 BC, authors complained that 'what has been said is repetition, and what has already been said is being said again. One cannot adorn oneself with the words of the ancestors, for the descendants will find out'.[1] Writing in ever more complex systems of textual dissemination has since produced ever more precious relationships between those who are speaking and those who are repeating, openly or furtively. Acknowledging this problem, much recent criticism on the history of plagiarism has sought to blur the distinction between author and plagiarist. Thus, Laura Rosenthal argues that originality is 'both relative and ultimately inconceivable'; therefore she is interested 'in cultural distinctions between legitimate and illegitimate forms of appropriation'. For her, 'to accuse someone of plagiarism' is 'to accuse him or her of repeating the literary property of another... in some kind of a public context'.[2] When originality has been reduced to a homeopathic dose, the 'public context', constructing cultural distinctions of legitimacy, provides the arbiter. One is an author – or plagiarist – only if others say so?

The author has become a mere Foucauldian function, determined by certain historical, social and cultural variables, and given the *coup de grâce* by Barthes.[3] Yet his death has proved a good career move. Academics still cannot adorn themselves with the words of their ancestors without due deference. The authors of the collapse of the author lead a happy afterlife in many a footnote. Reader, I quoted him.

Pure originality may be an unattainable ideal, yet the definition of an author's relationship to the plagiarist might reach beyond a reference to cultural convention. More mimicry than mimesis, the plagiarist's efforts prevent the audience from recognizing the source of his work. The author, on the other hand, may thrive on memory: interrelations to other works put him into context and may confer authority upon him, allusions rely on being detected. Augustan mock-heroic poems would be half the fun without recognizing the templates of *Iliad* and *Aeneis* therein. At worst an author may face an unfavourable comparison which may question his qualities as writer. His reviewers will – unless it be Gore Vidal reviewing Truman Capote – not go as far as to doubt his existence as author.

If we cannot determine the exact difference between author and plagiarist, we can at least observe when specific efforts were made to establish this difference in Western literature. The early modern period is seen as crucially important, for texts then circulated within an increasingly commercialized literary market and owning them meant profit.[4] Foucault sets the post-quem date after the emergence of copyright legislation and contracts in the eighteenth and early nineteenth centuries.[5] Such disciplining of those engaged in literary commerce, however, puts the punishment before the crime. Indeed recent work on English playwrights locates the problem in the later seventeenth century, decades before the first Copyright Act in 1710,[6] and the present study attempts to push the date even further back. In English usage, the word 'plagiary' appears in 1598;[7] yet we need to consider that its Latin equivalent may have been current among educated circles before that time. Annals from 1607, for instance, report how the master of Gonville and Caius College, Cambridge, had his play *The Destruction of Jerusalem* filched by a 'plagiarius', and earlier examples might exist.[8]

Scrutinizing the economic situation of writers in the seventeenth century, criticism perceives a text as a commodity, and 'author', 'plagiarist' and 'reader' as engaged in a kind of customer service relationship.[9] All materialism, the discourse of ownership and exchanged goods yet never makes it to materiality. It does not descend from an abstract vantage point to an empirical consideration of cultural hardware such as ink and paper – a way of thinking sanctioned by Foucault, who defines discourse itself as a result of procedures to 'sidestep gross, dreaded materiality'.[10] In this way, studies have addressed plagiarism as an economic-historical phenomenon of the printing revolution; they have described the privileges of publishers and appropriation strategies of individual writers. But they have sidestepped the question of how plagiarists and authors mediated and fashioned their texts in competition with each other. What did early modern customers see when they held books or manuscripts in their hands? How might the touch, feel, visual aspect of such a medium have influenced views on its content? Instead of asking how both legitimate and illegitimate owners went about packaging their texts, how works called upon customers 'buy me' or 'commend me to your patron', the assessment has so far been content with the aseptic vision of neutral transfer.[11]

None the less, texts are mediated by and dependent on hardware, whether vocal chords, paper or screen. The transfer of text from author to reader via plagiarist has a material side. The pageant from one owner to the next is not as insubstantial as made out in current criticism. The following case study illustrates how gross materiality might impose itself on the elegant flow of discourse.

II

In 1623 Shakespeare's First Folio edition materialized. This *annus mirabilis* in literary history may also be the year when a Western author accused, for the first time, a colleague of plagiarism *in public and in print* in order to reclaim the ownership of his text. What might be a milestone in the history of copyright and printing evolves from a dispute among professionals not commonly known for wielding the pen – dancers. The present study of François de Lauze, duped author and dancing master working in Jacobean England, explores how choreography could be perceived as a writing profession in the 1620s and how plagiarism could pose a threat here.[12] De Lauze composed a dance treatise in French, *Apologie de la danse*, which he dedicated to the Duke of Buckingham.[13] *Apologie* was published as a lavish quarto; in the prefatory section the author inveighs against a colleague who had stolen his work.

François de Lauze was a Renaissance all-round talent. Not an aristocrat, he yet belonged to an educated and mobile functional elite: next to dancing, other interests such as accountancy, literature, medicine and gardening seem to have filled the portfolio of this professional who attempted a career in both England and France. De Lauze spent most of his youth in Paris among musicians, married to the daughter of a sergeant-at-law. Young, urban, dynamic and professional, he left Paris for London before 1620 when he found that his talents were not matched by income.[14] The departure was a well-timed move, for during the reign of James I, French dancing masters and musicians had increasingly come into fashion in England's capital. In the hope of finding a patron in the courtly circles, de Lauze approached George Villiers, then Marquess of Buckingham, an enthusiastic sponsor of poets, masques and spectacles, and himself an expert dancer. Access to this powerful figure, however, was fraught with difficulties for someone newly arrived from France. Hence de Lauze gladly accepted the support of a colleague and compatriot, one Barthélemy de Montagut, who lived in London and belonged to Buckingham's household.

In order to attract Buckingham's attention, de Lauze started writing a treatise on the art of dancing, an innovative idea, for dance sources were extremely rare at the time. As far as we know, no English work on dance practice was produced at all during the sixteenth and the early seventeenth centuries. The only contemporary manuals circulating in print were Italian; and the last French author publishing on the topic had done so back in 1588. Among French manuscripts, only one source describing steps for music from Michael Praetorius' *Terpsichore* (1612) dates back to the early seventeenth century (leaving aside Montagut's cribbed *Louange*, of which later). Like his predecessors, de Lauze begins with a brief apology for the history and culture of dancing; some verbal step descriptions follow without any illustrations, so does some advice on how to comport oneself in better society. We do not know if de Lauze ever planned to have his tract translated into English, nor is it clear to what extent he – or his colleague Montagut – mastered the language.[15] A French book, of course, restricted the readership to an educated elite, such as the Inns of Court intelligentsia, or polyglot courtiers who, like Buckingham, the Earl of Carlisle or Sir Henry Wotton, had travelled abroad. It might also have attracted those among the French minority living in Westminster who were interested in the subject of genteel manners.

Montagut followed the undertaking with great interest and offers of advice. Soon, however, de Lauze came to doubt the sincerity of Montagut's motives and decided to withhold information on the progress of the book. Cut off from the project, Montagut fell back on an early draft of de Lauze's work, added a brief preface by himself and had all neatly copied. He called the resulting manuscript, a fine presentation copy, *Louange de la danse*, 'in praise of the dance', and presented it as his own work to Buckingham, who graciously accepted the chimæra. De Lauze protested to no effect, for Montagut emerged unharmed from the controversy.

Only a few years later, de Lauze was able to strike back by publishing *Apologie de la danse*. This book, a sumptuous quarto with woodcuts and engravings whose printer has not been identified, is both a technical treatise on the theory and practice of the dance, and an author's passionate vindication with a detailed, three-page introduction dwelling on Montagut's wrongdoings. Although de Lauze does not use the word 'plagiaire', a term which gained currency in French at the time of Diderot and Voltaire, his indictment is clear and unmistakable. His account is a singular early source in the history of plagiarism and so far remains, in the detail of its charges, unparalleled in the seventeenth century. It is unusual in that it names the plagiarist in public and in print and brims with authorial confidence. Yet de Lauze's ostentatious efforts seem to have failed to captivate Buckingham. There is no indication of subsequent patronage, while his rival kept devising entertainments for the marquess and later left for a soaring career at the English court. A Groom of the Privy Chamber in Queen Henrietta Maria's household, Montagut participated as dancer in masques, among them Ben Jonson's *Chloridia* and William Davenant's *Luminalia*. He even became the King's official dancing master.[16]

Did British entertainment culture turn sour on de Lauze? A failing career may have been the reason why we find him in later years in France at the courts of Louis XIII and Louis XIV, where his talents were more appreciated. He was responsible for the maintenance of the royal gardens and the health of the king (if 'médecin ordinaire du roi' and 'capitaine du parc' were not honorary titles only[17]) and participated in dance entertainments. De Lauze was involved in the balletic festivities in 1639 on the occasion of the celebration of the Dauphin's birth (and perhaps Louis XIV's first thespian appearance, as he was carried on stage). In 1641, de Lauze danced in *Le balet de la prospérité des armes de la France*, where he performed as a fury:

> Les sieurs de Looze, Montan & la Barre, representans les Furies tenans des serpens en leurs mains. Vn Aigle descend d'vne nuée, & deux Lyons sortent de leurs cauernes. Les Furies touchent de leurs serpens l'Aigle & les Lyons, pour leur inspirer la fureur. L'Enfer se referme, & la Terre paroist comme auparauant.[18]

While de Lauze was tending to both the dancefloor and the royal physique, Henrietta Maria arrived in Paris and established her exile court at St-Germain-en-Laye. Montagut was among her entourage. It is very likely that author and plagiarist met again decades after the affair.

III

François de Lauze's *Apologie* is his only known work. What interests us most here is, however, not his choreographic expertise but the three-page preface: how does Lauze signpost himself as 'author' and his rival

Montagut as 'plagiarist', and what arguments does he use to support his claim?

'Reader,' de Lauze begins, 'I realise the subject would merit a better pen than mine' – a view one is inclined to share, plodding through the long-winded book. Invoking the topos of feigned humility, de Lauze assures us that the book would never have left the darkness to which he had confined it, had not an 'over-ambitious character' forced him to publish his imperfect attempts in order to rescue his sullied reputation. The dancer Montagut played dirty on him. Thus de Lauze:

> I informed Sieur Montagut of my plan to prepare something on the dance, and, leaving him a copy of what I had already sketched, I asked him to consider it, and to advise me as a friend, if it was appropriate that I should continue. He had no sooner seen it, than, praising extravagantly my original decision to make a tract, he encouraged me by countless flatteries to continue with this work, whose completion he professed to desire impatiently,... whereupon I felt that his encouragement was directed only to his own advantage, and that his vanity was counting on my openness to yield readily to him all the credit which my labours could attract.... Telling him some months later that I had put the finishing touches, and also showing him a discourse which I had added in support of my subject, he used all his devices to obtain from me, and to print under his own name, that which I was not yet confident enough to have printed; but his pleas, his promises and all his attempts having no effect, he sought other means which I pass over, and of which those who know them can only speak to his discredit.... He finally had transcribed, without any change, the copy which he had had from me and expanded it with a certain discourse, which he called *Louange de la danse*....[19]

In this manner, Montagut presented as his own 'this singular mosaic to Monseigneur, the Marquess of Buckingham, thus giving to the whole Court (who knew of the deception) an occasion of entertainment for a while by this nice contrivance for fame'.[20] If references to plagiarism are rare in the seventeenth century, accounts of its reception are even more difficult to find. De Lauze's painful awareness of his audience provides a singular source for the views of certain circles in early modern London. Merely an amusing episode for Buckingham and the court, the affair has existential dimensions for de Lauze. A wide gap emerges between the individual author and his potential readers.

De Lauze takes solace in the fact that his colleague's literary efforts are clearly inferior to his own. Montagut admittedly is a brilliant dancer and deviser of spectacles, yet his *Louange* is imperfect, which the 'comparison between his book and mine' will soon reveal. Montagut promised, for example, extra chapters on certain dances and instructions for ladies but, unlike de Lauze, failed to deliver. De Lauze points out how Montagut missed out on final checks of his manuscript:

> all these things are visible signs that Sieur Montagut has been badly served for his money. He should never, for his honour, have had so much faith in that which left the hands of this copyist as to fail to review it, in order to efface from it at least that which could confirm the suspicions which he knew could well arise from this, his kindness towards me.[21]

What annoys de Lauze so much about *Louange* is the laziness of its perpetrator: Montagut had not even bothered to revise it in order to conceal its provenance, de Lauze, whom he was known to associate with. Montagut's literary egotism far surpasses that of plagiarists seeking to obliterate the traces of their sources. His attitude betrays the deepest possible contempt for the concept of authorship.

For the preface of *Louange*, de Lauze scoffs, Montagut is entirely indebted to Cornelius Agrippa's *Of the Vanity and Uncertainty of the Arts and Sciences*.[22] De Lauze thereby creates an ally. This leading figure of European humanism becomes a precedent to his own plight, a plagiarized ancestor. Agrippa's chapter on dance may well have inspired Montagut. Yet there are crucial flaws in de Lauze's argument. Montagut writes for, Agrippa against dancing. Second, far from being exclusive to Agrippa, Montagut's examples of dance history and mythology belong to a commonplace literary arsenal reaching back to Antiquity. Third, de Lauze fails to acknowledge that Montagut sometimes, if rarely, introduces a new idea. Montagut discusses the founding of the Order of the Garter (though not by Henry III, as he states with characteristic indifference to fact, but by Edward III) – a shrewd gesture, for Buckingham belonged to this exclusive, fashionable community, and Montagut was only too aware of this, addressing him as a Knight of the Garter in the preface of *Louange*.[23]

While Montagut never wastes time giving others credit, de Lauze seeks confederates in many disciplines. Turning to the dancing profession proper, he respectfully mentions Antonius Arena, a Provençal author of an early sixteenth-century dance history with practical instructions.

With respect to another writer, Thoinot Arbeau, de Lauze even intimates personal contact: 'Arbeau has promised me to refer to his *Orchésographie* in order to support me.'[24] De Lauze's mentioning of Arbeau is puzzling. Under this *nom de plume*, the cleric Jehan Tabourot had composed a treatise sympathetic to the art of dancing which had appeared in 1588. In the preface Arbeau tells his reader that he is 69.[25] The printer of *Orchésographie* states that its publication occurred 'long since' its composition.[26] Writing on *Apologie* in the 1620s, as he does, de Lauze gives Arbeau the unlikely lifespan of some 103 years! It is, of course, possible that the old cleric is, like the proverbial manuscript found in a chest, a biographic construct bearing little resemblance to reality. But if *Orchésographie*'s Arbeau is a fiction, then *Apologie*'s Arbeau is one even more so. No matter how we look at the problem, it raises questions about de Lauze's claim to have Arbeau's support in his present undertaking. A crucial difference appears in the strategies of de Lauze and Montagut. While Montagut obliterates his sources, de Lauze is so anxious to mention them that he lays false paths and invents connections. The plagiarist is a master of oblivion, whereas the author is an expert in the construction of false memory.

Some striking features of *Apologie* suggest that de Lauze took an active interest in the medium of his text and cared about its visual appearance. The engraved frontispiece shows Parnassus, the legendary home of Apollo and the Muses (see Figure 1). These are playing their instruments, observed by two poets or philosophers in the background. Pegasus is about to take off from this mountain of inspiration. The title-page of *Apologie* attests to de Lauze's ambitious literary claim: his work will make the heavenly horse soar.

The preface alludes to the imagery of the frontispiece and thereby confirms the hypothesis that de Lauze had a hand in its choice. A poem addresses Buckingham in the following terms:

> It is now time to shake off the restraints of [vain] expectation
> Fear no more to approach this magnificent power,
> Your book is the Parnassus where you give your lessons
> To the Nymphs eager to imitate your beautiful order
> Yet admit that even with your instruction,
> Their divine movements would fall into disorder
> If this great Buckingham were not their Apollo.[27]

The frontispiece, however, projects not only into the future – Buckingham as possible patron – but shows the way to the past as well. It is an

Figure 1:   F. de Lauze, *Apologie de la danse* (1623), title-page. By permission of the Canon of Peterborough Cathedral and the Syndics of the University Library, Cambridge.

imitation of a woodcut used by the French publisher Ballard. Ballard, a family business, controlled music printing in France for over two hundred years. In the course of its history, the house of Ballard used variants of the Parnassus motif for its title-pages (see Figure 2).[28] The Parnassus image both visualises the publisher's self-confidence and refers to the location of the printing house in Paris, Montparnasse. Since its foundation in the 1550s, a stupendous number of editions had been produced there. Thousands of works circulated throughout Europe by the time de Lauze published *Apologie*, and they were renowned for exquisite design.[29] De Lauze must have known what kind of associations his frontispiece would conjure up for readers all over Europe. He was an educated man; while in Paris, he lived in walking distance from Montparnasse, and he had many friends among musicians and the courtly circles.

Ben Jonson, too, owned Ballard books. His copy of *Le balet comique de la reine*, Baldassarino de Belgioioso's famous ballet which was staged at the Louvre in 1581 (see Figure 3) is a beautiful quarto with music scores and numerous illustrations, describing the actions of the ballet. Jonson signed the book in his customary manner: 'Sum Ben Ionsonii'.[30] The motto in the top right corner, 'tanquam explorator', 'like an explorer' or 'like a scout', Jonson gleaned from Seneca:

> Be careful, however, lest this reading of many authors and books of every sort may tend to make you discursive and unsteady. You must linger among a limited number of masterthinkers, and digest their works.... Select one [thought] to be thoroughly digested.... The thought for to-day is one which I discovered in Epicurus, for I am wont to cross over even into the enemy's camp, – not as a deserter, but as a scout.[31]

Talking about books and their makers, Seneca envisages a widely stretched landscape of learning, on which many authors have set up their camps. Some of these authors are as yet unknown, others may not be good for us to seek; yet an occasional foraging into foreign territory may benefit our intellectual development. Jonson takes up this very idea: the books in his library have been marked by the curious explorer. They need to be digested with discretion. 'Tanquam explorator' is an ambiguous motto for one's books. Does the *Balet comique* belong to the limited group of masterworks, a model spectacle inspiring Jonson's masques, or is it a trophy from the enemy's camp, a special-effects exponent of the mighty shows Jonson was so suspicious of?

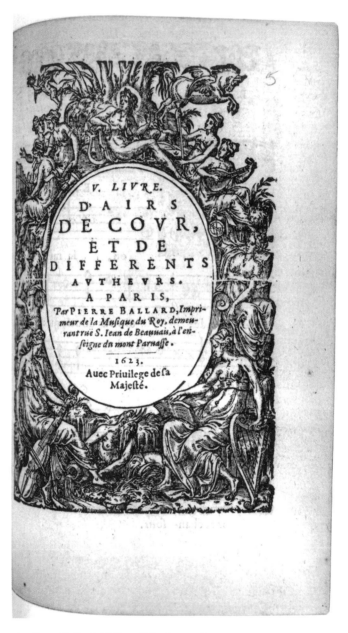

Figure 2:   Pierre Ballard, *V. livre d'airs de cour* (Paris, 1623), title-page. By permission of the Syndics of the University Library, Cambridge.

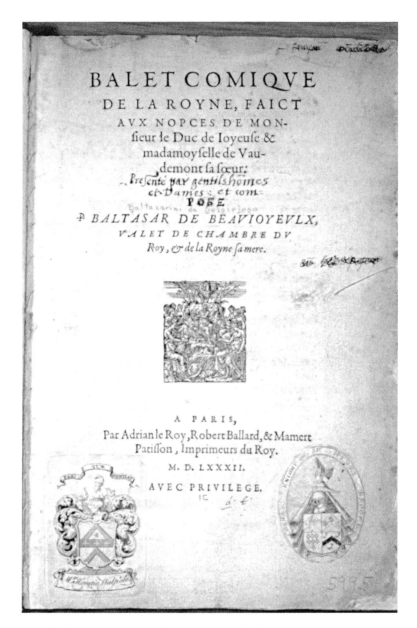

Figure 3:   Ben Jonson's copy of B. de Beaujoyeulx, *Balet comique de la royne* (Paris, 1582), title-page with Jonson's motto and signature crossed out. By permission of the New York Public Library, Music Collection, Drexel 5995.

Attracting an international community of connoisseurs, Ballard books were not only celebrated but copied. Printers in Lyons availed themselves of the Parnassus motif.[32] Early modern printers in London, too, were not above such methods. Thomas Tallis's and William Byrd's *Cantiones sacrae* (London, 1575) were printed by Thomas Vautrollier, who re-used the title-page from his edition of Orlando di Lasso (1570), which in turn was based on the title-page of the Ballard edition *Les meslanges d'Orlande de Lassus* (1570).[33]

Ballard was not the only house affected by copying. Often disseminated via the Netherlands, beautiful title-pages and ornaments of French and Italian origin found their way into new contexts. This practice would be encouraged when models for specific editions, such as sumptuous music prints, were lacking at home and when the printer looked abroad for suitable examples to imitate. Elegant composition and the resonance with prestigious publishers motivated the choice. In this way, Albion's publishers of the sixteenth and seventeenth centuries suggested to their readers urbanity and a cosmopolitan outlook. Their attempts look like a meek prelude to what was to come. In 1734, the publisher George Faulkner regarded title-pages as sellers pulling the audience. He not only lifted a frontispiece for Swift's *Works* from Fénelon's *Les avantures de Télémaque* (1730), but also found a supposed artistic author: instead of the ignominious figure of one P. Simms the famous George Vertue was claimed as the engraver in the publisher's advertisement.[34]

Apologie, then, might be considered an important, subtle precursor to eighteenth-century practice in attracting a readership. De Lauze was looking at a publisher who had already achieved a reputation for ballet books. The Ballard *Balet comique* is certainly the finest edition in this area. It makes sense that de Lauze chose the best available template for his own book, and knowingly introduced visual hints to a high-end editor of music and ballet livrets. As a consequence, the copious design of *Apologie* sets it above many contemporary English or French prose works in quarto. Notwithstanding some slight imperfections, its visual appearance recalls the splendour of Ballard editions.[35]

So much appreciation of one's models raises tantalizing questions. De Lauze condemns Montagut as plagiarist. Must his graphic borrowings be read as a compliment to Ballard and informed patrons, or do they represent an unacknowledged appropriation of a prestigious printer's device? We might answer that question by comparing, again, de Lauze's and Montagut's literary strategies. A crucial difference between Montagut's and de Lauze's attitudes to texts emerges. While Montagut left the early draft of *Apologie* to the copyist and could not care less about improving or changing it, de Lauze's *Apologie* has been revised, it includes the history of its genesis and a frontispiece which is similar but not identical to its French original. Rather than being a plagiarized copy or a forgery, this frontispiece might come across as a revised image. A plagiarized copy would seek to eliminate traces which might lead to the source of its inspiration. Here, however, there is no harm in readers recognizing the original and associating the book with France's most prestigious publisher; on the contrary, such effects are desirable. A forgery would seek the closest possible resemblance to the original. De Lauze's unknown artist, however, changed some of the instruments, inserted two philosophers in the background and slightly updated the apparel of the muses to match a more contemporary fashion style. The frontispiece might be another, visual way of de Lauze's pleasure at laying false tracks. In the same way that he introduces as personal acquaintances authorities who never spoke to him, publishers who never printed his book are impishly gestured at. Where Montagut forgets about his ancestors, de Lauze invents them.

Stephen Orgel argues that for the Renaissance artist 'invention was deeply involved with copying'. For Orgel, 'the question of the morality of literary imitation...starts to appear significantly in England only after the Renaissance'.[36] True, compared to de Lauze's diatribe, dismissive sixteenth-century remarks on upstart crows pluming themselves with their fellow writers' feathers seem epigrammatic quips only. Yet de Lauze's case also demonstrates that Orgel's theoretical framework might be extended by including foreign writers active in England at the time. Furthermore it highlights how an author experienced the distinction between *imitatio* and *furtum* as a personal injury and vocally protested against plagiarism some fourteen years before Jonson's death. Thus de Lauze provides some fine-tuning in the argument, in particular, if we consider his differentiated treatment of text and images, and if we compare his attitudes towards plagiarism to those of other contemporary writers.

English literary criticism has concentrated on Sir Thomas Browne's *Pseudodoxia Epidemica* (1646), published more than twenty years after de Lauze's book. Here, Browne pointed out that 'though great Authors may complain, small ones cannot but take notice' of plagiarism inflicted upon them.[37] Great rivers rob smaller brooks, and them the ocean. Browne wrote out of experience, for his own work had been plagiarized, yet he never took public action against the perpetrator. De Lauze represented a new, more aggressive and entrepreneurial antitype: he embarked on a costly publicity campaign to name and shame his plagiarist, even though the offending *corpus delicti*, Montagut's single *Louange* manuscript, was unlikely to have reached a mass audience.

IV

The plagiarist is in the eye of the beholder. What's aught but as 'tis valued? According to such logic, *Apologie* is worth nothing since there is no indication that it ever secured its author Buckingham's patronage. On the other hand, it greatly mattered to its author, who took great care to make it appear in the best possible light according to his means. It offered material, printed proof of his labours and the satisfaction of having his rival denounced before a wider public. De Lauze had a clear idea of who and what was a plagiarist independent of what others, notably Buckingham and the court, thought about the affair. *Apologie* did not gain legitimacy only from the regard in which its prospective consumer – Buckingham – held it.

The focus on the economic situation of writers needs to be widened. De Lauze's would-be Ballard edition might provide the starting point to consider the commercial identity of things in the early modern period, the engraved precursors of twentieth-century trade mark culture. Literary criticism needs to move beyond treating plagiarism as something proper to literature and philosophy only and realize that fruitful connections might be drawn to disciplines such as the visual arts, music and indeed craftsmanship.[38] Cultivating the high art of repetition and revision, de Lauze's *Apologie* demonstrates how to adorn oneself with the words and works of ancestors. It illuminates the sophisticated role the medium of a text plays in such an undertaking. François de Lauze shows us that the discussion about authors and plagiarists might profitably be extended – *tanquam explorator* – to other professions and to considerations of matter beyond pure text.

10
Originality and the Puritan Sermon
Harold Love

Despite Christopher Ricks's strongly put view to the contrary, what most of us would call plagiarism has not always been seen as wrongful.[1] No one would criticize an icon painter in the Orthodox tradition for the fact that a new work was closely modelled on approved predecessors with only the most subtle of personal inflections. By the same token a monastic writer in the medieval West would have expected praise not blame for building a new text out of the pre-existing words of venerated *auctores*. Both examples belong to inherited cultures of a deeply conservative kind which offered relatively little room for innovation. But in every culture and at every time there have always been certain texts that it was perfectly proper to plagiarize. An example in our own day would be orally transmitted jokes. Whatever one's moral position on the pinching of other people's poems, novels or essays (strongly against, I would hope), it would be regarded as strange if one were to address a friend 'I would like to tell you a funny story of unknown authorship which I heard from X' rather than 'Have you heard the one about . . .?'. Such stories are regarded as a universal possession. It might be argued that, situationally, no claim of personal authorship is made or assumed for such material. No one is ever going to say 'What a clever joke: however did you come to think of it?' But that too is to suggest that one has entered a free trade zone in which assumptions about the individual ownership of texts have never applied. In our own fiercely proprietorial world this is a relatively small zone. In other periods it has been much larger.

The cartography of such zones is itself likely to be variable at any given time, with certain groups wishing to draw their boundaries wider and others more restrictively. Today radical Internet libertarians represent one extreme position and embattled copyright owners the

other. Ricks counters Harold Ogden White's assertion that early modern
England was 'without any feeling analogous to the modern attitude
toward plagiarism' with the riposte 'his book is full of indictments of
plagiarism from classical and Renaissance times, that are entirely at one
with what he deplores as the modern attitude' (p. 156). This is a fair
objection but it does not deal with the possibility that, throughout the
sixteenth and seventeenth centuries, both the modern individualist
position and various enunciations of a much more liberal one existed
side by side, and were defended by arguments which those who held
them regarded as perfectly respectable.

Let us take some examples, beginning with an academic one. In
Oxford and Cambridge in the middle years of the seventeenth century
one would have found exponents of at least three distinct intellectual
traditions: medieval Scholasticism (still then the basis of the higher
curriculum), Renaissance Humanism and Cartesianism. Allegiance to
any one of these involved quite different views about the unacknowledged appropriation of others' words. The Scholastic, convinced that
the perfection of knowledge had been reached in the syllogistic method
of reasoning from universal axioms, would encourage a slavish adherence to precedent, training students in a technique of disputation so
formalized and derivative that it left virtually no room for personal
extension. The Humanist would encourage another kind of derivativeness based on the close imitation, shading over into direct appropriation, of revered ancient models. If Plutarch or Pliny had already given
perfect expression to what one wished to say, it was almost an act of
rudeness not to employ their words or, alternatively, a sign of ignorance,
suggesting one did not know where the perfect enunciation of a particular *topos* was to be found. And hadn't Seneca ruled 'Quidquid bene
dictum est ab ullo, meum est'? Only the Cartesian of the three would
have held a 'modern' view of literary ownership, grounded in the preference expressed in the *Discourse on Method* for artifacts 'on which one
individual alone has worked' over those which made use of 'old walls
which were built with other ends in view' or sciences composed of the
'gradually accumulated opinions of many different individuals'.[2]

Since each of these views was sincerely and coherently held, we
cannot come down in favour of any single one of them except by
aligning ourselves with it and perpetuating its discourse in our own.
The fact that plagiarism may have been both condoned and denounced
by people living in the same place at the same time is no more significant than that, in the 1850s, the inhabitant of a tropical island and a
European missionary may have had opposing views about the wrongful-

ness of cannibalism (a kind of comestory plagiarism). Both ethical systems were valid for those who embraced them. What ensues in such situations is sometimes called ideological debate and sometimes politics; but what concerns the history of ideas is not the views in themselves but the ways in which the difference between competing discourses was worked out through theory and action (e.g. by eating the missionary or seizing the island and enslaving its inhabitants). In considering plagiarism one will learn more by observing the debate than entering it.

Scribal and print authorship

One particular evolution in attitudes has been discussed by Paulina Kewes in connection with 'polite' literature of the late seventeenth and early eighteenth century.[3] Her analysis charts a movement from a situation in which transcription of other people's words into one's own text was seen by many as legitimate drawing on a common stock, to one in which there was a preponderant sense of words as individually owned property which could be disposed of in the literary marketplace. She demonstrates admirably that there was an enclosure movement in texts as well as land. Yet, this triumph of the owned original text was never a complete one; for example, the humanist close imitation of admired Greek and Roman models continued to be enjoined as a method of creating new works. The appropriative practice of Gray, Collins and Goldsmith, as illustrated in the footnotes of Roger Lonsdale's joint edition of these poets, goes beyond the provision of recognizable 'allusions' to become a fundamental technique of composition.[4] There can be no doubt that over this period the protectionist zone expanded its boundaries enormously at the expense of the free trade zone, but not to the extent of abolishing it.

We should note that such differences tended to be media-specific, with oral and scribal texts viewed from a more libertarian perspective than printed ones. This is not to say that there was not some conception that a spoken text might be plagiarized, as in the case of Mr Bayes in *The Rehearsal*:

Bayes. . . . My next Rule is the Rule of Record, and by way of Table-Book. Pray observe.
Johnson. We hear you Sir: go on.
Bayes. As thus. I come into a Coffee-house, or some other place where witty men resort, I make as if I minded nothing; (do you mark?) but

as soon as any one speaks, pop I slap it down, and make that, too, my own.

Johnson. But, Mr. *Bayes*, are not you sometimes in danger of their making you restore, by force, what you have gotten thus by Art?

Bayes. No, Sir; the world's unmindful: they never take notice of these things.[5]

Bayes's crime is that he is purloining from the free trade area of oral invention in order to construct a written text which will, by being performed and printed, become an owned article of commerce. But for an outraged wit, sword in hand, to demand the 'restoration' (by what means?) of his *bon mot* would be to assert a degree of proprietorship over the impromptu spoken word that was itself a crime against common communication. Mr Bayes was doing no more than dramatists and novelists have always done, and often confessed to, as when Synge writes in the preface to *The Playboy of the Western World*: 'A certain number of the phrases I employ I have heard also from herds and fishermen along the coast from Kerry to Mayo, or from beggar-women and ballad-singers nearer Dublin.'[6]

One finds a similar media-related distinction between works published through the press and works published or circulated scribally.[7] The printed word was an owned word, commercially owned by the bookseller who had entered it in the Stationers' Register, and morally owned by the writer whose name appeared on the title-page. The scribally circulated text tended to be anonymous to start with or, if it bore a name, that name was likely to be the result of some reader's private knowledge or guesswork. But even when the work was correctly attributed, this attribution was not regarded as conferring ownership. Instead, transcribers were free to alter the text in any way they liked, and frequently did. Arthur Marotti, in his important discussion of 'social textuality' in the manuscript system, cites several cases of compilers learning how to become poets themselves by first modifying poems they transcribed into a personal miscellany and then imitating them.[8] This lack of any strong sense of the scribally circulated text being individually authored is a mark of the 'chirographic' medium's closeness to the oral one. Ong uses the term 'residual orality' for this phenomenon.[9]

One signal example of this free trade attitude towards the handwritten text was the practice of compiling commonplace books under topic headings. While some compilers were careful to record their sources, many entered the thought or the verbal formulation alone, absorbing it as occasion required into their own future writings or preachings. In its original conception the commonplace book was intended as a step towards memorization. Minds trained in the subtleties of Aristotelian logic were well equipped for argument, but needed a subsidiary stock of instances and observations that might be drawn on in building an oration appropriate to any given occasion. The very name commonplace (*loci communes*) indicates their status as a universal possession. The authorial name was only significant, in such circumstances, when its prestige was used to give authority to what was said. In reclaiming written materials for oral employment speakers reactivated the freedom from ownership that had always attached to oral texts.

Dame Sara Cowper's commonplace books, written during the closing decades of the century, exemplify this sense of the commonplace as a universal possession.[10] As a woman she was not expected to undertake a career based on the arts of persuasion: instead, she tells us, her books, much of whose material was copied from the papers of Martin Clifford, were compiled for the pleasure and solace they offered to a fairly wretched life. They offer some wonderful examples of personal appropriation of gathered texts. She made print-published authors such as Sir Henry Wotton the subject of games in which phrases or whole sentences would be altered, combined and reapplied to subjects of her own choosing. Sometimes the source of these quotations was acknowledged but often not. Here there is at least some transformation; but what are we to say about her reuse of two manuscript letters of advice to a son, dating from a century earlier, that she copied into one of her volumes as 'A letter collected for my son Will' and 'A letter collected for my son Spencer'? The use of 'collected' may be an admission that these were not of her own composition but otherwise her behaviour in appropriating them for her own use is no different from that of many other parents of that and earlier times. As anonymous, scribally circulating documents they were regarded as available to all and no stigma attached to making use of them. A similar practice can be observed in the commonplace book of William Longueville. The first element in the book was copied from a similar book of observations by Samuel Butler, in this case mostly original; however, Longueville added entries of his own without making any attempt to distinguish the two. Clearly, he did not see Butler as having any proprietorial claim to this material, regarding it as part of the world's stock of freely available commonplaces.[11]

To turn from the printed to the manuscript page is to discover a totally different attitude to the ownership of texts existing contemporaneously with the early phase of the modern system of literary ownership. One cannot argue that because plagiarism was frowned upon in one discursive context it was abhorrent in all, nor that there were not (as there still are) areas of our written textual inheritance which constituted the unenclosed common.

Anglican and Puritan views of the sermon

A similar lesson might be drawn from the history of the seventeenth-century sermon, another genre ambiguously placed between oral, scribal and print-based notions of property. To begin with we need to note that conservative Anglicans, especially those in the Laudian tradition, and the people we will broadly call Puritans had strongly opposed attitudes towards the place of the sermon in worship.[12] For Puritans the sermon together with impromptu prayer were the central acts of divine service. For conservative Anglicans, on the other hand, the essential matter was the performance of the liturgy recorded in the *Book of Common Prayer*. As J. R. Tanner put it:

> The great ordinance of Puritanism was preaching, while the great ordinances of Anglicanism were the Sacraments. This difference in their conception of religious life was not a novelty of the seventeenth century, but had its roots further back in the reign of Elizabeth. The Queen herself hated preaching, and she had a short way with preachers.... The Puritans complained bitterly of 'dumb ministers' and the Puritan clergy carefully cultivated the art.[13]

The strength of this attachment to the liturgy, often questioned by historians, receives confirmation from Judith Maltby's *Prayer Book and People in Elizabethan and Early Stuart England*.[14] When a parish priest or curate was unwilling to preach or did it badly, his Puritan parishioners would go 'gadding about after sermons' or set up 'lectures', which were in effect a form of sermon detached from liturgy. Liturgist clergy were quick to denounce failure to take part in the common prayer as a form of immorality. A pre-Civil War parson at Milborne St. Andrew declared that all that went elsewhere to sermons in preference to attending his own services were 'bawdy knaves, drunken knaves, lecherous knaves and thievish knaves'.[15] Another, at Great Totham in Essex, told Puritans that 'their sins are greater than the sinnes of Sodome and Gomorrhe. They contemne or refuse the sacraments and service of God but do they thincke to escape the vengeance of God. No, I doubt not but fire and brimstone will come from heaven and consume them. Wee have them here today but wee shall not have them here againe foure or fyve sondaies followeing.'[16] According to the *Constitutions and Canons* of 1640, it was the mark of 'factious people' that they should refuse 'to joyn in the publique prayers, service and worship of God with the congregation, contenting themselves with the hearing of sermons onely'.[17] In opposition to this Puritan attitude, many Anglicans played down the importance of the sermon. A savage verse libel directed in 1605 at the recently deceased Archbishop Whitgift accuses him of being 'The dumb doggs patron'.[18] Under later canon law, the incumbent of a parish was supposed to preach every Sunday, or to supply a substitute 'if the Benefice will bear it'; but if the funds of the parish did not run to a substitute capable of preaching, the sermon could be dispensed with.[19]

A second point is that Puritans preferred their sermons to be improvised, and in that sense to be original: they were hostile to the notion of the read sermon (though notes might be permitted) and doubly so to the plagiarized one, because, almost by definition, a second-hand sermon could not be directly inspired by God. Printed Puritan and nonconformist sermons of the period were either transcribed after delivery or taken down in shorthand. The orthodox view was quite the reverse in respect of both reading and inspiration. In Elizabeth's reign parish clergy were encouraged to stick to a book of official sermons called the *Homilies*, making the sermon an extension of the printed liturgy. A writer of 1678 mentions a current proposal that 'only some select men in every Diocess' should be allowed to preach and the remainder be supplied with a privately printed collection containing a year's worth of sermons composed by these paragons.[20] Individual sermons by Andrewes or Donne may originally have been delivered from notes rather than from a fully written text; however, in the case of a Restoration master of the Anglican sermon, Isaac Barrow, we have his own carefully written-out texts, sometimes in several versions delivered on different occasions. He, clearly, was no subscriber to the notion of immediate inspiration. Both the grand oratorical effects and the biting wit of which he was capable were carefully scripted. Moreover, even an impromptu Anglican sermon was still likely to be highly derivative and packed with quotations and commonplaces. The standard model in which students at universities were trained was one of dividing the text for the day into its component words and phrases and explaining the significance of these in methodical order. William Chappell, Bishop of Cork's *The Preacher* (Latin 1648; English 1656) has not a word to say about inspiration, but presents the preparation of a sermon as an exercise in the application of Ramusian logic to the text considered as 'axiom', noting:

by this means the Preacher doth necessarily tye himself to the words of the Text, or at least will not erre in the foundation of his discourse; whereas contrarywise, this curb being taken away, there is a great way given to straying, making any thing of what you will, and applying some few general collections to any text, (sometimes to the connexion; before the Text itself be understood) and so without touching, but meerly neglecting the Text, to the filling of the ears and mindes of the hearers with impertinent (and peradventure dangerous) opinions in stead of Doctrines.[21]

The effect of an orthodox performance on the hearer should be that 'coming home, having opened the book, he may say, I have this day heard this part of holy writ expounded and applied' (p. 10). Despite the brilliant use that a great preacher like Andrewes or Donne could make of this method, it was essentially a mechanical one.

A preference for the composed sermon over the improvised one is evident in Hooker, who disparaged impromptu preaching as 'sermons without booke, sermons which spend theire life in theire birth and maie have publique audience but once'.[22] He also questioned whether there was anything in 'the best sermons beinge uttered, which they loose by beinge readd' (p. 107). In his long reply to Puritan arguments for the primacy of sermons in Book 5, Chapters 21 and 22 of *Ecclesiastical Polity*, he finds only one sentence of positive praise for them, and even this is suspiciously concessive:

So worthie a part of divine service we should greatlie wronge, if we did not esteeme preachinge as the blessed ordinance of God, sermons as keyes to the kingdom of heaven, as winges to the soule, as spurres to the good affections of man, unto the sound and healthie as foode, as physicke unto diseased mindes. (p. 87)

Yet for Hooker, sermons could never be inspired utterances but only products of 'the wit of man' and therefore prone to 'tast too much of that over corrupt fountaine from which they come' (p. 99). The word of God had been revealed to the prophets and apostles 'by immediate divine inspiration', but since that time there was 'no *word of God* but the Scripture' (p. 84). Inspiration could be encountered only through the study of the written Bible and its public reading, which for him was a species of preaching in no way inferior to sermons. His view of the sermon was the same as Chappell's – that it was not to be a substitute for scripture but to guide believers in their application of it.

By contrast, even today among Christian Churches, many kinds of (mainly) Protestant worship are built round impromptu oratory conceived as proceeding from unmediated divine inspiration. Speaking with tongues cannot be done from a script: it has by definition to be original. The seventeenth-century Puritan view ancestral to this position can be sampled in the diaries and memoranda of the Presbyterian Oliver Heywood (1630–1702). A conformist sermon was supposed to be 'studied' beforehand by reading commentaries and careful preparation of the text to be spoken. In March 1666, shortly after being ejected from his living under the Act of Uniformity, Heywood visited the home of an influential supporter:

> 4. on Wednesday we travelled together to Sr Thomas Stanleys of Auderley, where I being called to goe to prayer in that large family the first night we came, I had a temptation to study and speak handsome words with respect to the company, but reflecting, to whom I prayed, and that it was no trifling matter, I set myself in serious earnest to the work and god helpt me to speak to him seriously with respect of the state of their soules and the good of the family.[23]

Here study is so far from being a virtue that it becomes a temptation to be resisted. At another point God intervenes directly to prevent him from wasting time in study:

> that night being in my study snuffing my candle, I unawares snuft it out, being in the darke I set my self to meditation and secret prayer, and my spirit workt kindly betwixt god and my soul – oh it was a sweet time! that accident helpt me to spend that time immediately with god, wch otherwise I had spent in studying – blessed be god – (i. 285)

His successful sermons and impromptu prayers were accompanied by an experience of inspiration, for which he frequently uses the words 'liberty' and 'enlargement'. An example:

> at noone after dinner Mr Dinelaw (the gentleman of the place) moved me to preach in the afternoone, I told him I was willing if Mr Crosley was content, and if it might not prejudice them, they al unanimously desired it, and referred the consequences thereof to gods providence, that I took as a cal from god, and adventured to

preach, and the lord was graciously seen in giving me unwonted
liberty of speech and spirit, both in prayer, and preaching, and
affected the hearts of his people ... (i. 193)

Heywood is aware when he preaches with the aid of inspiration and
when he does not. A sermon without that particular 'liberty' was a
failure, even a badge of personal unworthiness. Conversely, the truly
inspired outpouring could have effects beyond its immediate one on its
auditors: believers recovered from sickness and women gave birth after
the intervention of inspired prayer. On one occasion Heywood recorded
that an experience of 'extraordinary assistance and enlargement' coincided with the collapse of the chamber floor at the Checquer Inn at
Halifax, in which agents of the local ecclesiastical courts who had been
persecuting him fell into the cellar among the beer barrels (no doubt a
prefiguration of an even steeper fall awaiting them!) (i. 191).

To a religious persuasion premised on the search for inspiration, and
for which the read or written sermon was an inferior substitute for the
impromptu one, the borrowed or plagiarized sermon was doubly abhorrent. No experience of 'enlargement' could attend the mechanical reading of another's words. Heywood notes in the case of a candidate
minister for his own former parish that

> he borrowed horse, money, bootes and is run away with all, and his
> sermon was found verbatim in a printed book so that he was traced
> by the sent of an intelligent hearer even as he was preaching it. (i.
> 189)

A similar denunciation of plagiarism, directed at the Conformist clergy,
was made about the same time by Ralph Wallis, 'the cobbler of Glouces-
ter':

> Another sort of this *Mystical Body*, are the *Rats* or *Cu-Rats*, who are set
> over the Flocks ... And they are so pestered in some places with
> *Phanaticks*, that they cannot filch a Sermon, as their Masters do, but
> they are found out. ... One Rat-master, having a Living of 150 *l. per
> annum*, saith, *that he can go to London, and buy Sermons to serve him all
> the year about for five pound, and bear his charges into the bargain*; which
> hath been his course.[24]

Wallis's main charge is explicitly one of unacknowledged derivativeness:
his 'Rat-master' is prepared to preach, but is incapable of producing his

own words. For Wallis, like Professor Ricks, this was inherently wrongful. But we have no reason to assume that the curate thought it so. His aim was presumably to produce the best kind of moral exhortation possible for his congregation, and if that could be done by a purloined or ghost-written sermon rather than one of his own he had a moral and professional duty to acquire these.

Ritualist Anglicans saw little difference between a borrowed sermon and an original one, provided it performed its allotted task as an extension of the liturgy. What emerged from the pulpit on Sunday was to be judged by its power to edify, not on its merits as an example of personal authorship. In addition, the pulpit was not the place for a declaration of authorship whether personal or otherwise. Like a leader in a newspaper written using the editorial 'we', the seventeenth-century Anglican sermon, while it might admit personal inflections, was ultimately to be delivered as the corporate opinion of the Church. Much as with our earlier example of the oral joke, it would have been neither proper nor relevant to begin a sermon by crediting it to someone else. What we have here are two contemporaneous systems of religious ethics which judged the presentation of borrowed texts from the pulpit from two very different viewpoints. Naturally not all conformist or nonconformist clergy held to one or other of the extreme views I have presented, but a substantial number of each did.

Of course the Church of England always had its great preachers – greater, on the whole, than those of their opponents, because they wrote their sermons for hearers with print-nourished expectations and in anticipation of recreating them as works for the press. The finest Jacobean sermons were in many cases composed for the personal instruction of that keen theologian and lover of language, James I. Their appeal was to the learned elite rather than to the people at large. Such sermons were also heavily dependent on 'study'. In the case of the virtuoso authored sermon intended for publication, theological plagiarism was itself an issue. P. J. Klemp has drawn attention to a case in which Lancelot Andrewes suffered the inconvenience of having the argument for a sermon appropriated by a fellow cleric, John Buckeridge, who preached on the same theme the day before Andrewes was to do so.[25] John Chamberlain's account was as follows:

> The fowre sermons at court passed with goode commendation, only Doctor Buckridge is somwhat toucht as a plagiarie, in that the bishop of Chichester having communicated with him what he meant to do, he comming immediatly before him preoccupated much of his matter.[26]

However, Klemp's account of the matter sees Buckeridge not as a thief but as an 'idolator' of Andrewes, whose plagiarism was an act of homage. He cites the funeral sermon Buckeridge was later to speak over Andrewes in which he said: 'He is the great *Actor* and *performer*, I but the poore cryer, *Vox clamantis*, He was the *Vox clamans*: he was the loud and great *crying Voice*, I am but the poore *Eccho*: and it is well with me, if as an *Eccho*, of his large and learned bookes and workes, I onely repeate a few of the last words.'[27] Klemp finds this unsatisfactory, arguing that Buckeridge had failed to learn certain important hermeneutic lessons that Andrewes had tried to teach him; but Buckeridge's behaviour made sense in terms of a culture of preaching which was in no way hostile to this kind of derivativeness. The point of the story for the present discussion is not Andrewes's presumed irritation but the fact that his devoted fellow cleric saw nothing harmful or unusual in such an act of appropriation. In any case, there could be no personal ownership of God's truth. Kemp in criticizing Buckeridge's 'inability to act on the distinction between an example and an idol or a voice and echo' (p. 35) is treating him as an individual rather than the representative of a deeply entrenched cultural formation.

Inspiration and originality

We have seen that the centrality of inspiration to Puritan worship encouraged one kind of originality, that of the impromptu sermon. It is time now to consider how this view may have contributed to the secular notion of literary originality that underlies the Copyright Act of 1710. To varying degrees among the sects (least among the Presbyterians, most among the Ranters and Fifth Monarchists), the commitment to inspirational preaching was an outcome of an ideal of religious truth as something progressively delivered through a process of continuing revelation. A sermon delivered in this belief would possess an authenticity of a certain kind that came from its deliverer attaining a prophetic status. However, the notion of inspiration and that of originality are not the natural bedfellows that they became in Romantic discourses on authorship. Indeed, there is a kind of epistemological Morton's fork at work in the matter. Judged from a secular perspective which denies the reality of divine intervention, the 'inspired' sermon is merely a reactivation of the traditional tropes of a particular discourse. This must also have been the view of many conformists who, while, like Hooker, accepting the reality of inspiration of the gospels, would not accept that it had been bestowed upon the Puritans. Satirical attacks on

Puritan preaching stress its repetitions of stock phraseology, its use of a nasal intonation and its reliance on the body language of the preacher to produce a suppositious excitement among the congregation. Roger L'Estrange in 1680 gave a list of Puritan terms which he dismissed as the 'the *Cant*, or *Jargon* of the *Party*'.[28] Swift's *A Tale of a Tub* and 'The mechanical operation of the spirit' locate the source of inspiration in the eruptions of corporeal wind. A machine cannot be original.

The other prong of the fork would deny originality in another way. Judged from the perspective of the sincere Puritan, there is a different problem attending the claim of originality for inspired discourse, in that it was not produced by the speaker as such, who had merely become the channel for a supernatural author. The inspired preacher was by definition a plagiarist, albeit from the best possible source. So by the same token was the inspired Puritan writer. The extension of this understanding of revelation – the kind that caused Richard Baxter to speak of himself as 'a Pen in God's hand' – to written texts is discussed by N. H. Keeble, who cites, among other passages, Thomas Ellwood's account of the writing of *An Alarm to the Priests* (1660):

> Fain would I have been excused from this Service, which I judged too heavy for me: Wherefore I besought the Lord to take this Weight from off me (who was, in every respect, but young;) and lay it upon some other of his Servants (of whom he had many) who were much more able and fit for it. But the Lord would not be entreated: but continued the Burden upon me, with great weight; requiring *Obedience* from me, and promising to assist me therein. Whereupon I arose from my Bed, and in the Fear and Dread of the Lord, committed to Writing what He, in the Motion of his *Divine Spirit*, dictated to me to write.[29]

The 'originality' of such a work does not arise from any operation of the writer's will, fancy or judgement but from its being the product of a particular extreme circumstance. Far from removing human authors from space and time, the trope of dictation from an external supernatural voice enmeshes them even more deeply in both. Consider, in a similar situation, Jeremiah in direct dialogue with Jehovah:

> The words of Jeremiah the son of Hilkiah, of the priests that were in Anathoth in the land of Benjamin: To whom the word of the LORD came in the days of Josiah the son of Amon king of Judah, in the thirteenth year of his reign. It came also in the days of Jehoiakim the son of Josiah king of Judah, unto the end of the eleventh year of

Zedekiah the son of Josiah king of Judah, unto the carrying away of Jerusalem captive in the fifth month.

Then the word of the LORD came unto me, saying, Before I formed thee in the belly I knew thee; and before thou camest forth out of the womb I sanctified thee, and I ordained thee a prophet unto the nations. Then said I, Ah, LORD GOD! behold, I cannot speak: for I am a child. But the LORD said unto me, Say not, I am a child: for thou shalt go to all that I shall send thee, and whatsoever I command thee thou shalt speak. Be not afraid of their faces: for I am with thee to deliver thee, saith the LORD.

Then the LORD put forth his hand, and touched my mouth. And the LORD said unto me, Behold, I have put my words in thy mouth. See, I have this day set thee over the nations and over the kingdoms, to root out, and to pull down, and to destroy, and to throw down, to build, and to plant.[30]

Jeremiah is very definite about the fact that his words were inspired by God, both in the general sense of his calling as a prophet and in terms of expressions and powers acquired in the dialogue here reported; however, he is also insistent on his own historical and family identity, asserting that the words are his as well as God's, and of the uniqueness of the moments and places of inspiration. This strong personal inflection was recognized by the seventeenth-century biblical critic, Richard Simon, for whom the language of Jeremiah had a highly individualistic character. 'Isaiah,' he writes, 'was a person of Quality' whereas Jeremiah was 'bred up in the Country among Peasants'.[31] The 'originality' of Jeremiah lies in a particular confluence of the personal and the universal, which requires that both be present in full measure at a particular place and at a particular time.

In the same way, Keeble sees the originality of Puritan 'inspired' writing not as proceeding *from* the author but as the product of the experience in which the human author took part. He notes 'the Quaker habit of presenting their writings as the irresistible and extemporaneous product of revelatory moments' (p. 183). A passage from John Philly's *The Arrainment of Christendom* (1664) is cited:

I JOHN, the Servant of the *most Hy God* ... Being a Prisoner, (*with my companion in travel* at a plâs caled *Great Gomara*, on a Certain Yland in *Hungaria*, the *East of Christendom*) For the Word of God, which liveth, & abydeth for ever, & for the Testimony of JESUS, which I held – on the 19 *Day* of the *fi[r]st Month* in the Year according to Christendoms account 1662. The *Living, Eternal, & pûr Power* of God moved in me, & revealed unto me that I should wryt...[32]

Keeble sees in this a 'combination of temporal and geographical accuracy, personal experience and revelation' that anticipates the blending of 'realism, subjectivity and visionary experience' in Wordsworth's *Tintern Abbey* (p. 183). But Wordsworth, as we know, wrote from recollection in tranquillity, whereas these nonconformist authors represent the act of writing as cotemporal with the experience of inspiration. Moreover, Wordsworth knew he was professionally responsible for his own inspiration, while the Quaker writers were convinced they were the mouthpieces of God. By this means they were able to extend the oral values of the inspired sermon into the medium of print, but only by pretending that writing was a kind of oral performance. Their opponents might deny their view of their inspiration but could not deny that a singular kind of personal experience had taken place. It is this that offers a path forward to secular notions of originality and rejections of plagiarism.

In practice, as we have seen, the average printed Puritan sermon, because of its fierce allegiance to the oral medium and the prophetic stance, is verbally a good deal less original than the highly polished works of the great Anglican sermon writers. Oral productions of this kind, like most improvised music, tend to be loosely structured, formulaic and repetitive. The Anglican sermon, solidly built on Ramus' 'method of differences' applied to the words of a Biblical text, generally offers a much more satisfactory reading experience. But the Puritan version does possess, or at least strive for, a particular kind of intensity which was denied to many of its premeditated orthodox counterparts. Certainly, by its own terms, it was inimitable, since its conceptions and words both belonged to that brief, singular period of inspiration. What attributing authorship to God took away from the idea of originality was repaid by the assertion of the historical uniqueness of the process by which the work came into existence.

In explicit reaction to Puritan inspirationism the orthodox Anglican sermon of the closing decades of the seventeenth century rejected the precedent of such great dandies of the pulpit as Donne and Andrewes in favour of a restrained reasonableness freed of all suspicion of 'enthusiasm'. The leading exponents of this manner were Barrow, Burnet, South and Tillotson, the last of whom was exalted as a model of English style by Dryden and Addison. Burnet praised Tillotson after his death in terms which perfectly sum up this new tendency:

He said what was just necessary to give clear Idea's of things, and no more: He laid aside all long and affected Periods: His Sentences were short and clear; and the whole Thread was of a piece, plain and distinct.... He read his Sermons with so due a Pronunciation, in so sedate and so solemn a manner, that they were not the feebler, but rather the perfecter, even by that way, which often lessens the Grace, as much as it adds to the Exactness of such Discourses.[33]

An achievement of this kind, considerable as it was, came at the cost of an erosion of personality, a flattening of affect, and a reduction in intensity: the qualities instanced by C. S. Lewis as characterizing early eighteenth-century 'rational Christianity'.[34] It also made the sermon infinitely re-usable: either Tillotson's methods or his actual words could be recycled endlessly through the eleven thousand parish pulpits of England, and frequently were. There is no evidence that moral disapproval would have attended such professional practice. Indeed a well-informed source from the last century suggests that the exchange of written sermons was still an accepted practice among Anglican clergy:

'Well, all I can say,' he cried, 'is that it's a bit thick! Preaching another man's sermon! Do you call that honest? Do you call that playing the game?'

'Well, my dear old thing,' I said, 'be fair. It's quite within the rules. Clergymen do it all the time. They aren't expected always to make up the sermons they preach.'[35]

What was lost in the acceptance of Tillotsonian values was the sense of the sermon having emerged from a fierce act of creativity, whether human or divine.

And yet the orthodox could not entirely surrender the notion of inspiration to the enemy. Their method of retrieving it involved two rhetorical moves. In the first, Puritan inspirationalism was condemned as a surrendering of the mind to the power of 'fancy' which, as Locke conveniently demonstrated, was closely allied to madness.[36] In the second move, fancy was to be redeemed by being put under the control of judgement. In this way it could be allowed to perform the regulated, subsidiary function of Dryden's 'nimble Spaniel' in the Preface to *Annus Mirabilis* of searching 'over all the memory for the species or Idea's of those things which it designs to represent'.[37] By this and other strategies, not here considered, it became possible to reconceptualize the inspired text from being something introduced into the mind from outside to something mysteriously generated from the mind's own resources. How that generation actually happened ceased to be a problem for theology and became one for psychology. It was in this form that the idea of inspiration came to be used as the basis of the new discourse of creativity whose negotiations are described by Kewes and which was to encourage the legislative choice of the individual author as the point of origin for literary ownership.

Taking back the debate over plagiarism to an earlier stage than that studied by Kewes establishes that it was a secularized continuation of a religious debate conducted between liturgists, whose values were communal and conservative and who encouraged the sharing of texts and words from texts, and those branded as 'enthusiasts' who regarded the privileged state of inspiration as the crucial feature of active worship and who saw this as embodied in the pulpit performance of the 'enlarged' preacher or lecturer. When this ideal was extended to writing, the way was open to a framing of the idea of literary creation as inhering in a particular, unrepeatable experience, an idea which, while distinct from later notions of proprietorial creativity, did at least endue the acts of preaching and writing with a historical inimitability. It also nourished a strong hostility to plagiarism. A realization of this fact allows us to place Professor Ricks's splendid harangue against the monstrous regiment of plagiarists in the finest Puritan tradition of English and New England sermonizing.

11
Theft and Poetry and Pope

Paul Baines

Writing in *The Daily Journal* of 18 March 1728, a gentleman, signing himself 'Philo-Mauri', registered the following complaint:

> Sir, – Upon reading the Third Volume of Pope's *Miscellanies*, I found five Lines which I thought excellent, and happening to praise them afterwards in a mixt Company, a Gentleman present, immediately produced a modern Comedy, publish'd last Year, where were the same Verses, almost to a Tittle. I was a good deal out of Countenance to find that I had been so eloquent in Praise of a Felony, and not a little in Pain lest I myself should be understood to be an Accomplice...[1]

The lines in question are, barring a few revisions, familiar enough:

> A Youth of Frolicks, and Old Age of Cards;
> Fair to no Purpose, artful to no End;
> Young without Lovers; old without a Friend:
> A Fop, their Passion; but their Prize, a Sot;
> Alive, ridiculous; and dead, forgot!

Something like these ended up in Pope's *Epistle to a Lady: On the Characters of Women*, published in 1735 (lines 244–8). In the *Miscellanies*, they form part of a poem to Martha Blount, 'To Mrs. M. B. Sent on Her Birth-Day'.[2] But something very similar had first appeared in print in James Moore Smythe's comedy *The Rival Modes* (1727), where a character called Sagely speaks them as a misogynistic soliloquy after the exit of the jilting coquette, Amoret.[3] Though Pope's poem to Martha Blount had been printed in versions without the offending lines in 1724 and

1726, the 1728 version thus appeared to contain lines plagiarized from an accessible public source: 'These gentlemen are undoubtedly the first plagiaries, that pretend to make a reputation by stealing from a man's works in his own life-time, and out of a Public print.'[4]

There was nothing particularly original in charging Pope with plagiarism; John Oldmixon had just published *An Essay on Criticism* in which Pope's (earlier) work of that exact title is alleged to be wholly drawn from Dryden and 'the French Criticks'.[5] Lady Mary Wortley Montagu told Spence that the *Essay* was 'all stolen'.[6] John Dennis had abused Pope's work as nothing but imitation, a sort of monkey-mimicking, as early as 1716, and Dunces such as James Ralph, Edward Ward, Thomas Cooke and Jonathan Smedley responded to their appearances in *The Dunciad* by renewing the charge that Pope had borrowed from the Dunces he attacked.[7] In modern terms, Pope is traditionally the poet of allusion, the king of intertextuality, the master of the parallel text.[8] Pope himself has less to say about plagiarism than one might expect of the poet who understood and pursued the legal and economic implications of the Copyright Act better than any other. He erases the supposedly novel style of Ambrose Philips by referring casually to his 'pilfer'd Pastorals', and in the four-book *Dunciad* he levels the traditional charge that Cibber has merely recycled other people's plays, mangling and degrading them in the process.[9] In 1738 he put into the mouth of the pusillanimous 'Friend' of the Epilogue to the *Satires* this contention:

> Decay of Parts, alas! we all must feel –
> Why now, this moment, don't I see you steal?
> 'Tis all from *Horace*: *Horace* long before ye
> Said, 'Tories call'd him Whig, and Whigs a Tory'

But since the parallel lines in Horace are actually very different from Pope's, the accusation serves only to show up the Friend as an 'impertinent Censurer', incapable of understanding Horace, and the art of formal imitation in general.[10] Pope had already, in the much-abused *Essay on Criticism* itself, defended Virgil's imitation of Homer on the grounds that 'Nature and Homer were, he found, the same' and invoked the 'Ancient Rules' as a specific model: 'To copy Nature is to copy Them'.[11]

None the less the controversy with Moore evidently did rankle, partly perhaps because the quotation of the lines besmirched a private tribute and turned into a curse what had been intended as a (negative) part of a tribute: as Pope put it to John Caryll, managing to vindicate both his property and his sincerity in one,

The Verses on Mrs Patty had not been printed, but that one puppy of our sex took 'em to himself as author, and another simpleton of her sex pretended they were addressed to herself....But indeed they are such as I am not ashamed of, as I'm sure they are very true and very warm.[12]

His public response to the accusation came in *The Dunciad* (1728). 'M – – –' (to rhyme with 'swore' and thus prompt the identification with Moore) appears as the phantom poet for whom the booksellers Curll and Lintot compete in Book II; but it was not until *The Dunciad Variorum* of 1729 that Pope got his story straight (or sufficiently crooked). Among the 'Testimonies of Authors' Pope confronts the charge of plagiarism by insinuating that certain people have got their priorities wrong: 'Next he is taxed with a crime (in the opinion of some authors, I doubt, more heinous than any in morality), to wit, Plagiarism'; but he goes on to rebut the charge anyway, with customary bibliographic exactness, re-printing the accusatory letter from 'Philo-Mauri' alongside a further letter from 'the inventive and quaint-conceited JAMES MOORE SMITH Gent...to our author himself', before the play was acted, acknowledging that the lines will be known as Pope's but hoping that Pope would not 'deprive' his comedy of them. Pope also cites the testimony of Bolingbroke, 'the Lady to whom the said verses were originally addressed', and Hugh Bethel, as witnesses to the original authorship of the lines.[13]

In the poem itself, the phantom poet is presented as Dulness's joke from the beginning:

> All as a partridge plump, full-fed, and fair,
> She form'd this image of well-bodied air,
> With pert flat eyes she window'd well its head,
> A brain of feathers, and a heart of lead,
> And empty words she gave, and sounding strain,
> But senseless, lifeless! Idol void and vain!
> Never was dash'd out, at one lucky hit,
> A Fool, so just a copy of a Wit;
> So like, that criticks said and courtiers swore,
> A wit it was, and call'd the phantom, More.
>
> (37–46)[14]

It is possible that Pope originally had his plump friend John Gay in mind for this portrait; the joke would have been that 'Joseph Gay' was a phantom author, a 'fictitious name put by *Curl* before several pamphlets, which made them pass with many for Mr. *Gay*'s'.[15] The change is one from substance to absence: the body is air, the words empty, the head feathers: it is an 'it' rather than a 'he', and only critics and courtiers would mistake it for a real 'Wit'. The hugely emphatic position of the name highlights its bathetic 'suggestions of redundancy, dropsical growth, tedious prolongation', as Pat Rogers puts it. The 'ponderous formula' of 'James Moore Smith' has been abraded: in 'stripping down this grandiloquent denomination, Pope robs its bearer of his pretensions. The monosyllabic ring of that word "More" has the effect of reducing the Dunce to a dehumanized cipher'.[16] More turns out to be less.

And yet more: when Curll, who wins the race, comes to seize his prize (itself an allegory of dispossession, the mechanisation of the author by the book-trader), the 'Idol void and vain' dissolves as mere illusion in a reverse transubstantiation:

> And now the Victor stretch'd his eager hand
> Where the tall Nothing stood, or seem'd to stand;
> A shapeless shade! it melted from his sight,
> Like forms in clouds, or visions of the night!
> To seize his papers, Curl, was next thy care;
> His papers light, fly diverse, tost in air:
> Songs, sonnets, epigrams the winds uplift,
> And whisk 'em back to Evans, Young, and Swift.
> Th' embroidered Suit, at least, he deem'd his prey;
> That suit, an unpaid Taylor snatch'd away!
> No rag, no scrap, of all the beau, or wit,
> That once so flutter'd, and that once so writ.
>
> (101–12)

Moore is disassembled much more radically than Swift's 'Beautiful Young Nymph'; a mere embroidered suit of clothes (he was something of a dandy, despite having run through his fortune), a pilferer of other men's paper.

Pope continues his erasure of Moore's claim to author-status in the notes. Noting first of all how appropriately the allegory suits the character of a Plagiary (note to l. 31), Pope avails himself of Curll's identification of 'More' as James Moore in the *Key to the Dunciad* in which Curll had obligingly filled in the blanks left in the 1728 poem, as if bibliographically clutching at the poets (note to l. 46):

it is probable . . . that some might fancy our author obliged to represent this gentleman as a Plagiary, or to pass for one himself. His case
indeed was like that of a man I have heard of, who as he was sitting in
company, perceived his next neighbour had stollen his handkerchief.
'Sir' (said the Thief, finding himself detected) 'do not expose me, I did
it for mere want: be so good but to take it privately out my pocket
again, and say nothing.' The honest man did so, but the other cry'd
out, 'See Gentlemen! what a Thief we have among us! look, he is
stealing my handkerchief'.

The papers and manuscripts which Moore had borrowed become an
article of dress, a social accoutrement, in an anecdote which nicely
transforms literary property into a filched respectability. Pope's note
goes on to list Moore's borrowings and the theft of Scriblerian papers,
which Moore claimed for his own; an epigram on Moore's plagiarisms is
reprinted; and a mock-bibliography of works ascribed to Moore but
really by someone else, is constructed, while a list of Moore's unacknowledged attacks on Pope (including the 'Philo-Mauri' letter) forms part of
one of the appendixes.[17]

However, Pope strips Moore of even this level of authorial claim:

Notwithstanding what is here collected of the Person imagin'd by
Curl to be meant in this place, we cannot be of that opinion; since our
Poet had certainly no need of vindicating half a dozen verses to
himself which every reader had done for him; since the name itself
is not spell'd *Moore* but *More*; and lastly, since the learned *Scriblerus*
has so well prov'd the contrary.

Scriblerus' note (to the same line) opines: 'It appears from hence that
this is not the name of a real person, but fictitious' and derives Moore's
name from the Greek word for stupidity, as punningly used by Erasmus
in the *Moriae Encomion* (1511). Moore appears to be stripped even of
property in his own person by a classicizing etymology which removes
family origin and identity to replace it with a classic source; at the same
time Pope invokes one of the originating models of the entire poem,
though the invocation is a good deal less playful than Erasmus's: Sir
Thomas More is as far from the actuality of stupidity as his name is close
to it. For James Moore, however, the etymology may stand.[18]

A Restoration culture of violence and vengeance is never very far from
the satire of Pope's era. In *Gulliveriana* (1728), Jonathan Smedley had
envisaged Moore cutting the nails off Pope and Swift, transformed into

dogs; Thomas Cooke imagined Moore and Welsted overcoming Pope in battle.[19] Moore continued hostilities by collaborating with Leonard Welsted on *One Epistle to Mr Pope* (1730), already advertised in *The Universal Spectator* (1 February 1729) as 'the due Chastisement of Mr. Pope for his *Dunciad*, by James Moore Smythe, Esq'. Moore appears to have been caned for this offence, by Arbuthnot (who was also abused in the pamphlet) or a relation of his, but Pope's vengeance is always a form of erasure.[20] Accused of malice, deceit, and (indeed) of pillaging and plundering 'every Dunce that writ before', Pope returned the charges on Moore through a series of epigrams and spoof letters in *The Grub-street Journal*.[21] In a mock epitaph, Pope for once spelt out Moore's full name, but immediately unpicked it by reference to the phantasmal nature of his identity:

> For *Jammie* ne'er grew *James*; and what they call
> *More*, shrunk to *Smith* – and Smith's no name at all.
> Yet dye thou can'st not, Phantom, oddly fated:
> For how can no-thing be annihilated?
> *Ex nihilo nihil fit* (*TE* vi.326–7 at p. 327)

Even the authorship of the *One Epistle* appears nebulous, for Pope tells Broome that the pamphlet was by Moore and others, but a month later tells Bethel 'James Moore own'd it but twas made by three others, and he will disown it whenever any man taxes him for it'.

In the *Epistle to Dr Arbuthnot* (1735) Pope seizes further possession of Moore's identity. Moore is one of those foolish poetasters who leave their proper job and imitate Pope: 'Arthur, whose giddy Son neglects the Laws, / Imputes to me and my damn'd works the cause' (23–4). Pope can make ironic reference to the plagiarism controversy by claiming as one of the signs of his humility that he has 'rym'd for Moor' (373). But the burden of his attack shifts to the abusive nature of Moore's complaints against him and his clan. The question of origin is relocated from literary plagiarism to the family name, where 'name' means not only identity and inheritance but reputation. It is of interest that Pope goes out of his way to avoid referring to Moore by the name which he put on the title page of *The Rival Modes*: James Moore Smythe (the aristocratic appendage was added when Moore came into his grandfather's property). To Pope he is J-my M-re, or Moore, or More, M-, or, at an ironically inflated pinch, 'Mr. James Moore Smith'. The fragmentation of his image and mis-citation of his name appear to deprive Moore of the title to property even as he is most inescapably identified.

II

Moore was, or ought to have been, a lawyer, as Pope noted: 'Arthur's giddy son neglects the laws.' He had done so not only by becoming a poet but by thieving verses from better poets, and Pope uses the readily available metaphor of criminal theft as part of his retaliation.[22] But what Pope and his contemporaries derive from criminalizing language is less a quasi-economic sanction, a judicial reapportioning of 'copyright' to owner, than a convenient image of brutal punishment for some less definable sense of theft – the noisy reclamation of the right to a poetic personality, or the abusive degradation of rival poets. In the long run, a more pervasive (or 'civil') sense of the 'law' of intellectual property does develop, but only after – perhaps as an equalizing response to – further controversy.

A more intense version of the appropriation of the law for poetic and critical purposes can be found in the case of William Lauder, who began his allegations about Milton's plagiarism three years after Pope's death, and who blamed his own consequent fall from grace on a passage in book iv of Pope's *Dunciad*. Lauder's claims began in a scholarly fashion, with the quotation of passages of *Paradise Lost* against their supposed source in Masenius, Grotius and others, in a series of articles in *The Gentleman's Magazine*, but a certain querulousness of delivery rapidly escalated into an accusatory and legalistic tone: this was quite explicitly a literary 'prosecution'.[23] Late in 1749, the articles were republished in an expanded form as *An Essay on Milton's Use and Imitation of the Moderns*, where Lauder provided 'indisputably clear and obvious evidence' of Milton's bad faith; 150 pages of summary and parallel quotation, 'a whole cloud of witnesses, as fresh vouchers of the truth of my assertion'. Lauder protested that Milton was 'criminal to the last degree . . . in honesty and open dealing . . . not inferior, perhaps, to the most unlicenced plagiary that ever wrote'.[24]

Paradise Lost was of course an icon of creativity, and thus imitated by hacks the world over, as Pope (who alluded to the poem throughout *The Dunciad*) noted in *Peri Bathous*; its own story of demonic thefts and arrogations of creativity covertly energized Lauder's case and its controversy. But battle was officially joined on precisely Lauder's ground of a juridical literary property, against which infringements were in effect criminal. The growing awareness amongst Milton scholars that what Lauder had printed as Milton's sources were for the most part actually bits of a Latin translation of *Paradise Lost* which had been spliced into the poet's supposed sources led eventually to the publication of *Milton*

vindicated from the CHARGE of PLAGIARISM, Brought against him by Mr.
LAUDER, AND LAUDER himself convicted of several FORGERIES and gross
IMPOSITIONS on the Public (1750; dated 1751). In this palendromic
turning of the tables John Douglas, a rising young clergyman, offered
an advocate's version of the evidence against Lauder's accusation; not
for nothing does the pamphlet conclude with the image of Justice, scales
in one hand and a sword in the other. Proceeding in an exact reversal of
Lauder's method, a scholarly opening gradually supplanted by forensic
rhetoric, parallel quotation larded with tendentious legalisms, Douglas
concludes that 'our conscientious Critic, whose Notions of Morality
taught him to accuse Milton of want of common Probity or Honor...
has, in order to be able to make good his Charge...had Recourse to
Forgeries – Forgeries perhaps the grossest that were ever obtruded on the
World'.[25]

It was scarcely necessary for John Bowle to whip up a Lear-like sense of
justice against Lauder ('Tremble thou wretch / That hast within thee
undivulged crimes / Unwhipt of Justice') for the public flagellation was
effective enough.[26] Public opinion was all on Douglas's side, and Lauder
was disgraced. Johnson, however, whose authorship of the preface and
postscript to Lauder's original pamphlet did not escape Douglas's detective's eye, ghosted an official apology on Lauder's behalf, which revealed
all the interpolation Douglas and his colleagues had failed to discover
and in effect asked for several other offences to be taken into consideration. In a dignified confession, Johnson discovers for Lauder a motive
for attacking Milton, in Pope's valuing of Milton against the Scottish
Latinist Arthur Johnston, whose version of the Psalms Lauder had
edited.[27] This set a kind of palliated criminal sentence or period to
Douglas's courtroom heroics. But Lauder proceeded to commit other
versions of his crime in new charges against Milton over the years
1751 to 1754, and in so doing succeeded in criminalising himself further.[28] He had already been mock-celebrated by Andrew Henderson for
his fractious Jacobitism in a pamphlet of 1748 called *Furius: or a Modest*
Attempt towards a History of the Life and Surprising EXPLOITS of the Famous
W. L. Critic and THIEF-CATCHER (1748) and his further efforts could not
rid him of the taint of rough justice.

It was an interesting moment to call a critic a thief-catcher. In 1751
Henry Fielding published *An Enquiry Into the Causes of the late Increase of*
Robbers, &c., dedicating it to Lord Hardwicke, one of the judges who had,
incidentally, kept an eye on the developing Lauder scandal.[29] Fielding's
dark analysis of the state of London, with its swamping commercialism,
stench-laden night-cellars, networks of alleyways, organized criminal

gangs, unruly mobs and corrupt legal officers, sometimes reminds one of *The Dunciad* and its concerns: the nauseous report of the promiscuous and criminal couplings allegedly endemic in the parish St. Giles Cripplegate (where Grub Street was to be found) is especially apposite. For Pope, Vice 'increases the publick burden, fills the streets and high-ways with Robbers, and the garrets with Clippers, Coiners, and Weekly Journalists', inspirational words for Fielding's own paranoia.[30] Fielding's account of the greatest thief-taker of them all, Jonathan Wild, obviously owed something to Scriblerian irony (and politics).[31] Even in his attempt to found a responsible and respectable police force to carry out surveillance work and replace the potentially corrupt system of rewards and thief-catchers, Fielding works up a mock-heroic account of the police function: 'What were *Hercules, Theseus,* and other the Heroes of old, *Deorum in Templa recepti* – Were they not the most eminent of Thief-catchers?'[32] Much of Fielding's argument about punishment is based on literary models; he cites Homer, Milton, Swift, Aristotle and Horace in favour of severe legislation and execution (pp. 122, 168–9). But his project as magistrate was to move beyond the brutality of mere punishment and reinvent the police as an instrument not only of apprehension and punishment, but of vigilance, control and the internalization of discipline.

Lauder had been pilloried by Douglas's coercive courtroom heroics; but what ensued was less thief-taking than a kind of saturation policing.[33] The Lauder controversy began a movement away from the satiric flail, by invoking a more evidential version of the charge of plagiarism. But the consequence was something more like surveillance: a pervasive version of literary policing and depluming in which the tracing of 'imitation' became increasingly part of the institution of scholarship. And the negative effects of this critical task force had not Milton but Pope for its main incriminated target.

III

One interested spectator of the Lauder débâcle was in fact William Warburton, whose *Letter from an author, to a Member of Parliament, concerning Literary Property* was published in 1747, the year Lauder began his crusade. Warburton wrote to Richard Hurd on 23 December 1749:

> I have just read the most silly and knavish book I ever saw; one Lauder on Milton's Imitations ... I think he has produced about half

a dozen particular thoughts that look like imitations. – But the matter of imitations is a thing very little understood.[34]

Their correspondence had begun earlier that year when Hurd sent Warburton his commentary on Horace's *Epistola ad Pisones*, otherwise known as the *ars poetica* which Pope is supposed to have plagiarized in his *Essay on Criticism*.[35] This commentary itself sought to raise the status of the *Epistola* by severing it from supposed dependence on Greek theory (v), and citing with approval Horace's own rules about acquiring a personal stake in what is already public property (Homer, and human nature).[36] The two men evidently discussed matters of imitation and plagiarism extensively, Warburton agreeing with Hurd, for example, that what Pope did with Horace by way of formal imitation was not plagiarism.[37] Warburton also asked Hurd (citing Lauder) to add a commentary on Horace's Epistles II.i, the 'Epistle to Augustus' of which Pope produced such a devastating version in 1737, and it was in that commentary (1751) that Hurd also responded to the implied invitation to decree on the matter of imitation.[38]

Hurd starts from the Platonic position that all writing is in effect an imitation of nature: 'all is *derived*; all is *unoriginal*'.

And the office of genius is but to select the fairest forms of things, and to present them in due *place* and *circumstance*, and in the richest colouring of *expression*, to the imagination. This primary or original *copying* is what, in our usual language, we call INVENTION. (p. 110)

Yet this 'shadowy ideal world, though unsubstantial ... yet glows in such apparent life, that it becomes, thenceforth, the object of other mirrors, and is itself *original* to future reflections' (p. 111). There is a difference between '*original*, and *secondary*, imitation' (p. 112). But Hurd argues further that it is very hard to tell the difference, because great minds think alike: everything has already been said, human nature remains the same, Homer's religious sentiment is like the Bible's not because he copied it but because piety is unvarying. For half the treatise the 'parallelist' who would quote Shakespeare and Virgil in order to convict the former of borrowing is reminded of nature's essential uniformity: 'Common sense directs us, for the most part, to regard *resemblances* in great writers, not as the pilferings, or frugal acquisitions of needy *art*, but as the honest fruits of genius, the free and liberal bounties of unenvying *nature*' (p. 136).

However, plagiarism rears its head at precisely the moment when Hurd most esteems the power of invention: ''Tis then in the *usage* and *disposition* of the objects of poetry, that we are to seek for proofs and evidences of plagiarism' (p. 159); the order and connection of words offer 'great room for *invention* to shew itself', and '*close and perpetual similarity*' might therefore constitute '*imitation*' in its 'secondary' or pejorative sense.

> An *identity of phrase or diction*, is a much surer note of *plagiarism*...There is no defending *coincidencies* [*sic*] of this kind...no one can doubt a moment of such *identity* being a clear and decisive proof of *imitation*. (pp. 183–4)

Hurd is in one sense a Popean, quoting Pope ('this original writer') from the Preface to the *Works* of 1717 on the problem of belatedness and advising 'men of genius...to apply themselves directly and without reserve to *imitation*, and not to perplex and torture their wits for the sake of attaining the envied *fame* of *inventors*'.[39] At the same time he praises Shakespeare for being uneducated and fears that when a poet 'tutored in the works of imitation, comes to address himself to invention, these familiar images, which he hath so often and so fondly admired, immediately step in and intercept his observation of their great original' (p. 191).

On such a cusp did Hurd leave the matter in 1751 – the year in which Samuel Johnson emerged from his involvement with Lauder to specify his own views on plagiarism in *The Rambler*, no. 143 (30 July 1751). Johnson used as his motto a well-known tag from Horace in which he advises a writer to borrow less from others,

> Lest when the birds their various colours claim,
> Stripp'd of his stolen pride, the crow forlorn
> Should stand the laughter of the public scorn.[40]

This was an image which Edward Ward had cited against Pope in claiming that Pope had plagiarized the Dunces; it had also been used (twice) by Lauder against Milton, and by Douglas to strip Lauder of the 'plumes' (or showy pen-feathers) of Johnson's involvement.[41] But initially for Johnson the charge of plagiarism is a kind of vexatious suit, a last resort to unpick the 'excellence' of some new composition (p. 394). Johnson finds that the 'accusation is dangerous, because, even when it is false, it may be sometimes urged with probability'. He cites Bruyère (as Hurd had done) to the effect that 'we are come into the world too late to produce any thing new, that nature and life are preoccupied, and that description and sentiment have been long exhausted'.[42] Supposed parallels between Virgil and Horace, Cicero and Ovid, and Cicero and Horace, derive more from the common experience of humanity than covert literary trafficking.

And yet: after all provisos, Johnson does offer a Hurdian strategy for detection of plagiarism, one which derives its essential lineaments from the Lauder controversy. 'No writer can be fully convicted of imitation, except there is a concurrence of more resemblances than can be imagined to have happened by chance; as where the same ideas are conjoined without any natural series or necessary coherence, or where not only the thought but the words are copied.' His first examples are from Pope: a thought from Ovid's *Tristia* in *Epistle to Dr Arbuthnot*, an expression from Cowley in the epitaph on Fenton. He has other examples, including a borrowing from Grotius, one of Lauder's alleged plagiarism victims; but it is striking that Pope heads the list. When Joseph Warton takes up the issue of Pope's originality two years later (*The Adventurer*, no. 63, 12 June 1753) he seems constrained to moderate the implications of what he is doing. Noting the inevitable drift of an imitative art towards resemblance, Warton quotes Boileau, translator of Lucretius and one of Pope's main sources, and Pope himself, to the effect that good sense is common sense across the ages. But though it is difficult, as Hurd and Johnson argue, 'to distinguish imitation and plagiarism from necessary resemblance and unavoidable analogy' Warton offers to his readers a curious collection of passages in Pope which 'seem evidently to be borrowed, though they are improved'. He parallels Popean formulations from a range of poems with 'origins' in some fairly dull places (Flatman, Palingenius, Charron, Wollaston) before getting to more creditable models (Pascal, Montaigne and Boileau).

> While I am transcribing these similarities, I feel great uneasiness, lest I should be accused of vainly and impotently endeavouring to cast clouds over the reputation of this exalted and truly original genius. (p. 378)

But such equivocations were not wholly convincing, and Johnson's next essay on the subject, in the same periodical, later in the same year, was a good deal more conservative than his earlier one (*The Adventurer*, no. 99, 16 October 1753). Eschewing parallel quotations altogether, Johnson reaffirms the essential unity of human nature and experience, and argues that 'the charge of plagiarism', which he calls 'one of the most reproachful, though, perhaps, not the most atrocious of literary crimes', cannot be easily made to stick. In the essay it is not made to stick at all. Johnson argues that historians, scientists and moralists (he says nothing of poets) necessarily say the same thing all the time, since their materials are immutable; but Johnson is further concerned to define how 'originality' might be achieved under the restrictions of belatedness. Johnson delivers a lecture in variety, the gradual shifts of manners and practices which coat the essentially unvarying nature of the world. Plagiarism is forgotten as possibilities for originality are opened up: 'the mutability of mankind will always furnish writers with new images, and the luxuriance of fancy may always embellish them with new decorations' (p. 429).

Warton's indictment of Pope, however, continued in 1756 when Warton published the first volume of his *Essay on the Writings and Genius of Pope*, which officially launched the slow decline of Pope's reputation. Lack of originality, of a kind of inner store of mental sublimity, was a prominent feature in the *Essay*. Warton found that Pope had failed to exceed his models in the *Pastorals*, and that this represented a 'barrenness of invention'.[43] When Johnson published his *Life of Pope*, just before Warton's second volume came out, he retorted, 'To charge these Pastorals with want of invention, is to require what never was intended'; he went on to defend Pope against several other supposed deficiencies of this kind.[44] None the less the writing was on the wall for Pope. The year after Warton's first volume, Hurd returned to the fray by adding a further dissertation 'On the Marks of Imitation' to his Horace commentary.[45] The emphasis shifted from the essential uniformity of nature which poets imitate, to the kinds of proof one might produce to ensure 'conviction' of imitation. It is effectively a detection manual for plagiarism hunters, with a dozen or so rules laid down within quotation marks at the end of each case history (p. 14).

We have arrived at the police state of literary history, in which the statutory economy of literary property has completely reconstituted the way literature in general is thought about: 'You see with what a suspicious eye, we who aspire to the name of critics, examine your writings' (p. 41). Poets have become highwaymen: 'A poet, enamour'd of himself, and who sets up for a great inventive genius, thinks much to profit by the great sense of his predecessors, and even when he steals, takes care to dissemble his thefts and to conceal them as much as possible' (p. 12); but 'whether the poet prevaricates, enlarges, or adds, still we frequently find some latent circumstance, attending his management, that convicts him of Imitation' (p. 54). Pope's disguised plagiarisms are everywhere: it is his particular talent (pp. 13, 55); he gets materials from Plato,

Cowley, Milton, Statius, Wollaston, Waller, Sheffield, Greville, and Manilius (pp. 11, 12, 27–9, 30, 43, 60, 66–9). He is, of course, as the dedicatee
of the volume (Pope's editor, Warburton) would wish, a great improver
of what he takes: 'his fine genius taught him to seize every beauty, and
his wonderful judgement, to avoid ev'ry defect or impropriety, in his
author' (p. 44). But of all canonical poets, he is the only professed
Imitator.[46]

Warton's *Essay* was dedicated to Edward Young, the poet whose flat-
tering *Two Epistles to Mr. Pope* (1728) had provoked Moore and Welsted's
vengeful *One Epistle to Mr Pope*. Young himself was composing *Conjectures upon Original Composition* at this time, and systematically erasing
references to Pope's genius at the behest of Samuel Richardson.[47] Genius
for Young is an Edenic fertility, organic, magical, masterful, against the
mechanical and material arts of imitation.[48] Young wants, like some
poetic Satan, to reclaim a paradise of the imagination: 'Born *Originals*,
how comes it to pass that we die *Copies*?' (p. 42). 'Hope we, from
Plagiarism, any Dominion in Literature; as that of *Rome* arose from a
nest of Thieves?' (pp. 24–5). Creativity is autotelic: it may be said to the
genius, 'as to *Eve* at the Lake, *What there thou seest, fair creature! is thyself*'
(pp. 50–1). Thus Milton is restored as the great original, alongside
Shakespeare: Pope is condemned for translating Homer into rhyme
and failing to carry out a self-born epic plan (pp. 57–69): 'Would not . . .
P*ope* have succeeded better in an *original* attempt? Talents untried are
talents unknown. . . . he was not only an avowed professor of Imitation,
but a zealous recommender of it also' (p. 65).

Debate about methodology went on. Edward Gibbon, himself later
the victim of a particularly vexatious plagiarism charge, thought Hurd
had not gone far enough, and that plagiarism was always more likely
than accident or coincidence in verbal resemblances; Edward Capell
thought that no similitude would prove plagiarism and only 'historical
evidence' of a writer being caught red-handed would do.[49] Hurd worried
about the resemblance of his methods to those of Lauder, as did Peter
Whalley and Richard Farmer in essays on Shakespeare's reading.[50] But in
general Pope was the loser. Robert Thyer, for example, the librarian who
had aided the detectors of Lauder, discovered in his edition of Samuel
Butler (also 1759) that Pope's satiric image (in the Epilogue to the
Satires) of courtiers recycling each other's flattery as Westphalian hogs
eating each other's excrement was itself recycled from Butler.[51] As Hurd
went on, or rather backwards, into the primitivism of *Letters on Chivalry
and Romance* (1762), with its privileging of origins, the romance of
power and lawlessness, and the emotional authenticity of fine fabling,

Pope became more and more belated.[52] That critical erasure, that Promethean theft of Pope's imaginative influence, was set to become one motor of the anxious self-surveillance which pervades the Romantic text.[53]

12
'In Pleasing Memory of All He Stole': Plagiarism and Literary Detraction, 1747–1785

Richard Terry

I

In his *Spectator* 542 (21 November 1712), Addison turned on his maligners. For some time, he had been nursing his frustration over those detractors who seemed 'so very willing to alienate from me that small Reputation which might accrue to me from any of these my Speculations', and he resolved to set aside one of his papers to expose two sorts of rumour that had been spread against him. The first of these was that the letters appearing in the *Spectator*, the credit for which Addison had seemed happy to take for himself, had in fact been written by real correspondents. In the face of this aspersion, Addison is delighted to 'mortifie the Ill-natured' by asserting his own authorship of most of the letters, and by explaining the reasons why 'I often chuse this way of casting my Thoughts into a Letter'. The conjectural reattribution of an author's works was a generic type of literary slander, and no less generic is the second imputation with which Addison feels obliged to take issue. This relates to some malign whisperings, which John Nichols later identified as coming from the bookseller Thomas Rawlinson, to the effect that Addison had plagiarized many of his sentiments from classical authors – that, as Addison puts it, 'I have translated or borrowed many of my Thoughts out of Books which are written in other Languages'. This accusation Addison dismisses as 'wholly groundless', pointing out moreover that in his fastidiousness in referencing his sources he has been 'scrupulous perhaps to a Fault'.[1]

It tends to be of the nature of allegations of plagiarism that there is more to them that meets the eye; just as there can be a pathology or opportunism in committing acts of plagiarism so there can be equal ones in alleging them or in bringing them to light. From the late seventeenth century, the charge of plagiarism had been taken up as an instrument of literary satire, a stock form of slander through which authors could needle one another.[2] In Pope's poetry, for example, the insinuation of plagiarism is regularly used to stigmatize duncely inadequacies, as those of Ambrose Philips who 'Steals much, spends little, yet has nothing left' and the reviled Colley Cibber, his eyes rolling over his books 'In pleasing memory of all he stole'.[3] That Pope dealt so enthusiastically in such aspersions makes it apt that he was on the receiving end of numerous ones himself, perhaps most famously in Lady Mary Wortley Montagu's caustic remark to Joseph Spence that she had at one time admired Pope's *An Essay on Criticism* 'because I had not then read any of the ancient critics and did not know that it was all stolen'.[4] Of course, the likelihood is less that more catholic reading had corrected Lady Mary's earlier naivety than that this casual accusation of plagiarism represents just one particular curdling of her longstanding hatred of Pope. That no writer of the time, not even a highly individualistic genius, was immune to anxieties over alleged plagiarism is evident from Swift's 'Verses on the Death of Dr. Swift, D.S.P.D.', where the poet recommends himself to posterity on the strength of a categoric denial of ever having plagiarized: 'To steal a hint was never known, / But what he writ was all his own'.[5]

This essay is concerned less with what plagiarism meant in the eighteenth century, the conceptual space that it occupied, than with the nature of the speech act being performed when the label of plagiarism was applied. My governing assumption is that an understanding of how 'plagiarism' was used in the past involves precisely the same as understanding the historical usage of any appraisive term. In some part, this does remain a matter of the *meaning* of the term, the particular criteria that need to be met, and have needed to be met, for an invocation of the term to be apposite. In the case of the now prevalent sense of 'plagiarism', these have to do with the fact of borrowing by one author from another, with the deliberateness of this borrowing, and with its perceived wrongfulness. But it would be misleading to assume that even if the understood meaning of the term 'plagiarism' is identical, say, in the eighteenth century and in our own day, as I think it is, this requires that the pattern of usage of 'plagiarism', or the working life of the concept of plagiarism, can also be assumed to be constant across time. For understanding how a word functions in history demands that we attend not just to its meaning but to the contexts that govern whether, or with what degree of qualification, that meaning will be applied to a given set of facts.[6]

Let me demonstrate the point with another appraisive term. A bank robber, having shot dead two security guards, flees, swag on shoulder, across the rooftops, leaping daringly between the dizzying heights. The making of these vertiginous leaps equates with what, in a strongly appraisive word, we might call 'courage': fearlessness, that is, in the face of an understood risk. Yet the word 'courageous', given the larger circumstance, is one that positively discommends itself. A thief; a murderer; a fugitive from the law: less 'courageous', we might think the manner of flight, than 'reckless' or (more probably) 'desperate'. This is not to question that those criteria apply in virtue of which 'courageous' might seem to be apposite term; the point is rather that the social condition for the application of that meaning, that it be invoked only in the context of strong approbation of an agent's actions, has failed to be met. To invoke the term 'courageous' in connection with the course of events would accordingly be to commit a linguistic error.

What follows is an investigation of how plagiarism was mobilized, the uses to which the concept was put (especially in connection with poetry), between 1747 and 1785, the initial date of my enquiry being established by the onset of William Lauder's campaign of defamation against Milton, and the terminal one by John Pinkerton's inflammatory attack on literary imitation in his *Letters of Literature*.[7] 'Plagiarism', unlike complex words such as 'literature' which archive within themselves a fluctuatory semantic history, is a straightforward term: the foremost sense of the word in the eighteenth century remains the foremost sense now.[8] What this fact, however, can sometimes mask is the variable way in which the concept has been apprehended. The story that I tell here can be simplified as one of rise and fall. The 1750s are a period in which the stock of plagiarism rode high, partly due to the scandal caused by William Lauder's fraudulent accusations of literary theft against Milton, which for a time made the motive of detraction inherent in alleging plagiarism more vilified than plagiarism itself; and partly as a result of the strong neoclassical adherence to imitation, which allowed plagiarism to be seen, if certainly as an offence, then as an understandable one, and one that was generally consistent with approved compositional principles. In the 1760s and 1770s, however, when the virtue of imitative writing increasingly gets called into question, plagiarism becomes seen as an intensification of what is suspect about imitative writing in general. Rather than plagiarism's being buoyed by its association with literary imitation, it finds itself being depressed by it. The key point that I want to impress is that this narrative of mid-eighteenth-century plagiarism does not yield itself to the en- quiry of what plagiarism meant or consisted of, but rather to the ques- tion of what it signifies that 'plagiarism' should be invoked in connection with a particular set of literary facts.

II

In January 1747, there appeared in the *Gentleman's Magazine* the first of a series of essays by William Lauder in which the author exposed, or claimed to expose, the widespread borrowing from modern Latin authors in Milton's celebrated poem *Paradise Lost*.[9] Lauder, educated and based in Edinburgh, was a Latin versifier and classical scholar, a self-styled 'teacher of humanity' and a querulous Jacobite. His vendetta, as it quickly became, against Milton seems to have been ignited by an incident that at first sight seems almost trifling. At the beginning of the 1740s, Lauder was involved in a controversy concerning the literary merit of the Latin poet Arthur Johnston, whose poems he had edited and championed. Lauder sought to enlist on his side of the argument the eminent voice of Alexander Pope, and he sent for Pope's consult- ation a copy of his edition of Johnston's work. To this correspondence, Pope, rather shabbily, declined to react, other than in the satiric manner of including in his *Dunciad* of 1742 a couplet in which he compared Johnston unfavourably with Milton.[10] From this unlikely pretext sprang Lauder's campaign of defamation against Milton, a campaign in which the allegation of plagiarism was to play an instrumental role.

The immediate idea behind Lauder's scheme was provided by an earlier, and entirely reputable, work that had come out in 1741, entitled *An Essay upon Milton's Imitations of the Ancients in his Paradise Lost*: Lauder's own method of procedure, however, departed from this precur- sor in some notable respects. Having luckily stumbled upon a Latin translation of *Paradise Lost* by the classical scholar William Hogg, Lauder hatched a plot to besmirch Milton by interpolating lines from Hogg's translation into a series of earlier Latin works by the likes of Masenius, Grotius, Staphorstius and others and then accusing Milton of having copied them. The whole project had a cunning circularity about it: Milton's own poem was to provide the lines which, in translated form, the very same author was to be accused of having stolen.

Given the shameless nature of the imposture, it is surprising that it remained so long undetected. Yet in 1750, three years after he had first put abroad his claims, Lauder felt sufficiently secure in his deceit to write up his allegations into a book, both the Preface and Postscript to which were written by Samuel Johnson. By this time, however, the chill wind of public scrutiny was already beginning to visit Lauder's dishonest pages. As early as January 1749, Richard Richardson had written to the *Gentleman's Magazine* pointing out that the lines Milton had supposedly lifted from Masenius and Staphorstius were in fact entirely absent from available printed editions of their work, and moreover, by an uncanny coincidence, were traceable to Hogg's Latin verse rendering of *Paradise Lost*. The magazine, however, declined to publish Richardson's offering, on the grounds of the sheer implausibility of Lauder's having practised an imposture so brazen as Richardson's findings seemed to indicate.[11] Though a close shave for Lauder, this was to be, as things turned out, only a temporary reprieve. His luck ran out completely in late 1750 when John Douglas responded to Lauder's volume of a year earlier with a work entitled *Milton Vindicated from the Charge of Plagiarism* (1751) in which he made public in irrefragable detail the nature of Lauder's methods.

Although Douglas's book proposed to vindicate Milton specifically against the charge of plagiarism, the extent to which plagiarism as such comes into the affair is not altogether straightforward. In part, this is because there was never general assent by those involved in the controversy that Milton would have been guilty of plagiarism *per se* even if he had done exactly what Lauder claimed he had. But it is also the case that Lauder was himself quite tentative in invoking plagiarism as part of his scheme for defaming Milton's reputation. The idea that it was specifically plagiarism, as opposed to a looser notion of derivativeness, that was at issue in the controversy he was fomenting seems to have occurred to him only as he went along.

Lauder's *Essay on Milton's Use and Imitation of the Moderns in his Paradise Lost* (1750) is indicative of the entire campaign of which it forms a part. It opens with Johnson's Preface, a contribution so innocent of Lauder's actual design that it seems inconceivable that Johnson had ever perused the manuscript. Johnson seems to have believed that Lauder's intention was that of tracing 'a progress of this mighty genius [Milton], in the construction of his work' by showing 'from what stores the materials were collected, whether its founder dug them from the quarries of nature, or demolished other buildings to embellish his own'.[12] That Lauder's investigations might have the effect of debunking, or at least detracting from, Milton's claim to the title of genius seems not to have entered his head.

Just as Johnson's Preface misleads about the controversial nature of Lauder's claims, so the early part of the book itself is characterized by a deceptive moderation of argument. The allegation that is initially made is that of Milton's 'consulting and copying' his sources, but as the book goes along Lauder inexorably cranks up his machinery of defamation. One part of this escalation is the charge of hypocrisy: Milton, so Lauder gets around to asserting, has not merely acquired in a questionable way the words of Masenius and others but he has also 'concealed his obligations' and accordingly fallen foul of his own 'high pretensions to truth and integrity'.[13] The highly calculated nature of the deceit is evident, moreover, in the poet's disingenuous claim to originality, to have written 'Things unattempted yet in prose or rhyme'.[14] Yet the reader still has to trawl through to page 159 to hear Lauder actually invoke '*Milton's* plagiarism' as such, though the word's appearance is anticipated earlier (p. 115), when, using a figure of speech which had an understood historical association with the act of plagiarism, Lauder asserts that '*Milton* has plum'd himself' with false feathers drawn from other writers. The argument finally comes to an ebullition on pages 162–3 with a tirade against the nefarious practices that have, and have alone, generated Milton's reputation as the 'BRITISH HOMER'. And Lauder prides himself that his own public-spirited offices have now 'reduced [Milton] to his true standard' and shown him in his true colours as 'the most unlicensed plagiary that ever wrote'.[15]

The accusations made against Milton, then, are actually various. He has copied the words of earlier authors; these appropriations have been 'unlicensed' (though in what ways theft from dead authors could ever be licensed, and whether, were it so licensed, it would then count as plagiaristic, is not clarified); he has conducted himself hypocritically in stealing from authors while protesting the originality of his methods; and he has exploited the advantage of plagiarism to secure from himself an unjustified priority in the canon of English poetry, to the detriment of more honest practitioners like Cowley, Waller, Denham, Dryden, Prior and Pope. The list of indictments is long and vociferous.

Lauder's attack on Milton, and the subsequent exposure of its fraudulence, are very constitutive of attitudes to plagiarism over the next two or three decades. For one thing, it stamped indelibly on literary sensibilities the fact that to speak of an occurrence of plagiarism was to speak of a charge being levelled to this effect and subsequently being proven or at least accepted. Plagiarism, that is, began with an aspersion, and aspersions of this kind, like aspersions of any kind, need not necessarily be well founded, a truism to which the whole Lauder affair stood as an outstanding case in point. Moreover, even in the event of an accusation of plagiarism standing up to outside scrutiny (as Lauder's so signally failed to do), this still provided no assurance of its not having been tarnished by an impurity of critical motive.

Misgivings of exactly this kind, indeed, are instrumental in defining Samuel Johnson's position on the subject. Having written the Preface and the Postscript to Lauder's book, Johnson inevitably felt compromised by the revelation of its fraudulence; and he it was who composed the letter of hand-wringing apology published in the aftermath of the controversy, to which Lauder was made to put his name. In the following year, when Johnson reflected more roundly on the subject of plagiarism in *Rambler* 143 (30 July 1751), he began with a paragraph laden with the lessons of the Lauder controversy:

> Among the innumerable practices by which interest or envy have taught those who live upon literary fame to disturb each other at their airy banquets, one of the most common is the charge of plagiarism. When the excellence of a new composition can no longer be contested, and malice is compelled to give way to the unanimity of applause, there is yet this one expedient to be tried, by which the author may be degraded, though his work be reverenced; and the excellence which we cannot obscure, may be set at such a distance as not to overpower our fainter lustre.[16]

It should be noted that Johnson sees plagiarism as a charge laid, in the ordinary way, against works and writers of established reputation, the effect of which is to call that reputation into question. But a second mischievousness inherent in plagiarism accusations is their disdain for, and defiance of, consensus, that 'unanimity of applause' by which the greatness of literary works is both confirmed and rewarded. Animated by a spirit of envy and subversiveness, such accusations, so Johnson maintains, are irrational and error-prone.

Johnson's attitude towards 'the charge of plagiarism', specifically his assignment of it to the psychologies of 'interest' and 'envy', is unsettling for us. To understand it, we need to appreciate the extent of his embarrassment by the Lauder brouhaha, but also his familiarity with contemporary debate about the ethical limits of literary borrowing and imitation. How much it was permissible to borrow from other works posed itself as a dilemma to be teased over by both poets and critics: Pope, for example, consulted early in his career with William Walsh, his poetic mentor, on precisely 'how far the liberty of *Borrowing* may extend'.[17] One common way of regulating the matter was to allow latitude in the case of borrowing from classical authors but to reserve the full opprobrium of 'plagiarism' for thefts committed against contemporaries. As well as being based on a simple differentiation between old and new writing, this resolution of the issue also took account of the amount of industry that had gone into an act of borrowing, no minor constituent of the technique of plagiarism being its sheer laziness. It was in light of this principle, for example, that the Abbé du Bos in his *Réflexions critiques* of 1719 ruled out the possibility of plagiarism between languages since the very fact of translation was incompatible with a true plagiaristic act.[18] In any event, no matter how it was arrived at, this moral distinction between borrowings from Ancients and Moderns gained broad (if not universal) acceptance. In 1713, for instance, Thomas Parnell, while being troubled by the servility of imitation in general, acknowledged resignedly that filching from classical authors 'we must agree together not to call Stealing', while in 1716 John Dennis advised that 'a Plagiary from living Authors is more profligately impudent' than one from classical writers.[19] The currency of this general line of argument, and of the conviction in which it invariably issued, can be seen from the way it surfaces in 1749 in Henry Fielding's *Tom Jones* (1749) which contains a wry chapter 'Showing what is to be deemed Plagiarism in a modern Author, and what is to be considered as lawful Prize', in which Fielding advocates unbridled pillaging of ancient authors but a more scrupulous acknowledgement of sources when modern authors borrow from one another.[20]

There were, though, other possibilities for regulation of the issue, the chief one being to distinguish the defensible from the indefensible in terms of the precise category of material being appropriated from an original. Arguments conducted in this area tended to found themselves on the very Augustan conviction of the inseparability of invention and imitation: the things of the world are simply too few, so it was maintained, for it not to be inevitable that literary works will furnish essentially the same ideas, images and observations. This supposition inevitably entailed that an author could be exculpated from the accusation of plagiarism not through not having copied, but through having copied only such material (as perhaps mere ideas or plot-lines) as was deemed permissible. This is, indeed, how John Douglas's *Milton Vindicated*, in the first instance at least, sets out to defend Milton, not by immediately disclosing Lauder's fraudulence but by denying that Lauder's claims, even if taken at face-value, amount to anything more than Milton's having stolen what it was perfectly legitimate for him to steal. On this basis, Douglas can confidently declare that 'There may be such a thing as an *original Work* without *Invention*, and a Writer may be an Imitator of others without *Plagiarism*'.[21]

Only a year after Douglas's exposure of Lauder, appeared another disquisition on the general topic of legitimate borrowing, Richard Hurd's *Discourse concerning Poetical Imitation*, printed as an appendix to his edition of Horace's *Epistle to Augustus*. Hurd agrees with Douglas on the matter of there being no firm distinction in literary matters between invention and imitation, invention's arising out of observation of the world, and the things of the world comprising 'a common stock'. Accordingly, even in a work of unimpeachable genius 'there will still be found the most exact *uniformity* of allusion, the same ideas and aspects of things constantly admonishing the poet of the same *resemblances and relations*'.[22] As regards setting a threshold for when these uniformities can legitimately be branded as plagiaristic, Hurd establishes this at the level of phraseology: 'An *identity of phrase or diction*, is a much surer note of *plagiarism*.' And he finesses this into a more categoric definition a few pages later: '*the same arrangement of the same words* is admitted as a certain argument of *plagiarism*'.[23]

Hurd's discussion pledges itself to the resolution of two questions: first, whether similarities between writers are natural and inevitable; and, second, whether the fact that a later work has borrowed from an earlier one should detract from its standing. Neither of these questions, it might be noted, broaches the issue of authorial intention; Hurd identifies plagiarism with the carriage of a particular type of material between works rather than with a deceitful intention lying behind that carriage. Six years later, however, in his *Letter to Mr. Mason on the Marks of Imitation* (1757), he was slightly to rescript his earlier arguments into a meditation on agency: how can one know, given the inevitability of overlap or uniformity between works, whether this similarity arises from chance or deliberate borrowing? how can we convert the 'suspicion of imitation ... into a proof'? Yet though these questions indicate a different line of approach, their point of resolution is scarcely different from that of the earlier work, with Hurd concluding that what alone can stand as proof of borrowing is an 'identity of *expression*' (as opposed to an 'identity of ideas' or of anything else). In other words, proof of the deliberateness of an act of copying is equated purely with the *kind* of material that the copying involves.[24]

The forensic tone of Hurd's *Letter*, and its insistence that only phraseological borrowing should count as plagiaristic, was especially unsettling for his close friend Thomas Gray, an habitual verbal borrower. In a letter to Edward Bedingfield of 27 August 1756, Gray listed some allusions embedded in 'The Bard' and then added with anxious resignation 'do not wonder therefore, if some Magazine or Review call me Plagiary'.[25] Yet, discomfiting though Hurd's conclusions must have been for Gray, they were for the most part exculpatory for those who might otherwise have been vulnerable to the accusation of plagiarism. After all, Hurd specifically exempts from the charge of plagiarism the copying of ideas, a concession that we tend not to make nowadays, nor that is allowed for in the *OED*'s definition of plagiarism as 'the wrongful appropriation... of the ideas, or the expressions of the ideas...of another'. Much the same attitude to the subject is struck by Johnson's *Rambler* 143 of the same year. Like Douglas and Hurd, Johnson doubts that any categoric distinction can be driven between invention and imitation, for even 'in books which best deserve the name of originals, there is little new beyond the disposition of materials already provided'; and, for this reason, writers furnishing themselves 'with thoughts and elegancies out of the same general magazine' ought not to stand in peril of being branded as plagiarists.[26] For Johnson, similarity between authors is the natural state of affairs, only amounting to a trespass when these uniformities occur in an extreme state: where the resemblances pile up so thick and fast as to defy the operation of chance; or where ideas, as an immediate result of being stolen, are pieced together in an idiosyncratic manner; or where 'not only the thoughts but the words are copied'.[27]

In discussing the ethics of borrowing, critics like Johnson and Hurd display a magnanimity towards plagiarism that cannot be attributed merely to their disinclination to admit the copying of ideas as constitutive of it. This is in some degree an issue of rhetoric: the question of what should count as plagiarism gets less assiduously pursued than the one of what ought not to count as it. There is a doubleness of attitude that condemns plagiarism but at the same time discounts it or disattends to it. Exactly such a mental posture can be seen, for example, in James Boswell's essay 'On Similarity among Authors', which appeared in the *London Magazine* in July 1779 and which, though written much later than the ones of Johnson and Hurd I have been discussing, expresses opinions much of a piece with theirs. Boswell's essay tries to discriminate among the three principal grounds of that 'sameness or similarity which we frequently find between passages in different authors', these being plagiarism, imitation and coincidence. He has no inhibition in branding outright plagiarism as a villainy ('a theftuous trick'), but when it comes to the practical application of the label of 'plagiarism', his argument slightly loses nerve. When we come across 'a passage of considerable length in one author, which we can discover in the very same words in another author', so Boswell resolves, 'we may without hesitation pronounce that it is *Plagiarism*'.[28] But notwithstanding the public disavowal of hesitation, this adjudication itself manifests hesitancy, in that it incorporates into itself two specific clauses of escape. Plagiarism is not merely the stealing of phraseology, which is where Johnson and Hurd had left the matter, but only occurs where in 'a passage of considerable length' the 'very same words' are used by an author as have been employed by an earlier one: it must be sustained and uninterrupted – nothing less will meet the severe demands that Boswell sets for the word's application. However much he might assert plagiarism's blameworthiness, Boswell is actually retreating from very often giving himself occasion to mete out that blame.

III

This gap between the definition of a concept and its practical application is also constitutive of perhaps the eighteenth century's most complex engagement with the issue of plagiarism, that of Dr Johnson. Johnson's *Dictionary* of 1755 called on him to legislate, along with a great deal else, on the word 'plagiary', and the gloss he produced is forthright and unemollient: 'A thief in literature; one who steals the thoughts or writings of another'. The definition compacts two ideas: the plagiarist steals from, and therefore offends against, another individual; but also his activities perpetrate an offence against the culture of learning in general, or 'literature' as it was then understood. Yet given that this is how Johnson understands plagiarism, his invocations of the concept nearly always tend in another direction, the bent of his rhetoric being towards admonishing not plagiarism itself so much as the precipitate levelling of the plagiarism accusation. Take these examples from his essay on the subject in *The Adventurer*:

> The allegation of resemblance between authors is indisputably true; but the charge of plagiarism, which is raised upon it, is not to be allowed with equal readiness.
>
> It is necessary... that before an author be charged with plagiarism... the subject on which he treats should be carefully consulted.
>
> Nothing, therefore, can be more unjust, than to charge an author with plagiarism, merely because he assigns to every cause its natural effect; and makes his personages act, as others in like circumstances have always done.[29]

It would be wrong to deduce from these remarks any attitude, extenuatory or otherwise, towards plagiarism *per se*; they merely specify certain proprieties that should be observed by those minded to allege plagiarism in others. Yet it remains that if the general subject of plagiarism throws up an injustice against which we particularly need to guard, then this, for Johnson, results not from the act of plagiarism but from its allegation.

How, though, does Johnson deal with plagiarism when it appears before him in incontestable form? The place where an answer can best be sought is his 'Life of Dryden', since Johnson was acutely aware of the notorious allegations of plagiarism made against Dryden nearly a century previously in Gerard Langbaine's *Account of the English Dramatick Poets* (1691), allegations to which Johnson returns a full five times in his biography.[30] Much as Johnson believed that Langbaine had sensationalized his case, he also accepted that Dryden was, in significant part, guilty of the charges levelled against him. At one point, indeed, he concludes that whatever Dryden's plays had 'of humorous and passionate', they received 'not from nature, but from other poets; if not always as a plagiary, at least as an imitator': not 'always as a plagiary', but, so it is implied, in very many places so.[31] And it comes as no surprise that Johnson accounts for Dryden's reluctance to challenge Langbaine's accusations on the grounds that he knew his defence against them was weak. Yet whenever Johnson raises the plagiarism allegation, and begrudgingly attaches credence to it, he almost at once retaliates with strong statements of the intrinsic value of the works concerned. So he mentions that Langbaine had indicted *Sir Martin Mar-all*, 'like most of the rest', as having been contaminated with plagiarism, but then points out that even Langbaine allowed that 'both the sense and measure are exactly observed'.[32] And later, bracketing together six of Dryden's plays, he remarks that even 'though all Langbaine's charges of plagiarism should be allowed' these plays demonstrate 'such facility of composition, such readiness of language, and such copiousness of sentiment as . . . perhaps no other author has possessed'.[33]

One position on the subject of plagiarism that seems convincing to us nowadays is that both author and work are implicated when an act of plagiarism occurs. The discovery of a counterfeit currency redounds prejudicially both on the counterfeiter and the currency; and it is natural to feel that the same principle ought also to apply to plagiarism. Yet, in the eighteenth century, this principle is not always upheld. Douglas, for example, in *Milton Vindicated* at one point suggests that even if Lauder's general allegations were to prove true, this would 'lessen our

Regard to the *Man*, but does not destroy his Reputation as a *Poet*'.[34] It is hard now to accept such a stance as tenable, yet it is one to which Johnson also seems to have subscribed. In *Rambler* 143, for example, he mentions the activity of plagiarism as an expedient through which an 'author may be degraded, though his work be reverenced'.[35] Similarly, even though he concedes the strength of Langbaine's accusations against Dryden, there is no hint of condemnation, nor any suggestion that a natural concomitant of this concession should be that he revise his estimation of Dryden's works.

Johnson's attitude towards plagiarism is to a high degree conditioned by its time, a time at which the impulse to exculpate plagiarism, and in particular to exculpate the works in which it occurs, was felt very strongly, perhaps uniquely strongly. What distinguishes Johnson's attitude, and differentiates it from our own (as I write), has not to do with what he thought the word 'plagiarism' meant, but rather with the predispositions that governed his application of the concept. First, he believed, as I have suggested, that it followed directly from the limited stock of things in the world that literary works would admit a considerable degree of duplication, the sole category of which that was culpable being duplication of phraseology. Of course, it might be retorted that this is much as we consider the matter nowadays (albeit not quite as 'plagiarism' is defined in the *OED*), but Johnson's subscription to this view reconciled him to the further conviction that true plagiarism was an exotic thing, scarce and seldom observed, and like a rare species of bird, invariably taken for its common cousin, legitimate imitation. Second, Johnson's attitude towards plagiarism was born out of his unfortunate embroilment in the Lauder scandal. His contemplation of the issue involved him in a powerful siege of contraries: much as he might have condemned acts of plagiarism where they stood in indisputable form, the Lauder episode had tutored him in the unreliability of plagiarism allegations, in the fact that even a charge rightly levelled might still be visited by the shadow of an impure motive, and in an appreciation that the literary polity might stand under more grievous disturbance and subversion by an erroneous accusation of plagiarism than by an act of plagiarism itself.

These circumambient factors belong to Johnson's time. It is only in Johnson's era that plagiarism yields itself so easily to being spoken of as a kind of imitation, therefore becoming eligible to benefit from the high cultural regard accorded to imitative writing. Although at all times, plagiarism comprises a breach (metaphoric or legal) of an author's property-rights, it is perhaps only at this time that those parts of a literary work over which it was felt an author could exercise a proprietorial role shrink down so severely to the merely phraseological. And it is only in Johnson's time, as part of the fall-out from the Lauder brouhaha, that the allegation of plagiarism looms as a more reproachable felony than plagiarism itself. These factors, as I have stressed, do not impinge on Johnson's understanding of the concept of plagiarism, but they do stay him from often invoking it, or from invoking it without reservation.

IV

Johnson's attitudes towards plagiarism in his 'Life of Dryden' are much the same as those he sets down thirty years earlier in his *Rambler* and *Adventurer* essays. But whereas in the 1750s, these views seem concordant with those of the day, in 1779 this is less the case. Two things, in particular, have changed, of which the first is that the admonitory impact of the Lauder controversy has now largely worn off. The second, however, has in a more far-reaching way to do with a change in the relationship between plagiarism and imitation. Whereas in the early and mid-eighteenth century, plagiarism is fortified by its relation to imitation (seen as a good thing), in the later decades its fortunes are depressed as imitative writing in general goes down in critical esteem. Plagiarism, as it were, loses its key alibi.

A landmark in this cultural shift has long been seen as Edward Young's *Conjectures on Original Composition* (1759). It would be wrong to see Young's essay as roundly hostile towards literary imitation; rather he tries to distinguish a technique of imitation (in particular of the classics) that could be seen as consistent with invention or creativity. What underpins the essay is Young's sensitivity to the ways in which our relation to the classical texts can turn to injury. We need to know the classics, admire them, improve ourselves through our acquaintance with them, but not capitulate to them: 'Let our understanding feed on theirs; they afford the noblest nourishment; But let them nourish, not annihilate, our own.' Moreover, to be nourished by Homer's example should not be construed as executing the same kind of work as Homer but rather as adopting the Homeric 'spirit' and 'taste' in pursuit of our own ends. The object in view is less to be Homer's 'descendant' than his 'collateral'.[36]

Young is unequivocally on the side of the Ancients but realizes that true, deferential emulation of them might be incompatible with straight imitation. 'The less we copy the renowned antients', he remarks, 'we shall resemble them the more', where the word 'copy' does not indicate theft of words or ideas, only imitating them in a lifeless way.[37] This distinction between the lively and the inert in imitative practices quickly catches on. In 1774, for example, Sir Joshua Reynolds chooses the subject of 'Imitation' for his annual Royal Academy lecture on painting (delivered 10 December), defining imitation as having to do with 'the following of other masters, and the advantage to be drawn from the study of their works'.[38] This 'following' of earlier artists, however, admits a distinction, between where a painter dryly assimilates an idea from a predecessor into his work so 'that it makes a part of it' and where he enters 'into a competition with his original' and bids 'to improve what he is appropriating to his own work'. This latter activity, far from being a servile copying, is 'a perpetual exercise of the mind, a continual invention'.[39] When both Young and Reynolds register their favouritism towards this particular kind of imitation they collocate it unabashedly with terms like 'invention' and 'emulation'. But what, then, to call the kind of imitation which they don't favour? The answer to this question is 'plagiarism'. So Young stipulates that the way that we can benefit from past authors is not 'by any particular sordid theft' but by a 'noble contagion', by letting our imaginations be kindled by their precedent. And he then asks the reproving question: 'Hope we, from plagiarism, any dominion in literature; as that of *Rome* arose from a nest of thieves'.[40] Similarly, when Reynolds praises the sort of competitive imitation that tries to outstrip its original, he contrasts this process of 'continual invention' with the 'servility of plagiarism'.[41]

Young and Reynolds speak about plagiarism in accents that are quite different from those of earlier commentators. For Johnson and others, plagiarism stood to be rebuked as a deceit: the plagiarist steals the words of another and passes them off as his own. But for Young and Reynolds, plagiarism is less a fraud than an ignoble office. It is a supine technique that, as Young puts it, rules out the achievement of 'any dominion in literature'. Similarly, Reynolds sees the difference between borrowing and plagiarism not as lying in the elementary distinction between honesty and deceit, but instead in 'the address with which . . . [the act of imitation] . . . is performed'.[42] It is this 'address', mainly seen in terms of the emulative nature of the imitation, that determines whether it will 'come under the charge of plagiarism, or be warrantable, and deserve commendation'.[43] This, however, is still only part of the change of attitudes towards plagiarism that is occurring. Earlier critics such as Johnson, Douglas and Hurd are united in seeing plagiarism as being a case of *what* (rather than *how*) a writer borrows from an earlier work. Borrowing at the level of plot, character and sentiments is condonable, the borrowing of phraseology not so. What circumscribes this general way of thinking about plagiarism is a conviction that all literary productions naturally tend to imitation, so that an author will have to wrestle determinedly with his material in order to throw it into an original shape. The import of Young's and Reynolds's essays is quite different. They emphasize that literary and artistic works, even those belonging to imitative kinds, possess the means, and moreover stand under an imperative, to be inventive. Once imitation becomes seen in this way as an inferior mode of artistic practice, distinct from, and perhaps incompatible with, the true exercise of poetic genius, then a term is needed to express its diminished credibility. What happens is that the word 'plagiarism', once used to name a reproachable sub-category of imitation, shifts over to refer to what is reproachable about imitation in general.

Only four years after Reynolds' lecture on painterly imitation, Percival Stockdale, the highly irascible essayist and critic, published *An Inquiry into the Nature, and Genuine Laws of Poetry; including a particular Defence of the Writings and Genius of Pope* (1778). As his title intimates, Stockdale is primarily intent on defending Pope against the disparaging tendency of Joseph Warton's *An Essay on the Writings and Genius of Pope* (1756, 1782), especially against the insinuation, mildly made in fact by Warton, that Pope had borrowed from earlier poets.[44] Stockdale's essay is a scattergun of tart observations about plagiarists themselves and about those (like Warton) whose malignancy or inadequacy has led them to make allegations of plagiarism against others. He begins by expressing his determination to silence the 'injudicious clamour' of accusations of plagiarism made against respectable authors, by distinguishing between the 'thievish plagiarist' and writers who merely seek to make 'a judicious, and moderate application of some striking, and expressive sentiments, which They recollect from books, and conversation'.[45] For Stockdale, the plagiarist is a creature of 'sordid spirit' who, conscious of his own shortcomings, still entertains an aspiration to be 'a conspicuous Author'.[46] Yet, notwithstanding the sharpness of tone, Stockdale still declines to recognize plagiarism as a moral wrongdoing. For him it constitutes a creative debilitation: what it affronts is not morality but creativity. The plagiarist is incapable of digesting his acquisitions from others, 'they do not coalesce, they do not incorporate with the little process of his own thoughts'; he fails to use them to ignite his own creativity; and is at a loss to improve on or embellish what he takes from elsewhere.[47] Moreover, though Stockdale allows that plagiarism has something to do with theft, he does not allow that it is on this ground that it becomes reprehensible. What stands to be condemned in the plagiarist is less that he cheats than that he is unskilled in carrying off the cheat:

> The splendid theft of our poetaster is obtruded in too improper a place, and it is too dissimilar from the bad company into which it is brought, not to discover the cheat: it stands prominent, and glaring from his flat, and inanimate page.[48]

The fault is not to have cheated but rather to have been unable to conceal the fact. Having decided on what is wrong with plagiarism, Stockdale goes on to delineate the positive type to which the plagiarist stands in diametric opposition: this he finds in 'the true poetical genius'. Moreover, when Stockdale tries to limn this august personage, his lineaments take form as those of Pope. Certainly, Pope avails himself of the words of others but these he 'incorporates, and harmonizes...with his own thoughts' and his acquisitions 'are selected by judgement, and adopted by fancy'.[49] Warton had charged Pope with being uncreative, and by dint of this with being something less than a 'poet' in the honorific sense of the word; Stockdale's retaliation is to redefine Pope's entitlement to be called a poet by reconstruing what poetry is to consist of. Henceforth, poetry is to be a verbal manifestation of creative originality or 'poetical genius', and 'plagiarism' becomes the anti-type, the negative wraith, against which these phenomena can be understood. More exactly, plagiarism comes to mean using an earlier work, or indeed using the contents of one's own remembrance, in a way that is mechanical and unfecund.

The tendency in Stockdale for 'plagiarism' to expand itself into an association with all writing of a weakly derivative nature is evident also in John Pinkerton's *Letters of Literature*, published in 1785 under the pseudonym of Robert Heron. The *Letters* were instantly controversial, causing a spate of aggressive contributions to the *Gentleman's Magazine*, in which the work was given unusually extensive coverage.[50] What caused the furore was the irreligiousness of some of Pinkerton's observations, his hostile attitude towards some Latin authors, especially Virgil, but also his derogation of the principle of literary imitation. Letter XLI, devoted to the topic of imitation, begins with a remark aimed at an interlocutor:

> YOU rightly observe that the fewness of original writers is greatly owing to the unjust esteem in which Imitation is held. Imitation is in fact only a decent and allowed plagiarism. When it appears in a

certain degree, it is pronounced literary theft, and justly held infamous: in other degrees, and in certain forms and dresses, it is called honourable: but in fact it only differs in the degree of disrepute.[51]

Pinkerton's essay is a paean to literary originality, calling for all young writers to be tutored in the inherent superiority of original works over those manifesting imitation or derivativeness: the young 'ought even to be told that there is more applause due to a bad original, than to the best of copies'.[52] Pinkerton, moreover, is opposed to copying and imitation of every kind, a general practice which he sees as so far removed from creativity as to be a mere 'academical occupation'; even the potential for imitative writings sometimes to surpass their originals, which had previously been allowed as a way that an imitation could boast creative credentials, is dismissed as of no consequence, for 'it is an easy matter to improve on the inventions of others'.[53] On this basis, Pinkerton sallies through the fields of literature, taking in view both the Ancients and Moderns, insouciantly inculpating some and exonerating others. Pope's 'Imitations of Horace', for example, are held up as an original, whereas Boileau's are 'poor copies'. Similarly, although Milton in his *Paradise Lost* traces, in some degree, the footsteps of Homer, he still deserves to be seen as a glorious original – this in contrast to Virgil who has followed Homer 'In every thing' and therefore deserves to be known as 'an infamous plagiary'.[54]

Pinkerton's treatment of plagiarism in his *Letters of Literature*, along with Stockdale's similar discussion of a few years earlier, complete the arc of this essay, one that I see as opening with the wary response to the plagiarism issue brought about by the Lauder controversy: a particular, graphic polarization of attitudes is between Boswell's nervous restriction of 'plagiarism' to occasions where 'over a passage of considerable length' the 'very same words' are used by a later writer as by an earlier one and Pinkerton's wild inculpation of Virgil as a plagiarist from Homer. For Johnson, 'plagiarism' is an appellation given to a subcategory of imitation, namely imitation of phraseology, that he and others deemed to be illicit, or, as the period itself expressed it, to be 'unlicensed'. What it is defined in opposition to are licit forms of borrowing between authors. For Stockdale and Pinkerton 'plagiarism' is the cognomen applied to all forms of imitation that are drab or uncreative; it stands antonymically to a category as spacious and monumental as 'poetic genius' itself.

In this essay, I have tried to spin these facts into a narrative of plagiarism's 'decline' – 'decline' in the sense of an increasing critical aggressiveness towards it. Johnson, it is true, defines plagiarism as a bad thing, yet

in practice he seems to feel that of those malefactions a literary person needs to ward against, the *act* of plagiarism is of lesser account than the malignant or erroneous accusation of it. It is Johnson, after all, who finds plagiarism, even in the slim ledger of purely literary crimes, to be 'one of the most reproachful, though, perhaps, not the most atrocious'.[55] Johnson is no friend to plagiarism, though in a notable way he is inclined to exculpate works in which it occurs; but nor is he an enemy to it either, in the sense of actively seeking to incriminate its perpetrators. After all, in Johnson's eyes plagiarism is only thinly partitioned from types of imitation that he feels happy in condoning or practising. For Stockdale and Pinkerton, however, plagiarism is not merely not adjacent to some condonable version of itself; it stands against poetic genius, not as its near neighbour, but as its implacable anti-type.

If there is a change that affects plagiarism in the eighteenth century, what precisely is this a change *of*? What I maintain here is that whatever does change, it is not the meaning of the word 'plagiarism'. The *OED* does not record an historical meaning of the term conversant with the particular application of it by Stockdale and Pinkerton, nor would the same authors have believed that they were inaugurating a construction of the term that ought properly to have been enshrined in a revised dictionary entry. The *OED*'s definition of plagiarism as 'The wrongful appropriation ... of the ideas, or the expressions of the ideas ... of another' does nicely for, and would serve the interests alike of, Johnson and Pinkerton. Nor should we be surprised by this, since it is in their rivalry over how the concept should be applied, rather than rivalry over what it consists of, that the difference between them lies, the nub of it residing in what actually makes for the 'wrongfulness' so constitutive of the *OED* definition. So much, of course, is in keeping with how all appraisive words work. Those people whom I particularly disesteem I label, authoritatively to my own mind, as 'idiots'; and my application of this term is untroubled by the fact that the objects of my disestimation will change over time and most likely will be different from those of other people. 'Idiot' is merely an empty semantic vessel into which I choose to pour my intolerance of certain other people. So also for 'plagiarism': what alone perhaps endures about the concept of plagiarism is that it is unswervingly invoked in connection with what a speech actor dislikes or is affronted by, but what varies is exactly what at different times makes different people take affront. For me the history of plagiarism in the eighteenth century is the history of a particular sort of disapprobation – this disapprobation has to do with what the *OED* designates as 'wrongful appropriation' but what counts as 'appropriation' or 'wrongful' in practice admits an almost indefinite elasticity. A history of 'plagiarism' as an appraisive term would look, as my essay has tried to do, at when plagiarism is invoked, and what colours, qualifies, incites or stays its invocation. Moreover, a history that did not view the phenomenon of plagiarism as issuing from and being sustained by a certain kind of utterance, and did not attend to the properties of that utterance, would fall short of historicizing it in the fullest way.

13
Lone Travellers: The Construction of Originality and Plagiarism in Colonial Grammars of the Late Eighteenth and Early Nineteenth Centuries

Richard Steadman-Jones

The colonization of India provided British subjects with enormous opportunities for personal self-advancement. In the late eighteenth century the term 'Nabob' passed into circulation as a way of describing the retired Servants of the East India Company who were then returning to Britain, weighed down with their accumulated fortunes. The Nabobs were often the sons of tradesmen – individuals whose prospects would have been far less enviable had they stayed in Britain. Yet by serving their time in India and applying themselves to private trade they had converted themselves into wealthy men, able to afford luxurious properties in the countryside and eager to infiltrate the ranks of the gentry. They were much ridiculed in the late eighteenth and early nineteenth centuries and were often represented as vulgar *arrivistes*. Yet ridicule goes hand in hand with envy and one can imagine that for characters such as John Zephaniah Holwell, who returned from India with a personal fortune of no less than £96,000, coping with the envy of others was a routine part of everyday life.[1]

Private trade was not the only means of self-advancement that the colonies offered. Texts and images of the Romantic period often emphasize the role of knowledge in the construction and maintenance of colonial regimes. The compliance of the colonized population was said to be predicated upon the benevolence of the administration and this, in turn, to be built upon a knowledge of native institutions and culture. Yet the task of making this body of knowledge fell largely to enterprising individuals. Of course the translation of a Sanskrit text would not result in the accumulation of wealth in the same way that trading in salt or tobacco would. But, by applying the instruments of the Western disciplines to an Asian reality, which the British frequently characterized as 'obscure' and 'unexplored', a Servant of the Company might build up a stock of symbolic capital. He might create for himself a reputation as a scholar. He might even, in the process, sell a few books to his colleagues in Calcutta or to a curious public back in London.[2]

In the late eighteenth and early nineteenth centuries knowledge of South Asian languages came to be seen as fundamental to effective colonial administration. What is more, the Company Servants involved in developing this body of knowledge clearly viewed their work in just these terms: as a means of self-advancement. The money one could make by writing a grammar would not buy an estate in Wiltshire. But it might be a welcome supplement to the income of an army officer or a Company surgeon. It might, furthermore, increase his symbolic capital and allow him to transform himself from the practitioner of a relatively lowly profession into someone with a literary or philosophical reputation. The possibility of developing such a reputation might be attractive, furthermore, even to someone with a more exalted position in life. Colonial grammars of the Romantic period are interesting, therefore, not only for the way they represent the languages of the colonies, but also for the fact that they are important sites in which individuals struggled to refashion themselves and represent themselves to their compatriots as scholarly and knowledgeable men. This is true not only of the grammars which emerged from the British community in Bengal, but also of others produced contemporaneously, by French administrators in West Africa, for example.[3]

An important aspect of such transformations was the depiction of the self as a lone traveller. If the colonies were 'obscure' and 'unexplored', then a powerful strategy for the colonial grammarian was to represent the making of his text as a lonely process, conducted in isolation, demanding a journey both physical and mental away from the centres of colonial power and into the 'unknown'. For this reason some of the grammarians to be discussed later in the essay go so far as to include an autobiographical preface in their work highlighting the isolation in which the work was produced, the hardships they endured, the extraordinary experiences they met with in the process. The important point here is that for a writer who has constructed himself in these terms, to find that his text has been plagiarized is a disaster. The uniqueness of the work is dangerously compromised because it is impossible for readers to know which text really constitutes the product of that original journey of discovery. To be accused of plagiarism is even more damaging because there is no ambiguity about the matter. The accused is the one who must justify his claims to originality.

This chapter will investigate two instances in which colonial grammarians explicitly discuss issues of originality and plagiarism. In one case the writer makes accusations against a commercial rival. In the other, a grammarian seems concerned that he may be on the receiving end of such an accusation and attempts to avoid this eventuality. For both writers it was clearly important to raise these issues in the minds of their readers. Their claims to have travelled to the frontiers of knowledge were so important to the self-representation of both men that they could not afford to leave the problem unexplored. The purpose of this chapter is to discuss their handling of these difficulties by examining the textual strategies through which they represented the literary crises in which they found themselves and the means by which they incorporated these representations into the framework of their texts. In the first case, a British grammarian of Urdu conducts his campaign through a barrage of figurative language. In the second, a French grammarian of Wolof adorns his text with philosophical discussion in order to position it away from a recently published description of the same language. In both cases the text is complicated in a way that enmeshes us as readers and demands that we acknowledge the true originality of the grammarian's work.

Hadley and Gilchrist: fables, emblems and classical myth

In 1782 a young Scot from Edinburgh arrived in Bombay and secured a position in the service of the East India Company. His name was John Gilchrist and at the age of fourteen he had been apprenticed to a surgeon in Falkirk. Subsequently, he had worked as a surgeon's mate in the Royal Navy. This job carried very little prestige in the late eighteenth century and Gilchrist's journey to India certainly represented a bid for self-advancement. A job as a surgeon in the service of the Company offered considerably better prospects than a similar position on a ship. But soon after arriving in India Gilchrist changed his plans. Having learned some Urdu to facilitate communication with the Indian soldiers, he resolved to produce a dictionary and grammar of the language for the use of Company Servants, both army officers and administrators.

A grammar of Urdu had already been published in London. This text was the work of Captain George Hadley, who had been an officer in the Company's army in the 1760s, and by 1784 it had reached a third edition.[4] Hadley's grammar described a kind of pidgin Urdu, which was often known as 'Moors' or 'Jargon'. Gilchrist was therefore able to present his projected work as wholly original because he intended to describe a more prestigious variety than the 'monstrous clack' to be found in Hadley's short and sketchy text.[5] It took Gilchrist some years to realize his aims, but between 1787 and 1790 his dictionary was published in instalments and in 1796 his grammar appeared. He clearly hoped to make money from this project and assumed that the superiority of his work would be evident to everyone. It proclaimed its seriousness through its size – three quarto volumes – and also through its high print quality, its frequent references to European grammatical authorities, and through copious citations from the Urdu poets.

In 1796, however, the very year that Gilchrist's grammar was published, a fourth and expanded edition of Hadley's text appeared in London and from what Gilchrist tells us it seems to have enjoyed a high degree of commercial success. In 1798, just a couple of years later, Gilchrist published two new works in which he explicitly discusses this new edition of Hadley's grammar. One of these texts constituted a kind of retrospective preface to Gilchrist's earlier publications and consists of a long and sprawling tirade of explanation and self-justification. It includes just the kind of biographical sequence mentioned earlier: a dramatic narrative in which Gilchrist depicts himself crossing Northern India in native garb, beset by sickness and self-doubt, but winning out and completing his project in the face of adversity. It also contains an accusation of plagiarism against Hadley and the terms in which this charge is couched are extremely interesting.[6]

Gilchrist's accusation concerns Hadley's treatment of the Urdu verbal system and in order to understand the dispute it is necessary to consider the difficulties which this part of the grammar presented to these early British grammarians. The issue hinges upon the derivation of one particular form of the Urdu verb: the perfect. One important use of the perfect form is the expression of past events which are now complete. So, for example, *dekhâ* is the perfect form of the verb *dekhnâ* ['to see'] and can be used to translate the English word 'saw'.

Today we would say that the vast majority of Urdu verbs form their perfects by adding *â* to the root. A few verbs undergo minor phonetic changes in the process. When the root of the verb itself ends in *â*, for example, the perfect is formed by adding *yâ* or, to put it more technically, a glide is inserted between the root and the perfect suffix. In addition a few verbs are irregular and have unusual perfects. Two important ones are *denâ* and *lenâ*, whose perfects are *dîyâ* and *lîyâ*. So, in summary, a few classes of verbs undergo minor phonetic changes in the formation of the perfect and a handful of verbs are anomalous. Generally, however, the verbal system is unusually regular and straightforward.

For various reasons Hadley's analysis was far less economical than this one. He was working with phonetic concepts different from those we use today and the relatively minor variations outlined here seemed much more problematic to him. The result was that, in the first three editions of his grammar, he divided the verbs of the Urdu language into five groups or conjugations.[7] The irregular verbs *denâ* and *lenâ* formed the first conjugation, for example, and verbs whose roots end in *â* were placed in the third conjugation. Hadley devised this classification by looking at the sounds which appear at the end of verbal roots and this method of analysis was undoubtedly borrowed from the Latin grammatical tradition where it produces a more efficient analysis than it does in the case of Urdu.

The important point is that when Gilchrist's grammar appeared in 1796 Hadley's analysis was called into question. Gilchrist insisted that the verbal system of Urdu was astonishingly regular. In fact, he produced an analysis very similar to the contemporary one outlined earlier. He points out that the insertion of a glide after roots which end in *â* is a relatively minor change, which simply has the effect of making the form easier to pronounce. This he sees as a virtue since it renders the language more euphonous.[8] Similarly, he insists it is not necessary to construct a whole conjugation merely to account for two irregular verbs, *denâ* and *lenâ*. He even speculates that their irregular perfects – *dîyâ* and *lîyâ* – must derive from two 'ancient' verbs which have fallen out of use, 'deena' and 'leena'. He clearly feels that, if this can be shown to be true, then *dîyâ* and *lîyâ* are not really irregular at all.[9]

There are several reasons why Gilchrist emphasizes the simplicity of the system to such a degree. First, it obviously makes the language less daunting to learners. More importantly, however, in the seventeenth and eighteenth centuries it was common for grammarians not simply to describe languages, but also to evaluate them with reference to criteria set by rhetoricians and philosophers. Did the properties of the language render it expressive? Was its grammar built upon sound metaphysical principles? Regularity was often presented as a positive feature of a language and this idea derives from the notion that there should be a simple one-to-one correspondence between words and things or, alternatively, between words and ideas. The notion of an action's being finished is a single idea so there should be a single way of deriving the perfect forms of verbs. Latin, for example, has a system of four conjugations and despite being a 'language of learning' it did not escape censure on these grounds. When John Wilkins published a proposal for a new philosophical language in 1668, for example, he was critical of the absurd proliferation of verbal forms to be found in the Latin language.[10]

By demonstrating the regularity of the Urdu verbal system Gilchrist was, therefore, revealing the excellence of the language as a vehicle of thought. Such a manoeuvre would clearly be advantageous to him because it would show that he was working on an object worthy of serious study. The contrast between his own economical analysis and Hadley's cumbersome system of conjugations also allowed him to construct himself as a lone traveller – the first European to have understood the true elegance of court Urdu and not to have settled for the 'monstrous clack' of Hadley's jargon.

Problems arose when Hadley published the fourth edition of his grammar in 1796, for in this text the discussion of the verbal system has been altered. The reader is now told that the Urdu language only has one conjugation and that such variations as exist in the formation of the perfect can be regulated with a small number of rules. Hadley had clearly had the opportunity to read Gilchrist's grammar before this new edition was published and it is not difficult to imagine how Gilchrist reacted to these new developments. When he published his retrospective preface in 1798 he condemned Hadley's work in no uncertain terms and he drew attention to this change of position on the verbal system, explicitly describing it as an act of plagiarism. How, then, did he do it?

Towards the end of the preface Gilchrist sets out an extended metaphor in which he draws a comparison between the learner's experience of reading his grammar and a journey through the Indian landscape. The rhetorical significance of this passage is clear. By developing this comparison, Gilchrist constructs himself as a lone traveller. He has visited these regions before; he has mapped them; and he can guide you through them. In a sense the metaphor of the journey constitutes a figurative recapitulation of the description of Gilchrist's actual journey, which appears towards the beginning of the preface. Different parts of the grammar are compared to different kinds of terrain. Significantly, the verbal system is presented as a beautiful meadow and the description is reminiscent of the picturesque paintings of the Gangetic plain which were being produced in this period by artists such as William and Thomas Daniell:[11]

[W]e may now make a long halt at the verbs, taking special care to string all the indispensable tenses in regular rosaries or garlands, at our finger ends [...]. No other section of this philological champaign can afford so much to admire and so little to censure.[12]

So the grammatical simplicity of the verbal system is metaphorically described in terms of a picturesque landscape and Gilchrist's attack on Hadley is inserted into this sequence, also in figurative terms:

> [This section of the philological champaign] teems with beauties even sufficient to have animated the tongue, and purged the nocturnal vision of one owl, who has long perched on the watch tower of Hindoostanee grammar, with an effrontery suited to the darkness of night, and with hootings ominous and fatal enough, to have far encroached upon the long secluded day. A charm so potent, and effects so wonderfully electrick, demand the confession of this luminous emblem of sapience in its own words.[13]

And Gilchrist goes on to quote the offending statement from Hadley's fourth edition: 'In the former three editions of the Work five Conjugations were given. But as they vary only in the formation of the Preterite, and rules are laid down to regulate it, this will be confined to *one.*'

This description of Hadley as an owl draws upon several sources of conventional imagery. First the description is fabular. Readers in the late eighteenth century would have been familiar with the owl, which because of its nocturnal vision, could not appreciate the beauty of the day. The story appears in Robert Dodsley's collection, *Select Fables of Esop and Other Fabulists*, which appeared in 1761 and was popular throughout the second half of the eighteenth century. In fact Gilchrist himself arranged for the first part of Dodsley's work to be translated into various oriental languages in 1803.[14] An important aspect of fables is their doubleness. Fables were very much part of eighteenth-century political discourse and the image has a seriousness which would not have been lost on contemporary readers. Hadley is like the foolish owl because for such a long time he has been unable to appreciate the beauty of the verbal system. But at another level fables are simply tales for children and, through the deployment of a fabular image, Gilchrist is also able to disavow the seriousness of his attack and suggest that Hadley is too ridiculous to be seriously discussed.

Gilchrist also trades ironically on the fact that in some contexts the owl is an emblem of wisdom or 'sapience' and the beauty of the verbal system has proved sufficient to transform Hadley from a foolish, fabular owl into a wise, emblematic one. In the space of a few lines we have

been invited to interpret Gilchrist's text in relation to the fabular tradition and then, ironically, by reference to the emblematic one. Before he
moves on, moreover, Gilchrist addresses the reader directly and invokes
a third frame of reference:

> If good reader! you ever detect me of similar, wilful plagiary, I shall
> submit to the same exalted station, and metamorphosis, now
> assigned to him *in terrorem* against all such insidious plagiarists.[15]

Now Hadley is the victim of a metamorphosis, condemned to live out
his life as a bird on a watch tower. He has been transformed into an owl
as a punishment for his plagiarism. And who is the agent of this transformation? It is Gilchrist, of course, who made the image through which
Hadley became an owl in the first place. The idea of metamorphosis as
punishment is reminiscent of the Ovidian tradition and there is a hint of
presumption in the idea that Gilchrist's textual strategies have rendered
him a classical god, capable of condemning his enemies to live out their
lives in the bodies of birds or beasts. But Gilchrist does defuse the
situation by offering to undergo the same transformation himself
should he ever be found guilty of the same crime as Hadley. Of course,
the implication of this promise is clear to everyone: such a thing is never
going to happen.

   Just as Gilchrist leads the reader through the landscape, then, and in
so doing through the linguistic analyses of the grammar, so he also leads
us through the present text, ostentatiously prescribing the interpretative
frameworks we should impose upon his imagery. Hadley meanwhile
does not act but is acted upon. He is the one who suffers change as the
interpretative frameworks shift. So through this metatextual strategy
Gilchrist ostentatiously dramatizes his own active role as creator and
renders Hadley a passive character within his text. Thus Gilchrist's
creativity and Hadley's alleged lack of it are figured in the text at every
level.

Hadley and Gilchrist: proverbs and innuendo

Gilchrist uses similar figurative strategies in the other text he published
in 1798, a concise introduction to the Urdu language entitled *The
Oriental Linguist*. In the preface to this work he is aggressively critical
of Hadley, describing his work as an 'insignificant, catch-penny production', 'a mere Tom Thumb', 'a pamphlet' and even as 'dog cheap trash'.
He states that he has been forced to produce a popular and 'conciliating'

text in order to compete with Hadley's work, which, ironically, is achieving wider circulation because it has itself been pirated. Gilchrist uses a range of terms which emphasize the material loss he has sustained as a result of Hadley's success. His rival is a 'poacher', a 'robber' and a 'thief'. What is more, he also identifies another specific act of plagiarism and frames it as a material theft by reference to another popular tradition of figurative language.[16]

All the editions of Hadley's work contain a vocabulary of Urdu. The one in the fourth edition, however, is more extensive than that in the third and also appears in reversed form so that the reader can either look up the meaning of an Urdu word or look up an English word and find an Urdu equivalent. Gilchrist claimed that the expansion of Hadley's vocabulary had been achieved by plundering material from his own dictionary:

> [G]uess my surprize, good reader! to find, that this boasted stock could be not other than the contents of my work, as I discovered on the first inspection, that he had extracted a vast number of words thence, in the very orthography too, which he had been condemning with considerable severity.[17]

Gilchrist notes, however, that Hadley has acknowledged the source of two of the words he has borrowed and his reporting of this fact is very interesting. The first of the words is 'k*oo*rtee' or 'coat' and Gilchrist claims to have an explanation for Hadley's 'candour' in admitting the source of this item. '[K]*oo*rtee, a coat, he probably conceived too barefaced a robbery'.[18] The first point to make is that Gilchrist's phrasing creates a certain ambiguity. Clearly what Hadley has appropriated is the lexical item 'k*oo*rtee', which appears in Gilchrist's dictionary. But one could equally well use Gilchrist's sentence to talk about the theft of a material object and Gilchrist could, in effect, be characterising Hadley as having stolen his jacket. English proverbial usage trades upon the fact that a person's coat is an everyday object, something familiar to him, indeed something more familiar than almost anything else. Thus in their collections of English proverbs both John Ray and Nathan Bailey indicate that to express the idea that particular information is reliable or secure one can proverbially say, 'As sure as the coat on my back'.[19] Thus to steal a person's coat would indeed be a 'barefaced robbery'.

But it is interesting that the familiarity of the coat as a material object leads to its proverbial use as an image of epistemological certainty. The humorous assertion that the theft of the material object is an act of extraordinary insolence leads us back, via the proverbial usage, to the idea that the coat represents knowledge – knowledge which, in this case, has been stolen. Clearly Gilchrist's use of figurative language is far less explicit in this case than it was in the image of the owl. Nevertheless, he is clearly making a joke when he says that appropriating a coat would have been a barefaced robbery and, in so doing, he sets up a series of associations which take us from knowledge to material possessions and back again to knowledge. So the joke serves to emphasize the material value which Gilchrist places on the linguistic knowledge he has acquired and the material loss he has sustained as a result of Hadley's stealing it. Once again a popular figurative tradition is exploited to create a deft but complex exposé of Hadley's dishonesty.

The second word that Hadley admits to having borrowed is 'ch*oo*t-muranee', which he translates as 'slut'. In this case Gilchrist takes exception to the way in which Hadley expresses his indebtedness. Next to the dictionary entry for 'ch*oo*tmuranee' Hadley asserts that '[t]his strange epithet is warranted by the Hindostanic Dictionary'.[20] The word 'strange' suggests that Hadley himself has not encountered the term before, presumably because when in India he did not himself consort with 'sluts'. The only evidence he has for its currency is the fact that it appears in Gilchrist's text, and the suggestion is clearly that Gilchrist would have more reason to be familiar with such a term than he would himself. Gilchrist responds by trying to turn the innuendo back on Hadley. He speculates that 'ch*oo*tmuranee, he perhaps deemed too precious an expression for embezzlement by a literary theft, and therefore allows, *that he found it* in my work.' This does not make much sense, however. Even if Hadley did enjoy the company of 'sluts' he would hardly find an Urdu word of much use in England, where he had been living since the early 1770s.

Once again Gilchrist seems to be pushing his readers to *interpret* the details of his text, not, this time, in relation to a figurative tradition but simply by reference to the ordinary language of gossip and innuendo. Once again, the debate over plagiarism is woven into broader issues of self-representation. Sexual propriety is clearly not a necessary condition of being an inventive or rigorous scholar. Nevertheless, Gilchrist's autobiographical profile does emphasise the self-denial which the acquisition of knowledge demands and the implication that he has spent his time consorting with prostitutes does work to undermine the austere picture he has painted of himself.

Grammar and philosophy

So far this chapter has discussed the ways in which colonial grammarians could represent existing disputes about plagiarism. In 1829, however, the French official, Jacques-François Roger, published a grammar of the Senegalese language, Wolof.[21] In the preface to his grammar, Roger depicts himself as a Romantic hero, escaping the trials of Paris and finding solace in Africa:

> My spirit weary, my heart bruised in the hurly-burly of public life, I had seen from too close a range the revolting game of jealous and avaricious passions; I had laid bare the fickle secrets of human activity. Social life had lost its attractions for me, and fleeing the world I had sought in the scalding climate of Africa, if not death, at least some solitude and distraction from my troubles.[22]

Roger's grammar is very much an act of self-representation. The material issues which are so central to Gilchrist are of virtually no importance to Roger. He is concerned rather to fashion an identity as someone apart from the crowd, someone whose familiarity with the language of the Wolofs has allowed him to look deeply into the 'African mind', and who has found there an image of natural wisdom which stands in contrast to the absurd sophistication of the metropolis. The problem, however, was that another French writer, an educationalist named Jean Dard, had already published a grammar of Wolof in 1826 and so Roger's text runs the risk of appearing derivative and not a new and startling journey into unknown Africa. In order to avert the possible charge of plagiarism, Roger constantly emphasizes that his text is work of a different kind from Dard's – a different genre of writing altogether. He states conventionally enough that his research was already complete by the time Dard published his book and he points to some minor differences in their analyses. But the main point of his argument is that the two works can exist side by side because his intention was not to produce a teaching grammar, but to provide philosophical insights for what he calls '*savants*', or scholars.[23]

This intention is signalled in the body of the text by a barrage of speculation and comparison which is signalled as rendering the work philosophical rather than simply pedagogical. Thus, when he talks about the nominal system, Dard simply tells us that Wolof nouns do not have gender but that it is possible to distinguish male from female individuals by adding the term '*gôre*' in the former case and '*dhiguéne*' in the latter.[24] He also points out that in French the signs of gender are the articles *'le* and *la'*. Roger, by contrast, tells us that the same lack of gender has been reported in the languages of Angola and in those spoken on the Gold Coast and he raises the question of how this is to be interpreted:

> I could consider whether the non-existence of genders, which introduces so much simplicity into the language and which does not hinder the expression of all the nuances of thought can be considered an advantage or a fault. However, one must leave the reader something to do.[25]

Roger does add some examples of what he considers the anomalous nature of the category in French and remarks that if similar features were found in the 'jargon of a primitive people' they would be severely censured. But, having raised the larger issue of how grammatical categories are to be justified, he does not provide any answer and the reader is left to do that alone. The discussion serves not so much to articulate any philosophical opinion as to signal the general philosophical character of the text and present us with a picture of Roger in the process of cogitation.

This is not to claim that the work is in some way bogus. Roger's grammar does articulate a particular Romantic view of an African language and, in doing so, realises its own aims. The important point is that it also provides a space for Roger's recreation of himself as a Romantic hero and this often demands that, when he comes to the same conclusions as a previous grammarian about what he calls the 'mechanism' of the language, he uses explicit textual means to demonstrate that he is nevertheless engaged in a different activity. He may not have a philosophical point to make about a particular feature of the language but, nevertheless, he is still deep in thought – still a philosopher.

Conclusion

The exploration of the 'unknown' colony provided the agents of colonial or colonising powers with major opportunities for the recreation of self. Despite his unpromising start as a surgeon's mate on a sloop of the Royal Navy, Gilchrist's grammatical work led to his being appointed the first Professor of Urdu at Fort William College Calcutta and when he returned to Edinburgh in the early years of the nineteenth century he was welcomed by no less a person than Robert Anderson, one of the leading lights of the literary community. In the marketplace of ideas, however, originality was at a premium and to maintain the impression of oneself as an explorer travelling beyond the frontiers of existing knowledge, it was sometimes necessary to negotiate the dangers presented by accusations of plagiarism.

The grammar appears a formal entity, highly codified and predetermined. Its surface seems too smooth to offer interpretative purchase and the idea that it might be emotive or playful seems difficult to accept. Yet colonial grammarians exploited a range of textual strategies to negotiate issues of originality both in the thresholds of their works, the notes and prefaces, and also in the body of the text itself, through the foregrounding of features unnoticed by previous writers and through the display of philosophical speculation. Figurative language is a particularly important resource, allowing several layers of comment to be compressed into a single image or sequence of images. And the self-conscious performance of a role as philosopher and *savant*, even when there is little substantive philosophy to express, allows the grammarian to keep reminding the reader of the originality of the work.

There is a certain irony in using such traditional forms of expression as emblems and proverbs to stake a claim to originality. This type of discourse is owned by everyone. Proverbs are common property and to use them is very much to conform to conventional patterns of communication. Similarly there is something of a paradox in demonstrating one's knowledge of an 'exotic' other by showing quite how easily it can be assimilated into a familiar framework of philosophical speculation. In both cases 'originality' is worked out in the details of a deeply conventional schema and as such is signalled in ways which are appropriate for the highly codified genre of the grammar.

The negotiation of traditional imagery to produce an impression of newness mirrors the work of the grammarian struggling to establish his own voice within the confines of a closely prescribed metalanguage. And so the textual strategies described in this essay dramatise the making of colonial knowledge in a way that is more complex than we might at first expect. Despite the grammarians' evocations of an 'unknown' world into which they are travelling for the very first time, everything here is strangely familiar. The European writer has littered the landscape with owls and watchtowers, sneak thieves and prostitutes, philosophers worrying away at the old chestnut of grammatical gender and *still* not solving the fundamental problem of its justification. The colony may offer a space in which the European writer can construct himself as an explorer, but his own ways of seeing limit what he can find there, and the struggle to appropriate commonly owned forms of expression, and make them speak, beautifully evokes the struggle to say anything new about this space in the common language.

Afterword

Bertrand A. Goldgar

Consider these comments: 'plagiarism is a phantom crime, impossible to commit' (Zsuzsa Baross, in *New Literary History*); 'plagiarism, then, is intellectual theft' (Joseph Gibaldi, in *MLA Handbook*).[1] Both remarks were written or published in the past three years, and though they are at opposite ends of some sort of moral spectrum, they illustrate a few of the difficulties of discussing plagiarism in a literary or academic culture in which postmodern theories exist side-by-side with traditional notions of authorship and morality. One sometimes finds the two in conflict even in sophisticated theorists who, though believing the author to be dead and the author function paralysed and the text gone from the classroom and originality a fiction, still occasionally have to deal with an actual act of plagiarism in the real world of either scholarship or teaching. My favourite example is an essay by a linguist, Ron Scollon, which argues that the idea of plagiarism arises from a faulty model of communication derived from 'the ideology of the rational, autonomous individual ... dominant in Europe since the Enlightenment'.[2] But then, at the end of his essay, he reports that his own work has been plagiarized, that despite his ideological position he was initially filled with 'rancour', but that he has now come to understand that the scholars who stole from him 'have done so from within a conceptual frame which I do not yet fully understand'.[3] Perhaps it takes a strong pleasure in paradox to reach that level of tolerance.

In a sense the central debate over plagiarism is very simple: either one believes that what the world still calls 'plagiarism' has some mode of existence and is a moral issue related to theft or acts of appropriation, or one thinks it is an illusion, a term rendered meaningless because there is no possibility of originality. 'Debate', however, is the wrong word, for these beliefs are like Kuhn's incompatible paradigms in that one cannot simply evaluate them and then choose the one which seems to be based on the best evidence. Some of the argument between them is bound to be circular and self-defeating, with no common language left with which to communicate. Given this situation, I think Brean Hammond makes a telling point when he suggests in the conclusion of his essay that perhaps both permissiveness about plagiarism and authoritarian reactions against it stem from the root insecurity of those in the world of letters about the 'death of literature' and the present nature of their discipline.

In any event, having sounded such a dark note, let me hasten to say that the issues just outlined are not really germane to this collection. The contributors concern themselves with issues perhaps less funda-mental but more capable of discussion and more useful to discuss. They have, for the most part, 'too much knowledge for the sceptic side', even Nick Groom, who does a little dance around a postmodern position and is the most antagonistic to the views of the keynote essay by Christopher Ricks. But no one else, it seems to me, whatever their arguments, comes close to saying outright that plagiarism is meaning-less in theory and impossible to commit in practice. None the less, though starting from some of the same fundamental assumptions, the essays make different claims and leave us with a diversity of attitudes about what seem to be the consistent questions in contemporary views of plagiarism. Let me elaborate on that point by focusing on a few of those questions or issues, as identified by Christopher Ricks in his provocative essay.

First, there is the matter of what the word 'plagiarism' means. Ricks uses the *OED* definition, wrongful appropriation, supplemented by Peter Shaw's crucial corollary, 'with an intent to deceive', and goes on to warn against letting 'grey areas' confuse us about the clarity and simplicity of that meaning. Clear and simple it may be, but in one way or another some of the responses to Ricks in this collection grumble about it slightly. Groom, who views plagiarism as only a bad metaphor, finds this definition a mere ploy, something set up to carry too much weight so that Ricks can relish its 'inevitable collapse'. Most of the other essays, however, take it as it was obviously intended, a serious statement of a strongly moral position, yet they worry over its applicability across time. Richard Terry, in his study of the term's meaning in the later eighteenth century, points out that contexts are what matter in such investigation and finds the sense of the word in our own day and in Johnson's to be substantially the same; but then he seems to throw away its moral implications by concluding relativistically that 'plagiarism' is just a word like 'idiot', an 'empty semantic vessel into which I choose to pour my intolerance of certain other people'. In contrast, Ian Donaldson, looking at the varieties of meanings and attitudes in the Renaissance and later, finds that what constitutes plagiarism and why it is condemned are 'more puzzling and variable' matters than one might have thought, yet none of the variations 'drains the offence of moral consequence' even while affecting our efforts to describe it historically. Thus Donaldson, whose essay I think should be a model for anyone writing an historical analysis of plagiarism, is able to recognize and describe shifts of meaning and usage without resorting to the time-honoured sophistic move of claiming that, because there is no clearly defined way to talk about something, or many competing ways to do so, therefore there *is* no way to talk about it, if indeed it even exists. Plagiarism, of course, is not the only moral issue to be evaded in that fashion.

The largest section of this volume is devoted to 'Contexts of Plagiarism', and it is in those chapters that it makes its most significant contributions. The modern myth, at least among literary scholars, has portrayed plagiarism as a cultural construct of a society dominated by ideas of private property and ownership. Indeed, the myth goes, and many of these essays show how much it is only a myth, there was no such thing until concepts of property came into dominance in the seventeenth century and then became extended to literary materials and then to the publishing industry with its copyright laws. There is a kind of innocence about all this, I think, as though these property-oriented scholars thought duplicity and fraudulent texts had been born with printing; I recommend Anthony Grafton's *Forgers and Critics* (Princeton, 1990) for a quick cure. At any rate, Ricks calls this particular evasion of moral responsibility the 'recent history' dodge: plagiarism is 'a recent construction in need of demystifying'. Paulina Kewes' earlier book had paved the way to demystifying that evasion itself, with her account of concepts of plagiarism, appropriation, and intellectual property in the crucial period at the end of the seventeenth and beginning of the eighteenth centuries.[4] All the essayists here seem pretty well agreed that in the seventeenth century attitudes towards plagiarism underwent a change. Certainly no one in this collection wants to argue that the idea of literary theft was *born* in the seventeenth century, much less in the eighteenth, although, again, one still encounters such claims in ahistorical postmodern writings. But where to fix its birth is still a tricky matter, and how to describe the changes in attitude continues to be a source of disagreement. Brean Hammond emphasizes that early modern and modern attitudes towards plagiarism are distinctively different from those in early periods because of the professionalization of writing, though he concedes that the concept of literary theft had been around for a long time. Stephen Orgel charmingly recants his earlier view that plagiarism wasn't taken seriously before the late seventeenth century, though, like Hammond, he says something *did* change after the Renaissance. Barbara Ravelhofer finds a case, perhaps the first, of an author in 1623 accusing a colleague of plagiarism in public and in print, and Andrew Hope pushes the examples as far back as the sixteenth century. In short, in this book so-called 'Modern' views of textual boundaries yield to empirical historical research and show up more than a century earlier than the first copyright law.

Yet no one can deny that attitudes change, and that complications remain. Harold Love, using property metaphors like 'free trade zone' that seem to beg a host of questions, argues that there have always been some texts that could properly be plagiarized; and he goes on to connect the debate over plagiarism to seventeenth-century religious debates between liturgists. His general point provokes thought: 'One cannot argue that because plagiarism was frowned upon in one discursive context it was not tolerated in another exactly contemporaneous context and that there are not ... areas of our written textual inheritance which constitute unenclosed common'. Perhaps, but for some readers might not this hint of relativism confuse the issue? Isn't it also the case that one can't argue, and so should not imply, that because practices that would be called plagiarism in most contexts are tolerated in certain other contexts (like oral traditions), there is no such thing as the condemnable practice itself? Like Love, Ian Donaldson charts the varieties and changes in views of plagiarism by tracking Ben Jonson's changing reputation with regard to literary thievery; and in so doing he reveals not only the shifting views of the term during almost two centuries, but also some of the 'contradictions which still beset our understanding' of it. But with Donaldson, as noted earlier, there is no glossing over of moral implications. Indeed his elaboration of Jonson's clothes-stealing scenes and images points to plagiarism as an act that, he says, is 'more than criminal' and 'disruptive to conventional notions of the stable individual self'.

Since Foucault, such efforts to treat plagiarism as a moral issue have of course been complicated by theory, by the disappearance of the author and the like. But in the same way another theory, imitation, once complicated the moral question during the early history of the concept 'plagiarism', and the confusion between the two continues to increase as time goes by. Ricks points to the way in which some 'unthinking' modern critics try to equate imitation with plagiarism, and many of the follow-up essays touch on the issue, citing the efforts of ancient critics to make a distinction between imitating and stealing, and filling out our understanding of imitative practices in historiography and in literature from the sixteenth through the late eighteenth centuries. Longinus's *On the Sublime*, mentioned only in passing, is a vital source, since in section 13 he distinguishes 'emulous' imitation from simple theft (the Greek text uses for plagiarism a word meaning 'stealing' or 'theft') in a passage that was highly influential as late as the eighteenth century. Richard Terry, in an especially interesting point, suggests that although plagiarism benefitted from its association (or confusion) with classical imitative practice in the early and mid-eighteenth centuries, as imitative writing fell out of favor, plagiarism too became regarded more severely: 'plagiarism, as it were, loses its key alibi'. A few of the essays are dependent on the early book by H. O. White, the value of which Ricks, quite rightly I think, has strongly questioned, and the entire matter of the role of imitation and its relation to plagiarism from the days of the Ancients to the late eighteenth century still seems to me insufficiently studied and in need of more research. Stephen Orgel writes, 'we all know and have always known that the crucial element in plagiarism is the intention to deceive'; but how long exactly, for how many centuries, have we known it? Somebody needs to write White's book all over again.

Other issues here which suggest future lines of work include the following: the common confusion between immorality and illegality (i.e. between plagiarism and copyright infringement), the effect (if any) of class and gender on attitudes toward plagiarism in the early modern period, and the moral difference (if any) between the plagiarism of professional writers and the cheating of undergraduate students (are professional writers to be regarded differently? and why?). The investigation of plagiarism in the early periods might be widened, Ravelhofer suggests, so that it covers the visual arts, music and craftsmanship rather than merely philosophy and literature. Scholars, she says, have concentrated on the economic ramifications of the print revolution but sidestepped the question of how, even in the early seventeenth century, 'plagiarists and authors mediated and fashioned their texts in competition with each other' so that the material nature of the product, its touch, look and feel, would play a significant market role. And why, she wonders, do we find so few authors charging others with plagiarism in the earlier seventeenth century?

Finally, an important and clear lesson from some of the essays is the folly of thinking of early modern plagiarism only in terms of property, either real or intellectual. De Lauze, the victim in the case Ravelhofer examines, gained nothing materially from exposing the thief, neither money nor patronage, yet he wanted the thief publicly exposed and his own labors demonstrated. In the same way the author-as-victim is the theme of the case described by Richard Steadman-Jones, where it is in particular the grammarian-writer's construction of himself, his crucial self-representation, that has been stolen. When Christopher Ricks asks what, exactly, the plagiarist steals, his answer is, of course, 'credit', reputation, honor, not money or property. I may seem to belabor the obvious, but a few passages in a recent essay by Max W. Thomas suggest the point bears repeating. After quoting Petrarch's expression of dismay, *not* over someone stealing his writing but over someone attributing to him the writing of another, Thomas comments, with an air of surprise, 'the primary value here is on something closer to honor than to intellectual property'.[5] Yes, indeed, and perhaps with plagiarism, in contrast to copyright infringement, such has often been the case. It's worth remembering that after the print explosion, when there was a new copyright law and entrenched concerns over property, and when the land was filled (in Pope's words) with 'imitating [and plagiarizing!] fools', writers like Swift and Pope complained almost as much about 'imputed trash' fathered on them by the likes of the bookseller Edmund Curll as they did about plagiarism itself.

Although I personally agree with Ricks's position, let me end with a seventeenth-century exculpatory passage on plagiarism by John Aubrey, one that again has to do with glory rather than profit. Aubrey condemns the motive and the deed of the perpetrator but at least finds some scholarly good to arise from the evil. It should be noted, however, that Aubrey himself was not one of the 'Inventors' whose work was appropriated:

> 'Tis certaine ... that John Wallis is a person of reall worth, and may stand very gloriously upon his owne basis, and need not be beholding to any man for Fame, yet he is so extremely greedy of glorie, that he steales feathers from others to adorne his own cap; e.g. he lies at watch, at Sir Christopher Wren's discourse, Mr. Robert Hooke's, Dr. William Holder, putts downe their notions in his Note booke, and then prints it, without oweneing the Authors. This frequently, of which they complain. But though he does an injury to the Inventors, he does good to Learning, in publishing such curious notions, which the author (especially Sir Christopher Wren) might never have the leisure to write of himselfe.[6]

Notes

Preface

1. Christopher Ricks, 'Plagiarism', this volume, pp. 21–40.
2. Richard A. Posner, 'On Plagiarism', *The Atlantic Monthly*, 289: 4 (April 2002), p. 23.
3. Laura J. Rosenthal, *Playwrights and Plagiarists in Early Modern England: Gender, Authorship, Literary Property* (Ithaca: Cornell University Press, 1996); Stuart Home (ed.), *Plagiarism: Art as Commodity and Strategies for its Negation* (n.p.: Aporia Press, 1987).
4. Marilyn Randall, *Pragmatic Plagiarism: Authorship, Profit, and Power* (Toronto: University of Toronto Press, 2001); Jack Stillinger, *Multiple Authorship and the Myth of Solitary Genius* (Oxford: Oxford University Press, 1991): Chapter V, 'Creative Plagiarism: The Case of Coleridge' (pp. 96–120); at the Conference on 'Plagiarism in History and Theory' (Institute of English Studies, November 1999), Professor Harold Love delivered a paper entitled 'Virtuous Plagiarism'. See also Stuart Cosgrove, 'In Praise of Plagiarism', *New Statesman & Society* 2, no. 65 (1 September 1989), pp. 38–9.

Chapter 1

1. W. A. Edwards, *Plagiarism: An Essay on Good and Bad Borrowing* (Cambridge: Gordon Fraser/the Minority Press, 1933), p. 115.
2. For a concise distinction between plagiarism and copyright infringement, see Alexander Lindey, *Plagiarism and Originality* (New York: Harper & Brothers, 1952), p. 2.
3. Christopher Ricks, 'Plagiarism', 1998 British Academy Lecture, in *Proceedings of the British Academy*, 97 (Oxford: Clarendon Press, 1998), pp. 149–68, reprinted pp. 21–40, this volume.
4. As does Laura J. Rosenthal, when she attributes a modern feminist sensibility to early modern women writers and appropriators. See her *Playwrights and Plagiarists in Early Modern England: Gender, Authorship, Literary Property* (Ithaca: Cornell University Press, 1996).
5. As does Harold Ogden White, when he contends, against the gist of his own documentation of recurrent charges of theft, that plagiarism was unknown in Renaissance England. See his *Plagiarism and Imitation During the English Renaissance. A Study in Critical Distinctions* (New York: Octagon Books, 1965).
6. Thomas Mallon, *Stolen Words. Forays into the Origins and Ravages of Plagiarism* (New York: Ticknor & Fields, 1989), p. xii.
7. *Pragmatic Plagiarism: Authorship, Profit, and Power* (Toronto: University of Toronto Press, 2001), p. 19.
8. *Of Dramatick Poesy: An Essay*, in *The Works of John Dryden*, ed. Edward Niles Hooker *et al.*, 20 vols. (Berkeley: University of California Press, 1956–), xvii,

p. 57. For discussion, see David Bruce Kramer, *The Imperial Dryden: The Poetics of Appropriation in Seventeenth-Century England* (Athens, GA: University of Georgia Press, 1994); and Ian Donaldson, '"The Fripperie of Wit": Jonson and Plagiarism', pp. 119–33, this volume. Randall provides a spirited overview of the conquest metaphor in *Pragmatic Plagiarism*, pp. 189–202.

9. John Florio, translation of Montaigne's *Essays* of 1603 (*STC* 17041), quoted in D. F. McKenzie, 'Trading Places? England 1689 – France 1789', in *The Darnton Debate: Books and Revolution in the Eighteenth Century*, ed. Haydn T. Mason (Oxford: Voltaire Foundation Ltd., 1998), pp. 1–24 at p. 10.

10. White, *Plagiarism and Imitation*, pp. 120–1. The Latin usage would have been familiar to all those with grammar school education. Those who knew French would have encountered the French equivalent, 'plagiaire', several decades prior to the appearance of 'plagiary' in English. The first recorded usage of 'plagiaire' dates from 1555: '*poëtes plagiaires*'. See *Le Grand Robert de la Langue Française*, rev. Alain Ray (2nd edn, Paris: Dictionnaires le Robert, 1985), VII: p. 446. Cf. *Riders Dictionarie Corrected*, 3rd edn (Oxford, 1612), sig. Lll3^r; *A Dictionarie of the French and English Tongues Compiled by Randle Cotgrave* (London, 1611), sig. 3P6^v; Thomas Blount, *Glossographia: or A Dictionary, Interpreting all such Hard Words, Whether Hebrew, Greek, Latin, Italian, Spanish, French, Teutonick, Belgick, British or Saxon, as are now used in our refined English Tongue* (London, 1656), sigs. 2G7^v–2G8^r.

11. See Anthony Grafton, *Forgers and Critics: Creativity and Duplicity in Western Scholarship* (London: Collins & Brown, 1990), pp. 36ff.

12. *Pseudodoxia Epidemica: or, Enquiries into Very many Received Tenets, And commonly Presumed Truths* 2nd edn (London, 1650), p. 16.

13. Frederic G. Kenyon, *Books and Readers in Ancient Greece and Rome* (Oxford: Clarendon Press, 1932), pp. 38ff. For a discussion of the changing reading practices and modes of textual transmission see the Introduction to Guglielmo Cavallo and Roger Chartier (eds.), *A History of Reading in the West*, trans. Lydia G. Cochrane (Cambridge: Polity Press, 1999), pp. 1–36; and Roger Chartier, *Forms and Meanings: Texts, Performances, and Audiences from Codex to Computer* (Philadelphia: University of Pennsylvania Press, 1995).

14. Lisa Jardine and Anthony Grafton, '"Studied for Action": How Gabriel Harvey Read his Livy', *Past and Present*, 129 (1990), pp. 30–78; Ann Moss, *Printed Commonplace-Books and the Structuring of Renaissance Thought* (Oxford: Clarendon Press, 1996); Arthur F. Marotti, *Manuscript, Print and the English Renaissance Lyric* (Ithaca and London: Cornell University Press, 1995).

15. Moss, *Printed Commonplace-Books and the Structuring of Renaissance Thought*, p. 259.

16. Love, 'Originality and the Puritan Sermon', pp. 149–65. See also Love's 'How Personal is a Personal Miscellany? Sarah Cowper, Martin Clifford and the Buckingham Commonplace Book', in *Order and Connexion: Studies in Bibliography and Book History*, ed. R. C. Alston (Cambridge: D. S. Brewer, 1997), pp. 111–26.

17. *Scribal Publication in Seventeenth-Century England* (Oxford: Clarendon Press, 1993). See also Marotti, *Manuscript, Print and the English Renaissance Lyric*.

18. See Felix Raab, *The English Face of Machiavelli: A Changing Interpretation, 1500–1700* (London: Routledge and Kegan Paul, 1964), pp. 52ff.

19. 'The Medium of Plagiarism: Rogue Choreographers in Early Modern London', this volume, pp. 134–48.
20. *Notebook of Thomas Gibbons*, f85* (British Library Harley 980), cited in Alan H. Nelson, *Records of Early English Drama: Cambridge* (Toronto, 1989), 2.864. For further examples of theft from authorial manuscripts, see Paulina Kewes, 'Plays as Property, 1660–1710', in *A Nation Transformed: England After the Restoration*, ed. Alan Houston and Steven A. Pincus (Cambridge: Cambridge University Press, 2001), pp. 211–40; and Kewes, ' "A Play, which I presume to call *original*": Appropriation, Creative Genius, and Eighteenth-Century Playwriting', *Studies in the Literary Imagination*, 34 (2001), pp. 17–47, at pp. 35–7.
21. J. W. Saunders has described this phenomenon in 'The Stigma of Print: A Note on the Social Bases of Tudor Poetry', *Essays in Criticism*, 2 (1951), pp. 139–64.
22. 'To my most dearly-loved friend Henery [*sic*] Reynolds Esquire, of Poets and Poesie', in Michael Drayton, *The Battaile of Agincourt . . . The Miseries of Queene Margarite . . . Nimphidia, the Court of Fayrie. The Quest of Cinthia. The Shepheards Sirena. The Moone-Calfe. Elegies upon sundry occasions* (London, 1627), p. 208.
23. 'Plagiarism', this volume, pp. 39–40.
24. *The Two First Comedies of Terence called Andria, and the Eunuch newly Englished by Thomas Newman. Fitted for Schollers Priuate action in their Schooles* (London, 1627), sig. A2^r.
25. For discussion, see chapters 1–3 of my *Authorship and Appropriation: Writing for the Stage in England, 1660–1710* (Oxford: Clarendon Press, 1998).
26. 'Typography and Meaning: the Case of William Congreve', in G. Barber and B. Fabian, eds., *Wolfenbütteler Schriften zur Geschichte des Buchwesens* (Hamburg: Hauswedell, 1981), pp. 81–123; Jerome J. McGann, *The Textual Condition* (Princeton, NJ: Princeton University Press, 1991).
27. D. F. McKenzie, *Bibliography and the Sociology of Texts*, The Panizzi Lectures 1985 (London: The British Library, 1986).
28. See Robert D. Hume, *Reconstructing Contexts: The Aims and Principles of Archaeo-Historicism* (Oxford: Clarendon Press, 1999), to which my discussion is substantially indebted.
29. In the 1690s we find eloquent denunciations of theft not only from literary and scholarly works but also from disquisitions on financial matters and journalistic projects. See *Mr. John Asgill His Plagiarism Detected; And his several Assertions, Of which he pretends to be the Author, proved to be taken out of Mr. Briscoe's Discourse on the late Funds* (London, 1696); *The Athenian Mercury* (vol. 7, numb. 12. Saturday, May 7, 1692); *The Lacedemonian Mercury: Being A Continuation of the London Mercury* (vol. i, no. 9, Monday, 7 March 1692).
30. 'Originality and the Puritan Sermon', this volume, pp. 153–4.
31. Love, 'Originality and the Puritan Sermon', pp. 154ff. Andrew Hope explores the intersection of ideas about translation and plagiarism *vis-à-vis* the transmission of the Bible in early modern England in his 'Plagiarising the Word of God: Tyndale between More and Joye', this volume, pp. 93–105.
32. Adrian Johns, *The Nature of the Book: Print and Knowledge in the Making* (Chicago: University of Chicago Press, 1998), chapter 7: 'Piracy and Usurpation: Natural Philosophy in the Restoration', pp. 444–542.
33. Johns, *The Nature of the Book*, pp. 504–10.

34. RS Ms. Boyle P. 36, fols. 9^v and 15^r, cited in Johns, *The Nature of the Book*, pp. 507–8.
35. Anthony Grafton discusses Thomasius' tract in *The Footnote: A Curious History* (London: Faber and Faber, 1997), pp. 13–14.
36. See Brean S. Hammond, *Professional Imaginative Writing in England, 1670–1740: 'Hackney for Bread'* (Oxford: Clarendon Press, 1997); Julie Stone Peters, *Theatre of the Book 1480–1880: Print, Text, and Performance in Europe* (Oxford: Oxford University Press, 2000), pp. 219–36.
37. See the essays by Nick Groom, pp. 74–89, Paul Baines, pp. 166–80 and Richard Terry, pp. 181–200 in this volume.
38. '"In pleasing memory of all he stole": Plagiarism and Literary Detraction, 1747–1785', pp. 181–200, this volume.
39. *Relation d'un Voyage en Angleterre* (Paris, 1664), p. 169. The tract was translated into English and printed together with Bishop Sprat's refutation of it in 1709. See Samuel Sorbière, *A Voyage to England, Containing many Things relating to the State of Learning, Religion, and other Curiosities of that Kingdom. As also Observations on the same Voyage, by Dr. Thomas Sprat, Fellow of the Royal Society, and now Lord Bishop of Rochester* (London, 1709).
40. See Michael Dobson, *The Making of the National Poet: Shakespeare, Adaptation and Authorship, 1660–1769* (Oxford: Clarendon Press, 1992); Gary Taylor, *Reinventing Shakespeare: A Cultural History from the Restoration to the Present* (New York: Weidenfeld and Nicolson, 1989); Margreta de Grazia, *Shakespeare Verbatim: The Reproduction of Authenticity and the 1790 Apparatus* (Oxford: Clarendon Press, 1991); Jonathan Bate, *Shakespearean Constitutions: Politics, Theatre, Criticism, 1730–1830* (Oxford: Clarendon Press, 1989); Robert D. Hume, 'Before the Bard: "Shakespeare" in Early Eighteenth-Century London', *ELH*, 64 (1997), pp. 41–75.
41. Kewes, '"A Play, which I presume to call *original*": Appropriation, Creative Genius, and Eighteenth-Century Playwriting', pp. 32 ff.
42. 'Plagiarism and Imitation in Renaissance Historiography', pp. 106–18, this volume.
43. J. G. A. Pocock, 'Texts as Events: Reflections on the History of Political Thought', in *Politics of Discourse: The Literature and History of Seventeenth-Century England*, ed. Kevin Sharpe and Steven N. Zwicker (Berkeley and Los Angeles: University of California Press, 1987), pp. 21–34.
44. '"In pleasing memory of all he stole": Plagiarism and Literary Detraction, 1747–1785', p. 183.
45. I am grateful to Rob Hume, Bill Sherman, William St Clair and Blair Worden for their trenchant comments on a draft of this essay.

Chapter 2

*© The British Academy 1998. Reproduced by permission from *Proceedings of the British Academy*, 97 (1998).
1. I am grateful to the friends who commented on a draft: Kenneth Haynes, Marcia Karp, Michael Prince, Lisa Rodensky and Christopher Wilkins.
2. To the Editor of the *Saturday Evening Post*, 3 November 1827; *New Essays by De Quincey*, ed. Stuart M. Tave (1966), p. 181.

3. Hillel Schwartz, *The Culture of the Copy* (1996), p. 311.
4. 'Plagiary', *The American Scholar* (Summer 1982), p. 327.
5. Marcel C. Lafollette, *Stealing into Print: Fraud, Plagiarism, and Misconduct in Scientific Publishing* (1992), p. 49.
6. H. M. Paull, *Literary Ethics* (1928), p. 126.
7. *New Yorker*, 20 January 1997, pp. 93–7.
8. Laura J. Rosenthal, *Playwrights and Plagiarists in Early Modern England: Gender, Authorship, Literary Property* (1996), p. 10.
9. Rosenthal, *Playwrights and Plagiarists in Early Modern England*, p. 13.
10. Ibid.
11. Paul Goldstein, *Copyright's Highway* (1994), p. 12.
12. Kincaid, *New Yorker*, 20 January 1997, p. 97.
13. Alexander Lindey, *Plagiarism and Originality* (1952), p. xiii.
14. Lindey, *Plagiarism and Originality*, p. 2.
15. *The Eighteenth-Century Hymn in England* (1993), p. 18.
16. Françoise Meltzer, *Hot Property: The Stakes and Claims of Literary Originality* (1994), p. 73.
17. Meltzer, *Hot Property*, p. 74. Meltzer goes on: 'Moreover, Goll's poem was published in New York in 1942, at a time (as Felstiner points out) when Celan was in a Rumanian labor camp and "hardly likely to have seen it".'
18. Martha Woodmansee and Peter Jaszi, eds., *The Construction of Authorship* (1994).
19. Epigrams i. 66; this translation by William Cartwright was published 1651.
20. Thomas Mallon, *Stolen Words* (1989), pp. 32–3.
21. Paull, *Literary Ethics*, p. 110.
22. Ibid., p. 332.
23. Harold Ogden White, in *Plagiarism and Imitation During the English Renaissance: A Study in Critical Distinctions* (1935), p. 202.
24. See also Schwartz, *The Culture of the Copy*, p. 311.
25. White, *Plagiarism and Imitation During the English Renaissance*, pp. 15–16.
26. Ibid., pp. 168–9.
27. Ibid., p. 128.
28. Mallon, *Stolen Words*, p. xii.
29. Ibid., p. 4.
30. Susan Stewart, *Crimes of Writing* (1991), p. 24.
31. Ibid., p. 30, quoting Constable.
32. Brean Hammond, *Professional Imaginative Writing in England, 1670–1740* (1997), p. 83.
33. Ibid., p. 21, my italics. This 'ur-conception' is later joined by 'prehistory', convenient to the historian, and by 'gestation': 'there is a prehistory to the conception of originality, at least in English culture, that suggests a longer gestation period than either [Martha] Woodmansee or [Mark] Rose allow' (p. 43).
34. Stephen Orgel, 'The Renaissance Artist as Plagiarist', *ELH: A Journal of English Literary History*, 48 (1981), 479.
35. Ibid., p. 482.
36. Ibid., pp. 482–3.
37. Ibid., p. 484.

38. Ibid., p. 483.
39. Ibid., p. 479.
40. Ibid., p. 480.
41. *Yorkshire Post; The Bed Post*, ed. Kenneth Young (1962), pp. 43–4.
42. Lindey, *Plagiarism and Originality*, p. 51.
43. *The Adventurer* No. 95, 2 October 1753.
44. Rosenthal, *Playwrights and Plagiarists in Early Modern England*, p. 3.
45. Schwartz, *The Culture of the Copy*, p. 313.
46. Ibid., p. 314. Another shady business is the use by politicians of ghost-writers; as for 'the most famous political plagiarist of our time', Senator Joseph Biden, see Thomas Mallon's acute pages (*Stolen Words*, pp. 127–30).
47. Kincaid, *New Yorker*, 20 January 1997, p. 94.
48. Young, *Conjectures on Original Composition* (1759), p. 7.
49. Kincaid, *New Yorker*, 20 January 1997, p. 97.
50. Neil Hertz, *The End of the Line* (1985), p. 144.
51. Ibid., p. 149.
52. Gerhard Joseph, 'Charles Dickens, International Copyright, and the Discretionary Silence of *Martin Chuzzlewit*', in *The Construction of Authorship*, ed. Woodmansee and Jaszi, p. 268.
53. Robert Scholes, *The Rise and Fall of English* (1998), pp. 98–9.

Chapter 3

1. Christopher Ricks, 'Plagiarism', *Proceedings of the British Academy* 97 (Oxford: Oxford University Press, 1998), pp. 149–68; Peter Shaw, 'Plagiary', *The American Scholar* (Summer, 1982), p. 327.
2. Brean S. Hammond, *Professional Imaginative Writing in England, 1670–1740: 'Hackney for Bread'* (Oxford: Clarendon Press, 1997).
3. In the Law Commission's Draft Criminal Code, '*mens rea*' is defined as: 'the state of mind expressly or impliedly required by the definition of the offence charged'.
4. *The Sunday Independent*, 9 February 1992 [The Art of Fiction series No. 36, 'Plagiarism'].
5. Roderigo (Ruy) Lopez is a real historical figure, who was accused of trying to poison Queen Elizabeth in 1593, and was hung, drawn and quartered at Tyburn in 1594. He has been suggested by some commentators as a possible model for Shylock.
6. *TLS*, 9 April 1982, p. 415.
7. Sir William Temple, *Essay upon Ancient and Modern Learning* (1690), repr. J. E. Spingarn (ed.), *Critical Essays of the Seventeenth Century*, 3 vols (Oxford: Oxford University Press, 1909), 3.55: 'There is nothing new in Astronomy to vye with the Ancients, unless it be the Copernican System; nor in Physick, unless it be Hervy's Circulation of the blood. But whether either of these be modern discoveries, or derived from old Fountains, is disputed: Nay, it is so too, whether they are true or no'.
8. Harold Ogden White, *Plagiarism and Imitation During the English Renaissance. A Study in Critical Distinctions* (Cambridge, Mass.: Harvard University Press, 1935, repr. New York: Octagon, 1965), p. 75.

9. See the entry under 'plagiarism' in *The Oxford Classical Dictionary*, ed. Simon Hornblower and Antony Spawforth (3rd edn, Oxford: Oxford University Press, 1996), p. 1188.
10. Paulina Kewes, *Authorship and Appropriation: Writing for the Stage in England, 1660–1710* (Oxford: Clarendon Press, 1998), p. 121.
11. John Dennis, *To the Spectator, on Criticism and Plagiarism* [1711], quoted from *The Critical Works of John Dennis*, ed. Edward Niles Hooker, 2 vols (Baltimore: Johns Hopkins University Press, 1943), 2.27.
12. Henry Fielding, *The History of Tom Jones*, ed. R.P.C. Mutter (Harmondsworth: Penguin Books, 1966, repr. 1980), p. 552.
13. Roy Strong, *The Spirit of Britain: A Narrative History of the Arts* (London: Hutchinson, 1999), p. 373.
14. Andrew Delbanco, 'The Decline and Fall of Literature', *New York Review of Books*, 4 November 1999, p. 10.
15. Ibid., p. 23.
16. I am grateful to Allison Coleman, Marie Hockenhull Smith and Bill Grantham for reading and commenting on early versions of this essay.

Chapter 4

1. *ELH* 48: 4(1981), 476–95.
2. See Peter Landesman, 'A 20th-Century Master Scam', *New York Times Magazine*, 18 July 1999, pp. 30 ff.
3. [Henry Killigrew], *Epigrams of Martial Englished* (London, 1695), numbered 67.
4. Peter Howell, *A Commentary on Book One of the Epigrams of Martial* (London: Athlone Press, 1980), p. 168.
5. Killigrew, *Martial*, numbered 73.
6. Thomas More, *The Latin Epigrams*, ed. Leicester Bradner and Charles Arthur Lynch (Chicago: Chicago University Press, 1953), no. 220.
7. *The Prose of Sir Thomas Browne*, ed. Norman Endicott (Garden City, NY: Anchor Books, 1967), p. 124.
8. Ibid., p. 55.

Chapter 5

1. Harold Ogden White, *Plagiarism and Imitation During the English Renaissance* (Cambridge, Mass.: Harvard University Press, 1935), pp. 120ff. See also Terry Eagleton, *Crazy John and the Bishop and Other Essays on Irish Culture* (Cork: Cork University Press, 1998), pp. 190–1. My essay is partly auto-plagiarized from 'Forgery and Plagiarism', *A Companion to Literature from Milton to Blake*, ed. David Womersley (Oxford and Cambridge, Mass: Blackwell, 2001), pp. 94–113; and *The Forger's Shadow: How Forgery Changed the Course of Literature* (London: Picador, 2002), pp. 25–31. I am grateful to Brean Hammond for his paper and suggestions, to Paulina Kewes, and to Mandana Ruane and Sally Bevan for legal advice.
2. John Dennis quoted by Roger Lonsdale, 'Gray and "Allusion": The Poet as Debtor', in *Studies in the Eighteenth Century IV: Papers Presented at the Fourth*

David Nichol Smith Memorial Seminar, ed. R. F. Brissenden and J. C. Eade (Canberra: Australian National University Press, 1979), pp. 31–55, 37; Horace, *Epistola ad Augustum*, ed. Richard Hurd (Cambridge: Thurlbourn and Woodyer, 1757), ii. p. 190.

3. Christopher Ricks, 'Plagiarism', *Proceedings of the British Academy*, xcvii (1997), *Lectures and Memoirs*, pp. 149–68, 151: pp. 21–40, 23 in this volume.

4. Ibid., pp. 152, 153, 164: pp. 24, 25, 37 in this volume.

5. Plato, *The Republic*, trans. H. D. P. Lee (Harmondsworth: Penguin Books, 1955), p. 385.

6. See Brean Hammond, *Professional Imaginative Writing in England, 1670–1740: 'Hackney for Bread'* (Oxford: Clarendon Press, 1997), *passim*.

7. Hammond, p. 43, this volume.

8. See Martha Woodmansee, *The Author, Art, and the Market: Rereading the History of Aesthetics* (New York: Columbia University Press, 1994), and Martha Woodmansee and Peter Jaszi (eds), *The Construction of Authorship: Textual Appropriation in Law and Literature* (Durham, NC: Duke University Press, 1994).

9. In the *OED*, the earliest usage is credited to Ben Jonson, 1601, but it also appears in John Hall's *Virgidemiarum* of 1598.

10. *Oxford Classical Dictionary* (Oxford: Clarendon Press, 1949), 'Plagiarism'; Anthony Grafton, *Forgers and Critics: Creativity and Duplicity in Western Scholarship* (Princeton: Princeton University Press, 1990), pp. 78–9.

11. William Hazlitt, *Lectures on Drama and Literature* (London, 1820), p. 257; Ricks, p. 164: p. 37 in this volume.

12. Robert Burchfield, 'Dictionaries New and Old', *Encounter* (Sept.–Oct. 1984), pp. 10–19.

13. See also *Rambler* 121, *Adventurer* 95, and James Boswell, *Boswell's Life of Johnson (Together with Boswell's Journal of a Tour to the Hebrides and Johnson's Diary of a Journey into North Wales)*, ed. George Birkbeck Hill, rev. L. F. Powell, 6 vols, 2nd edn (Oxford: Clarendon Press, 1934–50), i. p. 334.

14. John Bowle, *Reflections on Originality in Authors* (London, 1766), p. 64. Boswell claims in *Life* that the 'richness of Johnson's fancy' and 'the strength of his memory' made him 'less liable to the imputation of plagiarism than, perhaps, any of our writers' (i. p. 334).

15. Dionysius Longinus, *On the Sublime*, trans. William Smith (London: J. Watts, 1739), p. 37.

16. Lonsdale, 'Gray and "Allusion"', p. 38.

17. Henry Fielding, *The History of Tom Jones*, ed. R. P. Mutter (Harmondsworth: Penguin Books, 1985), pp. 551–3.

18. Hammond, p. 52 in this volume.

19. Horace, *Epistle*, ii. 106; pp. 158–9. See Linda Zionkowski, 'Aesthetics, Copyright, and "The Goods of the Mind"', *British Journal for Eighteenth-Century Studies* XV (1992), pp. 163–74.

20. 'A Letter to Mr. Mason on the Marks of Imitation' (1757): Lonsdale, 'Gray and "Allusion"', p. 43.

21. Horace, *Epistola*, pp. 23–4; Thomas Percy, *Reliques of Ancient English Poetry*, ed. Nick Groom (London: Routledge/Thoemmes Press, 1996), i. xvi.

22. Edward Young, *Conjectures on Original Composition. In a Letter to the Author of Sir Charles Grandison* (London, 1759), p. 12, see also pp. 40–1.

23. Quoted by Lonsdale, 'Gray and "Allusion"', p. 33.

24. Bernard Dupriez, *A Dictionary of Literary Devices*, trans. Albert W. Halsall (New York, etc: Harvester Wheatsheaf, 1991), p. 227.
25. See James L. Clifford, 'Johnson and Lauder', *Philological Quarterly* LIV (1975), pp. 342–56. See also the essays by Paul Baines and Richard Terry in this volume.
26. Quoted by Clifford, 'Johnson and Lauder', p. 349.
27. John Nichols (ed.), *Illustrations of the Literary History of the Eighteenth Century*, 6 vols (London: Nichols, 1817–58), ii. p. 177.
28. *Gentleman's Magazine* xvii (1747), p. 423.
29. Samuel Johnson, *Lives of the English Poets*, ed. George Birkbeck Hill, 3 vols (New York: Octagon, 1967), i. p. 124.
30. Johnson, *Lives*, i. 194; see Groom, *The Forger's Shadow*, pp. 205–8.
31. Samuel Johnson, *Works*, ed. Arthur Murphy, 12 vols (London: Nichols, etc., 1816), viii. p. 2.
32. *Gentleman's Magazine* xvii (1747), p. 24.
33. Ibid., p. 67.
34. Ibid., p. 68.
35. See Nick Groom, 'Forgery or Plagiarism? Unravelling Chatterton's Rowley', *Angelaki* 1.2 (1993), pp. 41–54.
36. Stewart Home, *Neoism, Plagiarism & Praxis* (Edinburgh and San Francisco: AK Press, 1995), pp. 49–50.
37. Hillel Schwartz, *The Culture of the Copy: Striking Likenesses, Unreasonable Facsimiles* (New York: Zone Books, 1996), p. 314.
38. Home, *Neoism, Plagiarism & Praxis*, p. 49.
39. Jacques Derrida, *Monolingualism of the Other; or, The Prosthesis of Origin*, trans. Patrick Mensah (Stanford: Stanford University Press, 1998), p. 61.
40. Nichols, *Illustrations*, iv. 429; Johnson, *Lives*, i. pp. 110–11.

Chapter 6

1. Gregory the Great, *Moralia in Job*, praefatio, *Patrologia latina*, edited by J.-P. Migne (Paris: 1844–64), vol. 75, cols. 517A–519A, quoted in A. J. Minnis, *Medieval Theory of Authorship* (2nd edn, Aldershot: Wildwood House, 1988), p. 37.
2. Minnis, *Medieval Theory of Authorship*, pp. 28–9, 79, 81, 94–8.
3. H. O. White, *Plagiarism and Imitation During the English Renaissance: A Study in Critical Distinctions* (1935, reprinted New York: Octagon Books, 1965).
4. Augustine of Hippo, *City of God*, chapter 18, part 43. See also R. Loewe, 'The Medieval History of the Latin Vulgate' in *The Cambridge History of the Bible*, ii: *The West from the Fathers to the Reformation*, edited by G. W. H. Lampe (Cambridge: Cambridge University Press, 1969), pp. 102–54 at pp. 107–8.
5. G. R. Evans, *The Language and Logic of the Bible: The Road to Reformation* (Cambridge: Cambridge University Press, 1985), p. 72.
6. *The Cloud of Unknowing and The Book of Privy Counselling*, ed. P. Hodgson, Early English Text Society, original series, no. 218 (Oxford: Oxford University Press 1944, reprinted 1981). See 'Introduction', p. lxxi, and text chapters 12 (pp. 38–9) and 17–21 (pp. 47–55).
7. *English Wycliffite Sermons*, vol. 2, ed. P. Gradon (Oxford: Oxford University Press, 1988), pp. 291–2. On the other hand, two sermons in the cycle edited

by G. Cigman have 'better party': sermon 14 at 214–15, and sermon 16 at 215–17. *Lollard Sermons*, Early English Text Society, no. 294 (Oxford: Oxford University Press, 1989), pp. 181, 201.

8. R. Loewe, 'The Medieval History of the Latin Vulgate' in *The Cambridge History of the Bible*, II: *The West from the Fathers to the Reformation*, ed. G. W. H. Lampe, pp. 148–52; Evans, *The Language and Logic of the Bible: The Road to Reformation*, pp. 71–2.

9. J. H. Bentley, *Humanists and Holy Writ: New Testament Scholarship in the Renaissance* (Princeton, NJ: Princeton University Press, 1983), pp. 92, 98, 121–2.

10. J. H. Bentley, *Humanists and Holy Writ: New Testament Scholarship in the Renaissance*, pp. 70–111, especially pp. 100–7.

11. See *Erasmus' Annotations on the New Testament: The Gospels. Facsimile of the final Latin text (1535) with all variants (1516, 1519, 1522 and 1527)*, ed. A. Reeve (London: Duckworth, 1986), p. 189. Of the six major English Bible translations up to 1611, Luke 10: 42 is translated 'best' in the two translations from the Vulgate (Wyclif and Rheims). Tyndale, the Great Bible, Geneva, and the Authorized Version, being derived from Erasmus's Greek, have 'good'.

12. C. A. L. Jarrott, 'Erasmus' *In principio erat sermo*: A Controversial Translation', *Studies in Philology*, LXI (1964), pp. 35–40; M. O'R. Boyle, *Erasmus on Language and Method in Theology* (Toronto: University of Toronto Press, 1977), pp. 5–31; R. H. Bainton, *Erasmus of Christendom* (London: Collins, 1972), p. 174.

13. There were editions in 1484, 1490, 1494 (2), 1506, 1507, 1517, 1525, and 1530. There were then editions in 1606 and 1622 (*STC2* sv. Bonaventura). Eamon Duffy's observation in *The Stripping of the Altars: Traditional Religion in England, c.1400–1580* (New Haven: Yale University Press, 1992, p. 79) that Love's work 'went a long way towards satisfying lay eagerness for knowledge of the Gospels' would seem to be ill founded.

14. Cologne fragment A ij. See *Records of the English Bible*, ed. A. W. Pollard (Oxford: Oxford University Press, 1911), pp. 111–12. In all quotations 'i' and 'j' and 'u' and 'v' have been silently amended to follow modern usage, and some minor adjustments made in punctuation.

15. C. C. Butterworth and A. G. Chester, *George Joye 1495?–1553: A Chapter in the History of the English Bible and English Reformation* (Philadelphia: University of Pennsylvania Press, 1962), pp. 20–1.

16. Ibid., pp. 48–50.

17. *STC2*, no. 2370.

18. On the responsibility of de Keyser rather than Johannes Hoochstraten for the Tyndale 'Marburg' imprints, see P. Valkema-Blouw, 'Early Protestant Publications in Antwerp, 1526–30: The Pseudonyms Adam Anonymous in Basel and Hans Luft in Marlborow', *Quaerendo*, 26/2 (1996), pp. 94–110. Hoochstraten is suggested in M. E. Kronenberg, *Verboden Boeken en Opstandige Drukkers in de Hervormingstijd* (Amsterdam: P. N. van Kampen & Zoon, 1948), pp. 93–111.

19. Butterworth and Chester, *George Joye 1495?–1553: A Chapter in the History of the English Bible and English Reformation*, pp. 55–6.

20. 1 Corinthians 14: 29–30. 1 Corinthians 2: 15 is also drawn upon in this passage: 'But he that is spretuall, discusseth all things: yet he him selfe is judged of no man'. From *The New Testament Translated by William Tyndale*

1534, ed. N. Hardy Wallis (Cambridge: Cambridge University Press for The Royal Society of Literature, 1939), pp. 349, 366.

21. *The New Testament Translated by William Tyndale 1534*, ed. N. Hardy Wallis, p. 3.
22. Ibid., p. 15.
23. Tyndale believed that the conventional position derived from the joining of 'the spiritual doctrine of Christ and the fleshly doctrine of the philosophers', *An Answer to Sir Thomas More's Dialogue*, ed. H. Walter (Cambridge: Cambridge University Press for the Parker Society, 1850), p. 181. The dispute does not concern purgatory as suggested by D. Daniell, *William Tyndale: A Biography* (New Haven: Yale University Press, 1994), pp. 324–5.
24. *The New Testament Translated by William Tyndale 1534*, ed. N. Hardy Wallis, p. 15.
25. Ibid.
26. Ibid., pp. 15–16.
27. Ibid., p. 16
28. i.e. badger's.
29. *The New Testament Translated by William Tyndale 1534*, ed. N. Hardy Wallis, p. 18.
30. Ibid., pp. 18–19.
31. Ibid., p. 17.
32. G. Joye, *An Apology made by George Joy, to satisfy, if it may be, W. Tindale (1535)*, ed. Edward Arber (The English Scholar's Library, no. 13, 1882).
33. Ibid., p. 12.
34. Ibid., p. 22.
35. Ibid., p. 28.
36. Ibid., p. 23.
37. Ibid., p. 23.
38. Ibid., p. 42.
39. Ibid., p. 43.
40. For examples see *Contemporaries of Erasmus: A Biographical Register of the Renaissance and Reformation*, ed. P. G. Bietenholz (3 vols, Toronto: University of Toronto Press, 1985, 1986, 1987).
41. M. Dowling, *Humanism in the Age of Henry VIII* (London: Croom Helm, 1986), pp. 37–57. However, it is difficult to concur with Richard Rex in 'The English Campaign against Luther in the 1520s', *Transactions of the Royal Historical Society*, 5th series, XXXIX (1989), 85–106, at p. 100, when he describes Erasmus as the 'linchpin of the English response to Luther's attack on Henry', since Erasmus' correspondence suggests this was precisely the role Erasmus was at pains to avoid.
42. T. More, *Responsio ad Lutherum*, ed. J. M. Headley, trans. S. Mandeville (*The Yale Edition of the Complete Works of St Thomas More*, v. New Haven and London: Yale University Press, 1969), part 1, pp. 98–101. See also 'Introduction', part 2, pp. 736–7.
43. More, *Responsio ad Lutherum*, part 1, p. 251.
44. T. More, *The Confutation of Tyndale's Answer*, ed. L. A. Schuster, R. C. Marius, J. P. Lusardi and R. J. Schoeck (*The Yale Edition of the Complete Works of St Thomas More*, viii. New Haven and London: Yale University Press, 1973), part 1, p. 150.

45. M. D. Hooker, 'Tyndale's 'Heretical' Translations', *Reformation*, 2 (1997), 127–42; R. C. Marius, 'Thomas More's View of the Church', in T. More, *The Confutation of Tyndale's Answer*, ed. L. A. Schuster, R. C. Marius, J. P. Lusardi, and R. J. Schoeck, part 3, pp. 1349–61. Marius notes however (p. 1351) that More does cite a note by Erasmus in his criticism of Tyndale's translation of 'senior' for 'priest'.

46. T. More, *A Dialogue Concerning Heresies*, ed. T. M. C. Lawler, G. Marc'hadour and R. C. Marius (*The Yale Edition of the Complete Works of St Thomas More*, vi. New Haven and London: Yale University Press, 1981), part 1, p. 285.

47. Q. Skinner, *The Foundations of Modern Political Thought*, ii: *The Age of Reformation* (Cambridge: Cambridge University Press, 1978), pp. 71–3.

48. James VI and I believed scripture to have been dictated by the Holy Spirit: 'The whole Scripture is dyted by Gods Spirit . . . to instruct and rule the whole Church militant to the end of the world'. Moreover, James apparently believed that the Holy Spirit had a recognizable authorial voice: 'And as to the Apocryphe bookes, I omit them, because I am no Papist . . . ; and indeed some of them are no wayes like the dytement of the Spirit of God'. King James VI and I, *Political Writings*, ed. J. P. Sommerville (Cambridge: Cambridge University Press, 1994), pp. 14–15.

49. M. Coverdale, 'Dedication and Prologue to the Bible' (1535, 1537, 1550, 1553), reprinted in *Remains of Myles Coverdale, Bishop of Exeter*, ed. G. Pearson (Cambridge: Cambridge University Press for The Parker Society, 1846), pp. 12–13. Joye was of a similar belief, and claimed to find support in St Augustine. G. Joye *An Apology made by George Joy, to satisfy, if it may be, W. Tindale (1535)*, ed. Edward Arber, p. 29.

50. J. Nielson and R. Skousen, 'How Much of the King James Bible is William Tyndale?', *Reformation*, 3 (1998), pp. 49–74.

51. Joye, *An Apology made by George Joy, to satisfy, if it may be, W. Tindale (1535)*, p. 44. On Tyndale's low historiographical profile in the English reformation see P. Collinson, 'William Tyndale and the Course of the English Reformation', *Reformation*, 1 (1996), pp. 72–97.

52. I wish to thank Paulina Kewes for her part in the genesis of this chapter and Guido Latré, Carol Percy, Gergely Juhász and members of the conference for discussion, responses and suggestions. I have discussed the theological issues at stake in 'What Happens When We Die? The Tyndale–Joye Controversy' (forthcoming).

Chapter 7

1. This chapter is concerned predominantly with formal literary historiography rather than antiquarian research or the English Chronicles.

2. *Sir Francis Bacon his Apologie, in certaine imputations concerning the late Earle of Essex* (London, 1604), pp. 34–5.

3. L. Richardson, 'Sir John Hayward and Early Stuart Historiography' (unpublished PhD thesis, two volumes, Cambridge, 1999), I, pp. 35–82; II, pp. 1–76. Individual components of Savile's volume are referred to separately below.

4. Ibid., I, pp. 63–6, 68, 79–82, 77–82, 84.

5. Hayward, *First Part*, p. 44; Tacitus, *Histories*, p. 148.
6. Hayward, *First Part*, p. 56; Tacitus, *Ende of Nero*, p. 11.
7. Richardson, 'Sir John Hayward', I, pp. 66–7.
8. Ibid., I, pp. 58–63.
9. His efficiency in dismembering and reassembling Savile's text suggests that he may have compiled a well-organized commonplace book of the kind recommended by historiographical commentators in the period, from which he could select material exactly appropriate for any historical event or individual (ibid., I, p. 50, note 72).
10. Some material not used in the *First Part* appeared in Hayward's later histories, particularly his *Second Part* of Henry IV (Richardson, 'Sir John Hayward', I, pp. 113–16, II, pp. 77–117).
11. Richardson, 'Sir John Hayward', I, pp. 88–90, 92–3; I, 90, notes 301–2, 104, note 359.
12. Ibid., I, pp. 113–28, 146–57, 170–3, 191–205; Hayward, *The Life, and Raigne of King Edward the Sixt* (London, 1630), pp. 40–3; Nicholls, *The hystory writtone by Thucidides* (London, 1550), fols 59^r-60^v.
13. R. H. Martin, 'Tacitus and his Predecessors', in T. A. Dorey, ed., *Tacitus* (London: Routledge & Kegan Paul, 1969), pp. 127–30, 133.
14. R. S. Sylvester, ed., *The Complete Works of St Thomas More* (15 vols, New Haven and London: Yale University Press, 1963–97), II, pp. lxxxii–xcviii; T. S. Freeman, 'From Catiline to Richard III: the influence of classical historians on Polydore Vergil's *Anglica historica*', M. A. Di Cesare, ed., *Reconsidering the Renaissance* (Medieval and Renaissance texts and studies, 93. Binghampton, NY, 1992), pp. 192–214.
15. Richardson, 'Sir John Hayward', I, pp. 256–62. Camden, R. N[orton], trans. *Annals, or, The Historie of the most Renowned and Victorious Princesse Elizabeth* (London, 1635), pp. 348–9; More, *The Union of the two noble and illustre famelies of Lancastre & Yorke*, ed. E. Hall (London, 1550), Edward V, fol. 24^v. Camden, *Annals*, p. 46; T. Danett, trans., *The Historie of Philip de Comines* (London, 1596), pp. 64–6.
16. E. P. Read and C. Read, eds, *Elizabeth of England. Certain Observations Concerning the Life and Reign of Queen Elizabeth by John Clapham* (translations and reprints from the original sources of history. Third series, vol. 6. Philadelphia, 1951); Richardson, 'Sir John Hayward', I, pp. 249–55.
17. Heylyn, *Augustus*, pp. 64–70, 92, 97; Tacitus, *Agricola*, pp. 257–8 (and 241), 96–7.
18. Heylyn, *Augustus*, pp. 123, 194, 220, 145–6, 148; Tacitus, *Agricola*, pp. 238, 249, 254, 265; *Annales*, p. 101.
19. For example, Heylyn, *Augustus*, pp. 25, 7, 30–1; Tacitus, *Histories*, pp. 7, 5; *Ende of Nero*, p. 16.
20. Quoted by H. O. White, *Plagiarism and Imitation During the English Renaissance. A Study in Critical Distinctions* (Harvard Studies in English, XII. Cambridge, Mass.: Harvard University Press, 1935), p. 41.
21. Ibid., pp. 71–3.
22. Ibid., pp. 20–1.
23. Ibid., pp. 26, 116–17.
24. Ibid., pp. 10, 16.
25. Ibid., pp. 76, 78.

26. Ibid., pp. 146–8. Accusing rival writers of plagiarism was a common commercial strategy (ibid., p. 112). The only other well-substantiated accusation of historiographical 'fellonie' in this period was Richard Grafton's implicit claim, in his *Manuell of the Chronicles of England* (London, 1565), that John Stow had plagiarized his *Abridgement of the Chronicles of England* (London, 1562). This was part of the ongoing conflict between Grafton and Stow caused by the direct competition of the *Abridgement* with Stow's *Summarie of English Chronicles* (London, 1565).

27. White, *Plagiarism and Imitation*, p. 56.

28. Ibid., p. 7. Sir Richard Baker also 'excused' that he 'may seeme rather to transcribe then to write' by describing the past as 'common stocke': *A Chronicle of the Kings of England* (London, 1653), sig. A2^r.

29. Clapham, *The Historie of Great Britannie* (London, 1606), p. 104.

30. Clapham's *Historie of Great Britannie* was partially (and unhistorically) Tacitean too (for example, Clapham, *Historie*, p. 184; Tacitus, Savile's 'A. B. to the Reader', sig. ¶3^r).

31. R. Williams, Hayward ed., *The Actions of the Low Countries* (London, 1618), sigs. A^{r-v}, ¶3^v-4^r.

32. Hayward, Camden and Clapham all transcribed from Tacitus (Richardson, 'Sir John Hayward', II, pp. 1–2; I, pp. 257–8; I, p. 249, note 4). Camden appropriated Polybius and Cicero, and Clapham Dio (ibid., I, 256, note 46, 249, note 3). Hayward also borrowed from Cicero, Quintilian, the younger Pliny and even Diodorus of Sicily, whom he regarded as a purveyor of 'most senselesse fictions' and 'country womens tales' (ibid., II, pp. 1–2; Williams, *Actions of the Lowe Countries*, sig. ¶4^r).

33. *An Apology for Poetry*, ed. G. Shepherd (2nd edn, Manchester: Manchester University Press, 1973), p. 105.

34. British Library Additional Manuscript 57336.

35. *The First Part of the Historie of England* (London, 1612), p. 3.

36. Richardson, 'Sir John Hayward', I, pp. 228–47.

37. White, *Plagiarism and Imitation*, p. 6.

38. Richardson, 'Sir John Hayward', I, pp. 8–34, 82–8.

39. Ibid., I, pp. 64, 66, 68.

40. Hayward, *First Part*, pp. 50, 84; Tacitus, *Agricola*, p. 264.

41. Hayward, *First Part*, p. 112, and implicitly p. 100; Tacitus, *Histories*, p. 202, *Agricola*, p. 263. See also, for example, *First Part*, pp. 99, 95; *Ende of Nero*, pp. 1–2, *Histories*, p. 235.

42. Hayward, *First Part*, p. 135; Tacitus, *Histories*, p. 265.

43. Richardson, 'Sir John Hayward', I, pp. 116–19.

44. For example, Tacitus, *Ende of Nero*, pp. 13, 11, *Agricola*, p. 265, *Histories*, p. 90; Hayward, *First Part*, pp. 130, 60, 41, 39. Tacitus, *Agricola*, p. 246, *Histories*, pp. 172–3, 20; Hayward, *First Part*, pp. 4–5, 49.

45. 'Sir John Hayward', II, pp. 32–9. Mucianus is the *Histories*' most treacherous character (pp. 101–2, 176, 117–18, 145–6, 198; 100, 6, 235 as exploited by Hayward at *First Part*, pp. 10, 130, 95). Hayward regarded Richard III as a 'tyrant and usurper' (*First Part*, p. 134) and very few contemporary readers would even have demurred.

46. I have found only two early modern readers who recorded their identification of Hayward's use of Tacitus: Bacon, and one 'Tho[mas] Carleton' who

marked two of Hayward's Tacitean transcriptions 'Savile' in his fourth edition of the *First Part* in the 1630's or thereafter: Oxford, Bodleian Library, Douce HH 222, pp. 125, 131 (Savile's 'A.B to the Reader', sig. ¶3ʳ and *Ende of Nero*, pp. 6–7).

47. This, Hayward's most stylistically accomplished Tacitean history, was also his bestseller.
48. R. R. Bolgar, *The Classical Heritage and its Beneficiaries* (Cambridge: Cambridge University Press, 1954), pp. 266, 267, 269.
49. Hayward, *Davids Teares* (London, 1623), sigs. A7ʳ-8ʳ. A judgement echoed, rather harshly, by R.S. Sylvester, who declared Hayward 'a superficial humanist, content to echo a particular author... monotonously' (*Complete Works of St Thomas More*, II, p. lxxxiii).
50. White, *Plagiarism and Imitation*, p. 10.
51. Ibid., p. 17.
52. G. W. Pigman III, 'Versions of Imitation in the Renaissance', *Renaissance Quarterly*, XXXIII (1980), pp. 5–6; White, *Plagiarism and Imitation*, p. 10.
53. White, *Plagiarism and Imitation*, pp. 12–13, 18.
54. M. F. Tenney, 'Tacitus in the Middle Ages and the early Renaissance and in England to about the year 1650' (unpublished PhD thesis, Cornell University, 1931), pp. 171–2, 246.
55. A. Momigliano, 'Pagan and Christian Historiography in the Fourth Century AD', *Essays in Ancient and Modern Historiography* (Oxford: Wesleyan University Press, 1977), pp. 119, 115–17. Thus Hayward's historiography bemused and irritated at least one ecclesiastical historian, while he considered their documentary methodology 'not regarded by most imitable writers' and 'fruitlesse & improper for a true caryed history' ('Richardson, 'Sir John Hayward', I, pp. 219–20).
56. M. W. Brownley, *Clarendon and the Rhetoric of Historical Form* (Philadelphia: University of Pennsylvania Press, 1985), p. 4.
57. Clarendon, *History of the Rebellion and Civil Wars in England* (3 vols, Oxford, 1702–4), *passim*; May, *The History of the Parliament of England* (London, 1647), *passim*, and, for example, sig. A3ʳ; II, 99. May also cited additional documentary sources for the further information of interested readers (ibid., for example, II, p. 54; III, p. 53). Peter Heylyn also adopted the new polemic methodology, including only a single, explicitly identified, quoted and italicised allusion in his (anonymous) *Short View of the Life and Reign of King Charles* (London, 1656), pp. 95–6.
58. It had always been customary, even in literary historiography, to quote and cite authorities for polemic argument. Even Hayward had done so (*First Part*, pp. 101–6). White, *Plagiarism and Imitation*, p. 13. John Selden had tried to protect his painstakingly attributed *History of Tithes* from the inevitable wrath of ecclesiastical interests by anticipating attack and explicitly denying that 'any piece of it' had been 'stolne from any other mans notes'; but Bishop Montagu still seized upon the disclaimer itself, demanding whether Selden was 'afraid to be challenged for plagiarisme'? (ibid., pp. 179–81).
59. P. B. Craddock, *Edward Gibbon: Luminous Historian* (Baltimore: Johns Hopkins University Press, 1989), p. 9. Gibbon's 8, 362 notes amounted to a quarter of his history (Roy Porter, *Edward Gibbon: Making History* [London: Phoenix, 1995], p. 72).

60. D. Womersley, *The Transformation of "The Decline and Fall of the Roman Empire"* (Cambridge Studies in Eighteenth-Century English Literature and Thought. Cambridge: Cambridge University Press, 1988), p. 84; Craddock, *Edward Gibbon*, pp. 122–30.

61. *Transformation*, pp. 85–8, 170–3.

62. For example, E. Badian, 'Gibbon and War', and F. Paschaud, 'Gibbon et les sources historiographiques pour la période de 363 à 410', P. Ducrey, ed., *Gibbon et Rome à la Lumière de l'Historiographie Moderne* (Geneva: Droz, 1977), pp. 119, 229–30.

63. P. B. Craddock, ed., *The English Essays of Edward Gibbon* (Oxford: Clarendon Press, 1972), pp. 313, 381, note 7.

64. J. M. Levine, *Humanism and History: Origins of Modern English Historiography* (Ithaca: Cornell University Press, 1987), p. 191; *The History of the Decline and Fall of the Roman Empire* (6 vols, London, 1776–88), VI, p. 433.

65. Critics have identified unacknowledged allusions to sources ranging from Plato, Tacitus and Sallust, to Machiavelli and Montesquieu, Milton and Dryden, and Addison, Reynolds and Hume. J. A. W. Bennett, *Essays on Gibbon* (Cambridge: Bennet, 1980), pp. 30–2. H. L. Bond, *The Literary Art of Edward Gibbon* (Oxford: Clarendon Press, 1960), p. 137. G. W. Bowersock, 'Gibbon on Civil War and Rebellion in the Decline of the Roman Empire', G. W. Bowersock, J. Clive and S. R. Grabaud, eds, *Edward Gibbon and the Decline and Fall of the Roman Empire* (Cambridge, Mass.: Harvard University Press, 1977), p. 31. A. H. T. Clarke, 'The Genius of Gibbon II: Gibbon the Historian', *The Nineteenth Century and After*, XIX–XX (1910), 682–3. Craddock, *Edward Gibbon*, p. 9. D. P. Jordan, *Gibbon and his Roman Empire* (Chicago: University of Illinois Press, 1971), pp. 174, 178–9, 181. J. G. A. Pocock, 'Between Machiavelli and Hume: Gibbon as Civic Humanist and Philosophical Historian', in Bowersock, Clive and Grabaud, eds, *Edward Gibbon*, pp. 107–9. Womersley, *Transformation*, pp. 44, 53–4, 209–10; 'Gibbon's "Memoirs": Autobiography in Time of Revolution', *Edward Gibbon: Bicentenary Essays* (Oxford: Voltaire Foundation, 1997), pp. 383–4; ed., *The History of the Decline and Fall of the Roman Empire* (3 vols, Harmondsworth: Penguin Books, 1994), I, p. lxx. Even Gibbon's most enthusiastic admirer described these 'plagiarisms' as 'incessant': literary sources were 'openly plundered...to varnish the circumstances of Gibbon's narrative' (Clarke, 'The Genius of Gibbon II', pp. 681–2).

66. Craddock, ed., *English Essays*, p. 277; Jordan, *Gibbon*, pp. 124–5, 140. Hayward, Clapham and Bacon also all described themselves as arrangers and polishers of raw materials gathered by other historians (Richardson, 'Sir John Hayward', p. 180, note 5; Clapham, *Certain Observations*, p. 12; D. R. Woolf, 'John Selden, John Borough, and Francis Bacon's *History of Henry VII*, 1621', *Huntington Library Quarterly*, 47 [1984], 47–53).

67. Craddock, *Edward Gibbon*, pp. 124, 9.

68. After five printed editions and additional scribal publication on request 1599–1638/9, the work appeared only in increasingly polemic contexts (Richardson, 'Sir John Hayward', I, p. 19; II, pp. 243–60, and Oxford, All Souls College, Manuscript 131). See also, for example, ibid., I, pp. 215, 219–20, 183, note 19; I, p. 6, note 18).

Chapter 8

1. On Renaissance doctrines of imitation, see in particular G. W. Pigman III's 'Versions of Imitation in the Renaissance', *Renaissance Quarterly* 33 (1980), pp. 1–32; Thomas M. Greene, *The Light in Troy: Imitation and Discovery in Renaissance Poetry* (New Haven and London: Yale University Press, 1982); Stephen Orgel, 'The Renaissance Artist as Plagiarist', *ELH* 48 (1981), pp. 476–95; David Quint, *Origin and Originality in Renaissance Literature: Versions of the Source* (New Haven and London: Yale University Press, 1983); and Harold O. White, *Plagiarism and Imitation During the English Renaissance* (Cambridge, Mass.: Harvard University Press, 1935).

2. *Discoveries*, 2466ff. On the borrowings, see *Ben Jonson*, ed. C. H. Herford and P. and E. Simpson, 11 vols: (Oxford: Clarendon Press, 1925–52), xi. p. 282. All quotations from this edition: i/j and u/v spellings and upper case/lower case regularized.

3. Horace, *Epistles*, I. xix. 21–2; see Horace, *Satires and Epistles*, trans. and intro. Niall Rudd (Harmondsworth: Penguin Books, 1973). The trope is also found in Lucretius, 1. 926, Virgil, *Georgics*, 3.8f., Propertius, 3. 1. 18, 3. 3. 26, Manilius, 2. 50, 2. 138, Callimachus, *Aetia*, fr. 1. 25ff; cf. Callimachus, *Epigram* 28. 1f., *Epigram* 7. I owe these references to Dr Philip Hardie.

4. Robert Burton, *The Anatomy of Melancholy*, ed. Nicolas K. Kiessling, Thomas C. Faulkner and Rhonda L. Blair (Oxford: Clarendon Press, 1989), i. pp. 8–9.

5. *Sir Thomas Browne's Pseudodoxia Epidemica*, ed. Robin Robbins, 2 vols (Oxford: Clarendon Press, 1981), i. pp. 34–5.

6. Cf. Martial, I.liii.11–12: 'indice non opus est nostris nec iudice libris; / stat contra dicitque tibi tua pagina "Fur est"': 'My books need no title or judge to prove them; your page stares you in the face, and calls you "thief".' Martial, *Epigrams*, trans. Walter C. A. Ker, Loeb Classical Library, 2 vols (Cambridge, Mass. and London: William Heinemann, 1968).

7. 'Hoc faciat animus noster: omnia, quibus est adiutus, abscondat, ipsum tantum ostendat, quod effecit': *Epist.* 84.7, Seneca, *Ad Lucilium Epistulae Morales*, trans. Richard M. Gummere, Loeb Classical Library, 3 vols (Cambridge, Mass. and London: William Heinemann, 1917–25).

8. Macrobius, *Saturnalia*, 1. Praefatio, 7.

9. Pigman, 'Imitation in the Renaissance', pp. 4–10.

10. Christopher Ricks, 'Plagiarism', Inaugural British Academy Lecture, 97 (Oxford: Oxford Univeristy Press, 1998), pp. 149–68, this volume, pp. 21–40.

11. See, for example, Mark Rose, *Authors and Owners: The Invention of Copyright* (Cambridge, Mass. and London: Harvard University Press, 1993); Joseph Loewenstein, 'The Script in the Marketplace', in Stephen Greenblatt, ed., *Representing the English Renaissance* (Berkeley: University of California Press, 1988), pp. 265–78.

12. Ben Jonson, *Poetaster: Or, The Arraignment*, ed. Tom Cain, The Revels Plays (Manchester: Manchester University Press, 1995), Introduction p. 19 and n. 41; Ian Donaldson, *Jonson's Magic Houses* (Oxford: Clarendon Press, 1997), pp. 206–7.

13. *Poetaster*, ed. Cain, note to I. i. 43–84.

14. *Hero and Leander*, i. 199–202, in *The Works of Christopher Marlowe*, ed. C. F. Tucker Brooke (Oxford: Clarendon Press, 1910). Jonson introduces some textual variants.

15. John Florio, *Queen Anna's New World of Words* (London: Melch. Bradwood for Edward Blount and William Barnet, 1611), 'Parodia'.
16. Donaldson, *Jonson's Magic Houses*, pp. 203–4.
17. The *OED*'s first example of 'playwright' is from 1687. If Jonson did not invent the word, it was certainly new at the time he wrote this poem. Cf. 'Cygnus' (Hugh Holland?) speaking of 'common playwrights' in his commendatory verses on *Sejanus*, 1605 (Herford & Simpson, xi. 314), and Henry Fitzjeffrey on Webster as a 'playwright-cartwright', in *Notes from Blackfriars*, 1617.
18. Many of Jonson's early co-authored plays are no longer extant: e.g. *Hot Anger Soon Cold* (1598, with Henry Porter and Henry Chettle), *Page of Plymouth* (1599, with Thomas Dekker), *Robert II the King of Scots' Tragedy* (1599, with Dekker and Chettle).
19. In *The Second Part of the Return From Parnassus* Jonson himself was characterized as 'a mere empiric, one that gets what he hath by observation, and makes only nature privy to what he indites': *Three Parnassus Plays*, ed. J. B. Leishman (London: Ivor Nicholson & Watson, 1949), p. 244. In *Poetaster* (IV.iii.104–7) Jonson ironically allows Demetrius (Dekker) to make the same criticism of Horace (Jonson): 'Alas, sir, Horace! He is a meere spunge; nothing but humours, and observation; he goes up and downe sucking from every societie, and when hee comes home, squeazes himself drie againe'. Jonson was more often praised by his contemporaries, however, as an original artist: see for example Nathan Field's verses on *Volpone*, quoted by Herford and Simpson, xi. 323.
20. See Peter Stallybrass, 'Worn Worlds: Clothes and Identity on the Renaissance Stage', in *Subject and Object in Renaissance Culture*, ed. Margreta de Grazia, Maureen Quilligan and Peter Stallybrass (Cambridge: Cambridge University Press, 1996), pp. 289–320; Ann Rosalind Jones and Peter Stallybrass, *Renaissance Clothing and the Materials of Memory* (Cambridge: Cambridge University Press, 2001).
21. *The Critic*, 3. 1. 25, 29–32, in *The Dramatic Works of Richard Brinsley Sheridan*, ed. Cecil Price, 2 vols (Oxford: Clarendon Press, 1973), vol. I, p. 541.
22. 'An Essay of Dramatic Poesy', in *John Dryden, Of Dramatic Poesy and Other Essays*, ed. George Watson, 2 vols (London: J. M. Dent & Sons; New York: E. P. Dutton, 1962), I, pp. 31, 69. This had long been a defence of Jonson's style of imitation: cf. the tributes of Jasper Mayne and William Cartwright, Herford and Simpson, xi. 454 and 458. Peter Whalley was to return a similar verdict in his assessment of Jonson's 'character as a writer' in 1756: 'What he borroweth from the antients, he generally improves by the use and application, and by this means he improved himself, in contending to think, and to express his thoughts like them; and accordingly those plays are the best, in which we find most imitations or translations from classical authors; but he commonly borrows with the air of a conqueror, and adorns himself in their dress, as with the spoils and trophies of victory': *The Dramatic Works of Ben Jonson and Beaumont and Fletcher*, 4 vols (London: John Stockdale, 1811), vol. I, Preface, pp. x–xi.
23. *The Complete Works of Thomas Shadwell*, ed. Montague Summers, 5 vols (New York: Benjamin Blom, 1927/1968), V. 254; *Mac Flecknoe*, 183–6, in *The Poems of John Dryden*, ed. Paul Hammond, 4 vols (London: Longman, 1995–), vol. I;

Edward Pechter, *Dryden's Classical Theory of Literature* (Cambridge: Cambridge University Press, 1975), p. 93.

24. Dryden, *Preface to An Evening's Love* (1671), in *Of Dramatic Poesy*, ed. Watson, I. 154.

25. Gerard Langbaine, *Momus Triumphans: or, the Plagiaries of the English Stage* (London: Printed for N. C., sold by S. Holford, 1688 [1687]), sig. a2ᵛ (italic and roman reversed); Paulina Kewes, *Authorship and Appropriation: Writing for the Stage in England, 1660–1710* (Oxford: Clarendon Press, 1998); James M. Osborn, *John Dryden: Some Biographical Facts and Problems* (New York: Columbia University Press, 1940), pp. 218–24.

26. Edward Young, *Conjectures on Original Composition*, ed. Edith J. Morley (Manchester: Manchester University Press, 1918), p. 36.

27. T. W. Baldwin, *Shakespere's Small Latine and Lesse Greeke*, 2 vols (Urbana, Ill.: University of Illinois Press, 1944); Emrys Jones, *The Origins of Shakespeare* (Oxford: Clarendon Press, 1977).

28. *Reflections on Originality in Authors*, published anonymously (London: R. Horsfield, 1766), p. 64.

29. Richard Cumberland, *The Observer*, vol. IX, no. CIX (1788), p. 136.

30. *The Dramatic Works of Richard Brinsley Sheridan*, ed. Price, II. 468–71.

31. [Richard Hurd], *Q. Horatii Flacci, Ars Poetica*, 2 vols. (London: W. Thurlbourne, 1753), I. 84. Hurd is weighing Jonson's practice against Horace's precepts in *Ars Poetica*, p. 131. Hurd's 'Discourse on Poetical Imitation', contained in the second volume of this edition, considers more closely the nature and status of literary plagiarism.

32. William Hazlitt, 'On Shakespeare and Ben Jonson', *Lectures on the English Comic Writers* (1819), in *The Complete Works of William Hazlitt*, ed. P. P. Howe, after the edition of A. R. Waller and Arnold Glover (London and Toronto: J. M. Dent & Sons, 1931), vol. VI, p. 38.

33. *Diary, Reminiscences, and Correspondence of Henry Crabb Robinson*, ed. Thomas Sadler, 3 vols (London: Macmillan, 1869), III. pp. 167, 107; Malcolm Elwin, *Landor: A Replevin* (London: MacDonald, 1958), pp. 69–70.

34. Langbaine, *Momus Triumphans*, sig. A4ᵛ.

35. See E. B. Partridge, 'The Symbolism of Clothes in Jonson's Last Plays', *Journal of English and Germanic Philology*, 56 (1957), pp. 396–409.

36. 'Of the Institution and Education of Children; To the Ladie Diana of Foix, Countesse of Gurson', *Montaigne's Essays*, trans. John Florio, 3 vols (London: J. M. Dent & Sons, 1965), p. 183 (The First Booke, chap. xxv).

37. Donaldson, 'Jonson's Duplicity', ch. 2 in *Jonson's Magic Houses*.

Chapter 9

1. Complaint of the sage Kacheperreseneb. Plaque, British Museum 5645 recto, perhaps eighteenth dynasty, *ca.* 1500 BC, lines 2–7. The composition may go back as far as 1900 BC. Transcribed in Alan Gardiner, *The Admonitions of an Egyptian Sage* (Leipzig: Hinrichs, 1909), pp. 96–8. Gardiner provides a literal version; my translation has partly been inspired by that of Erik Hornung cited in Jan Assmann, *Das kulturelle Gedächtnis* (München: Beck, 1992), p. 97. For a history of the Latin '*plagiarius*' since the Roman Empire, see Christopher

Ricks, 'Plagiarism', *Proceedings of the British Academy*, 97 (Oxford: Oxford University Press, 1998), pp. 149–68; reprinted this volume, pp. 21–40. *'Plagiarius'* means 'kidnapper', *'plagiaria'* prostitute.

2. Laura J. Rosenthal, *Playwrights and Plagiarists in Early Modern England: Gender, Authorship, Literary Property* (Ithaca and London: Cornell University Press, 1996), p. 10.

3. Michel Foucault, *L'Ordre du discours* (Paris: Gallimard, 1971), p. 28.

4. Plagiarism, the appropriation of another's text as one's own without due acknowledgement, is commonly perceived as gaining momentum in literary discourse from the late seventeenth century onwards; it becomes increasingly important at the expense of the Renaissance concept of imitation. Earlier references to literary theft do not resonate with the same urgency. The problem was discussed at the conference 'Plagiarism in History and Theory', Institute of English Studies, University of London, 5 and 6 November 1999.

5. Michel Foucault, 'What is an Author?', in *Language, Counter-Memory, Practice. Selected Essays and Interviews*, ed. Donald F. Bouchard (Oxford: Blackwell, 1977), pp. 113–38, at p. 125.

6. Paulina Kewes, *Authorship and Appropriation: Writing for the Stage in England, 1660–1710* (Oxford: Clarendon Press, 1998), ch. 3. Kewes addresses a general development: 'the idea of proprietary authorship has its genesis not in the eighteenth century but in the later seventeenth.... The concept of the author as 'owner' of his or her text was constructed in the critical literature and in the commercial practice of the half-century between the Restoration of Charles II in 1660 and the Copyright Statute of 1710' (p. 2). As the present case study shows, the concept existed prior to 1660.

7. The usual date given is 1601, according to *The Oxford English Dictionary*, prepared by J. A. Simpson and E. S. C. Weiner, 2nd edn, 20 vols (Oxford: Clarendon Press, 1989): 'Why? the ditt' is all borrowed; 'tis Horace: hang him plagiary' (Jonson's *Poetaster* (1601), IV.iii). Joseph Hall, however, includes the word in *Virgidemiarum. First Three Bookes* (London, 1598), lib.IV, satire 2, ll. 80–82: 'As a Catch-pols fist vnto a Bankrupts sleeue; / Or an, Hos ego, from old Petrarchs spright / Vnto a Plagiarie sonnet-wright.'

8. The *OED* does not record the first mention of the Latin *plagiarius*. This source is a random example and others before this time might be found. John Caius, *The Annals of Gonville and Caius College*, ed. John Venn (Cambridge: Cambridge Antiquarian Society, 1904), p. 214, on the dramatic efforts of Thomas Legge, entry July 1607: 'altera de excidio Hierosolymitano, quamdiu vixit, horis subsicivis sub lima polivit, quo elimatiorem eam tandem proponeret spectandam; cumque jam omnibus numeris absoluta esset, plagiarii nescio cujus piceatis manibus spes nostra misere frustrata erat.' Here, it seems, *'plagiarius'* is used in the sense of 'kidnapper', somebody stealing an author's intellectual offspring.

9. See note 11.

10. Foucault writes, 'dans toute société la production du discours est à la fois contrôlée, sélectionnée, organisée et redistribuée par un certain nombre de procédures qui ont pour rôle d'en conjurer les pouvoirs et les dangers, ... d'en esquiver la lourde, la redoutable matérialité'; *L'Ordre du discours*, pp. 10–11.

11. There are, of course, countless studies of material culture and printing history; yet the approaches of D. F. McKenzie, Peter Stallybrass, Margreta de

Grazia or Malcom Smuts have not had an impact on discussions of seventeenth-century plagiarism *per se*. The products of the printing press, however, deserve attention beyond the standard acknowledgement that printing revolutionized the literary market and rendered plagiarism and piracy a profitable option. Rosenthal's œuvre on appropriation employs vocabulary such as 'property', 'ownership', 'market economy', 'consumer's position' and 'cultural capital' but completely ignores the materiality of the texts she discusses. Christopher Ricks is interested in the ethical aspect of plagiarism, not its medium. The conference on plagiarism was concerned with the blurring of boundaries between imitation, plagiarism and originality but did not address the presentation of texts at all. Kewes only begins to touch on such questions when she discusses, for instance, how late seventeenth-century compilers of anthologies reflected on the medium of printing (on John Cotgrave, p. 110). In his meticulous study of piracy, John Feather concentrates on the legal and institutional history of publishing before 1710, not the design of books; see his *Publishing, Piracy and Politics: An Historical Study of Copyright in Britain* (London: Mansell, 1994).

12. For a detailed account of this affair see B. de Montagut, *Louange de la danse*, ed. B. Ravelhofer (Cambridge: RTM Publications, 2000). The present article draws upon the section 'Plagiarism and Imitation' and seeks to address some of the questions left open in the argument.

13. François de Lauze, *Apologie de la danse* (1623).

14. *Louange*, pp. 2–3.

15. Presumably Montagut at least spoke it fairly well since he spent some twenty years of his life in England.

16. Montagut instructed Charles I in 1631, for which he was paid £160. PRO London, E 403/2191, p. 42.

17. *Louange*, p. 3.

18. *Ballet de la prospérité des armes de la France* (1641). Fourth entreé of the first 'acte'. I am most grateful to Rose Pruiksma for forwarding the information on the 1639 and 1641 court ballets as well as the text passages to me.

19. '... ie communiquay au sieur Montagut le dessain que i'auois de faire quelque chose sur la danse, & luy laissant vne coppie de ce que i'en auois desia trassé, le priay de la considerer & me conseiller en amy s'il seroit à propos que ie passasse outre: Il ne l'eut pas si tost veuë que loüant infiniment ma premiere resolution il me tentoit par mille flateuses paroles a la poursuitte de cest œuure, dont il protestoit souhaitter l'accomplissement auec impatience, & qui seroit indubitablement (disoit-il) bien veu de tout le monde, me faisant deslors sentir que ses persuasions ne tendoient qu'à son aduantage, & que sa vanité se promettoit cela de ma franchise que ie luy cederois aisement tout l'honneur qui se pourroit tirer de mes peines. ... Quelques mois apres luy disant que i'y auois mis la derniere main, & mesme luy faisant voir vn discours que i'y auois adiousté en faueur de mon subiect, il n'oublia pas vn de ses artifices pour tirer de moy & faire imprimer en son nom ce que ie n'auois pas assez d'asseurance de donner au public; Mais ses prieres, ses promesses & toutes ses importunitez demeurans nulles, il recherca d'autres moyens que ie tais, & desquels ceux qui les sçavent ne peuuent parler qu'à sa confusion. En fin la longueur du temps non plus que la raison n'ayant peu matter ceste ambition qu'il auoit de triompher du merite d'vn autre, il fist dernierement transcrire sans aucune

alteration, la coppie qu'il tenoit de moy & la feit grossir d'vn certain discours qu'il intitule *Loüange de la Danse...*', *Apologie*, Advertissement, pp. 1–2.

20. '... il a presenté comme sienne ceste rare piece de rapport, à Monseigneur le Marquis de Buckingham, donnant par là subject à toute la Cour, (qui cognoist la fourbe) de s'entretenir pour vn temps sur ceste gentille inuention de gloire...', *Apologie*, Advertissement, p. 2.

21. *Apologie*, p. 3.

22. Agrippa's book was first printed in 1530 and widely available in several translations. See Catherine M. Dunn's edition of the same (Northridge, California: California State University Press, 1974) and *Louange*, pp. 48–9.

23. *Louange*, pp. 89, 109.

24. *Apologie*, preface, pp. 9–10.

25. Thoinot Arbeau [Jehan Tabourot], *Orchesography* [*Orchésographie*], intro. Julia Sutton, trans. Mary Stewart Evans (Langres: des Preyz, 1588/89; New York: Dover, 1967), p. 18.

26. Jehan des Preyz to Guillaume Tabourot, *Orchésographie*, p. 10.

27. *Apologie*, preface, sig. π3ʳ. 'IL est temps de briser les liens de l'attente / Ne crains plus d'approcher ceste grandeur puissante, / Ton Liure est le Parnasse ou tu fais la leçon / aux Nymphes curieuses d'imiter ton bel ordre / Aduoue toutesfois qu'auec ton instruction, / Leurs mouuemens diuins s'en yroient en desordre / Cy ce Grand Bᴠᴄᴋɪɴɢʜᴀᴍ N'estoit leur Apolon'. 'Liens de l'attente' literally means 'ties of waiting'. For a more adventurous reading of the poem, see Martha Schwieters, 'Deciphering de Lauze', *Proceedings of the Twenty-Second Annual Conference of the Society of Dance History Scholars, University of New Mexico, Albuquerque, 10–13 June 1999* (Stoughton, Wisconsin: Society of Dance History Scholars, 1999), pp. 69–78.

28. *Louange*, p. 61; and F. Lesure, G. Thibault, *Bibliographie des éditions d'Adrian le Roy et Robert Ballard (1551–1598)* (Paris: Société Française de Musicologie, 1955). I am indebted to Laurent Guillo for a comprehensive history of Ballard's Parnassus title-pages. Accordingly, the specific frontispiece close to *Apologie* was used from as early as 1565 until the end of the seventeenth century. Its artist is unknown, it was only used by the Ballard workshop, and only as a woodcut (private communication).

29. *Louange*, pp. 59–62, summarizes literature on Ballard.

30. 'I belong to Ben Jonson.' It has been erased by the subsequent owner. The few annotations in this book are all written in French, a habit Jonson was not known for.

31. Seneca, *Ad Lucilium epistulae morales*, ed. Richard Gummere, Loeb Classical Library, 3 vols (London: William Heinemann, 1917–25), I, pp. 7–9, no. 2. I am grateful to Ian Donaldson for this reference.

32. Laurent Guillo drew my attention to the title-page of Sieur Despinelle, *Les muses ralliées* (Lyons: Thibaud Ancelin, 1606). He also refers to Jean le Royer and Pierre de Saint-André, who apparently cribbed ornate initials used by Ballard in the 1570s. See *Les éditions musicales de la renaissance lyonnaise* (Paris: Klingsieck, 1991), p. 100; *Louange*, p. 60.

33. *The Collected Works of William Byrd*, gen. ed. Philip Brett, 17 vols (London: Stainer & Bell, 1977–91), I, p. xv; and Joseph Kerman, 'An Elizabethan Edition of Lassus', *Acta Musicologica*, 27 (1955), pp. 71–6. I am deeply grateful to Thomas Elias for providing these references. For a facsimile of the Ballard

title-page, see Orlando di Lasso, *Kompositionen mit französischem Text I: die vierstimmigen Chansons aus 'Les meslanges d'Orlande de Lassus', Paris 1576*, ed. Horst Leuchtmann, *Sämtliche Werke*, new series, vol. 12 (Wiesbaden: Breitkopf & Härtel, 1982), p. xliii.

34. All information on the dubious frontispiece in Swift's *Works*, volume II, from Margaret Weedon, ' "'Quivis speret idem" – a Frontispiece by N.-N. Coypel Plagiarized', *Swift Studies*, 12 (1997), pp. 103–7.

35. On closer inspection flaws in the setting and choice of initials may be noticed – this, together with the modified frontispiece, is the reason why the book cannot have been produced by Ballard. See *Louange*, pp. 66–7.

36. Stephen Orgel, 'The Renaissance Artist as Plagiarist', *English Literary History*, 48 (1981), 476–95, especially pp. 479, 483–5. Orgel has in the meantime conceded to Ricks the point that plagiarism has been an ethical issue since classical times; yet the question remains why we find so few seventeenth-century authors accusing plagiarists with specific charges in public.

37. Sir Thomas Browne, *Pseudodoxia Epidemica*, ed. Robin Robbins, 2 vols (Oxford: Clarendon Press, 1981), I, book I, ch. VI, p. 35; II, p. 670, commentary on p. 35. See Ian Donaldson's essay ' "The Fripperie of Wit": Jonson and Plagiarism' in the present collection, pp. 119–33. I am grateful to Ian Donaldson for forwarding the references to Browne and his plagiarist Philipot. See also *Louange*, pp. 45–6.

38. Stephen Orgel's discussion of the problem, for instance, is among the few looking at painting; see also Richard Steadman-Jones's essay in this collection, pp. 201–14.

Chapter 10

1. Christopher Ricks, 'Plagiarism', *Proceedings of the British Academy*, 97 (Oxford: Oxford University Press, 1998), pp. 149–68; reprinted this volume pp. 21–40.
2. René Descartes, 'Discourse on Method', in *The Essential Descartes*, ed. Margaret D. Wilson (New York: New American Library, 1969), pp. 113–14.
3. *Authorship and Appropriation: Writing for the Stage in England, 1660–1710* (Oxford: Clarendon Press, 1998).
4. (London: Longman, 1969).
5. George Villiers, 2nd Duke of Buckingham *et al.*, *The Rehearsal*, ed. D. E. L. Crane (Durham: University of Durham, 1976), p. 6.
6. J. M. Synge, *Collected Works*, gen. ed. Robin Skelton (Oxford: Oxford University Press, 1962–8), iv. p. 53.
7. This distinction is more widely discussed in my *Scribal Publication in Seventeenth-Century England* (Oxford: Oxford University Press, 1993; repr. as *The Culture and Commerce of Texts: Scribal Publication in Seventeenth-Century England* (Amherst: University of Massachusetts Press, 1998).
8. *Manuscript, Print and the English Renaissance Lyric* (Ithaca: Cornell University Press, 1995), pp. 135–208.
9. Walter J. Ong, *Orality and Literacy* (London: Methuen, 1982), pp. 115–16.
10. Discussed in my 'How Personal is a Personal Miscellany? Sarah Cowper, Martin Clifford and the Buckingham Commonplace Book', in *Order and Connexion: Studies in Bibliography and Book History*, ed. R. C. Alston (Cambridge: D. S. Brewer, 1997), pp. 111–26.

11. Samuel Butler, *Prose Observations*, ed. A. de Quehen (Oxford: Oxford University Press, 1979), pp. xvii–xviii.

12. For a reasonable working definition of 'Puritan', see J. A. Sharpe, *Early Modern England: A Social History*, 2nd edn (London: Arnold, 1997), p. 240. To professed separatists Sharpe would add those conformists who wished to retain the spirit of the 1559 church settlement.

13. *English Constitutional Conflicts of the Seventeenth Century 1603–1689* (Cambridge: Cambridge University Press, 1957), p. 14.

14. (Cambridge: Cambridge University Press, 1998). An extreme case was the funeral of Charles I, which was conducted in silence because the use of the liturgy had been forbidden. See on this Lois Potter, *Secret Rites and Secret Writing: Royalist Literature 1641–1660* (Cambridge: Cambridge University Press, 1989), pp. 168–9.

15. Quoted in David Underdown, *Revel, Riot and Rebellion: Popular Culture in England 1603–1660* (Oxford: Oxford University Press, 1985), p. 90.

16. Cited in Laura Gowing, *Domestic Dangers: Women, Words and Sex in Early Modern London* (Oxford, 1996), pp. 55–6 from a consistory court case of 1613. The division into sentences is my own.

17. *Constitutions and Canons Ecclesiasticall* (London, 1640), sig. E1^r.

18. Alastair Bellany, 'A Poem on the Archbishop's Hearse: Puritanism, Libel and Sedition after the Hampton Court Conference', *Journal of British Studies*, 34 (1995), p. 138.

19. Richard Grey, *A System of English Ecclesiastical Law* (London, 1743), p. 116.

20. *A Seasonable Defence of Preaching* (London, 1678), p. 62.

21. William Chappell, *The Preacher, or the Art and Method of Preaching* (London, 1656), pp. 10–11.

22. Richard Hooker, *Of the Laws of Ecclesiastical Polity. Book V*, ed. W. Speed Hill (Cambridge, Mass.: Harvard University Press, 1977), p. 84. For Robert South's even stronger views, see N. H. Keeble, *The Literary Culture of Nonconformity in Later Seventeenth-Century England* (Leicester: Leicester University Press, 1987), pp. 243–4. The Hookerian caution was restated in the last century by Canon F. A. Simpson, for whom it was 'better to hear a good sermon twice than a bad sermon once'. Following the logic of this principle, he increasingly restricted himself to a single 'remarkable' sermon, on the Good Samaritan. (*A Last Eccentric*, ed. Eric James [London: Christian Action, 1991], p. 88.)

23. *The Rev. Oliver Heywood: His Autobiography, Diaries, Anecdote and Event Books*, ed. J. Horsfall Turner, 4 vols (Brighouse and Bingley, 1882–4), I. 223.

24. *More News from Rome or Magna Charta, discoursed of between a Poor Man & his Wife* (London, 1666), pp. 22–3.

25. P. J. Klemp, 'Lancelot Andrewes, Plagiarism, and Pedagogy at Hampton Court in 1606', *Philological Quarterly*, 77 (1998), pp. 15–39.

26. *The Letters of John Chamberlain*, ed. Norman Egbert McLure (Philadelphia: American Philosophical Society, 1939), I. 232–3.

27. *A Sermon Preached at the Funerall of the R. R. Father in God, Lancelot Late Lord Bishop of Winchester* (London, 1629), p. 16.

28. *The Casuist Uncas'd*, 2nd edn (London, 1680), sigs. A2^v–A3^r, quoted in Keeble, *Literary Culture*, p. 247.

29. pp. 77–8; quoted in Keeble, *Literary Culture*, pp. 182–3.

30. Book of Jeremiah, 1: 1–17 (King James version).
31. *A Critical History of the Old Testament* (London, 1682), p. 35.
32. p. [1]. Cited in Keeble, *Literary Culture*, p. 183.
33. Gilbert Burnet, *A Sermon Preached at the Funeral of the Most Reverend Father in God John ... Lord Archbishop of Canterbury* (London, 1694), pp. 14–15.
34. In 'Addison', *Essays in the Eighteenth Century Presented to David Nichol Smith*, ed. James Sutherland and F. P. Wilson (Oxford: Oxford University Press, 1945), pp. 1–14.
35. P. G. Wodehouse, 'The Great Sermon Handicap', *The Inimitable Jeeves* (Harmondsworth: Penguin Books, 1953), p. 140.
36. *An Essay Concerning Human Understanding*, II. xi. 13.
37. *The Works of John Dryden*, ed. Edward Niles Hooker *et al.*, 20 vols (Los Angeles: University of California Press, 1956–), i. p. 53.

Chapter 11

1. Quoted in Norman Ault, *New Light on Pope with Some Additions to His Poetry Hitherto Unknown* (London: Methuen, 1949), pp. 198–200. See also J. V. Guerinot, *Pamphlet Attacks on Alexander Pope 1711–1744: A Descriptive Bibliography* (London: Methuen and Co., 1969), pp. 104–7, 116–22.
2. Quoted here from Guerinot, *Pamphlet Attacks*, p. 106. For the text and bibliography of the poem, see *Twickenham Edition of the Poems of Alexander Pope*, gen. ed. John Butt, 11 vols (London: Methuen, 1939–1969; hereafter *TE*), vi. pp. 244–7.
3. *The Rival Modes* (1727), pp. 24–5; the lines are printed in italic, perhaps to indicate a quotation.
4. As quoted by Pope in the *Dunciad Variorum*: *TE*, v. 33–4.
5. Guerinot, *Pamphlet Attacks*, pp. 102–3.
6. John Barnard, ed., *Pope: The Critical Heritage* (London: Routledge and Kegan Paul, 1973), p. 86.
7. Guerinot, *Pamphlet Attacks*, pp. 87–8, 99, 118–19, 124–7, 145, 157, 196, 240–1, 249–50, 255–6, 287–8, 302.
8. See, however, Roger Lund, 'From Oblivion to Dulness: Pope and the Poetics of Appropriation', *British Journal for Eighteenth-Century Studies* 14: 2 (Autumn 1991), pp. 171–89.
9. *Epistle to Dr Arbuthnot*, 179–94, *Dunciad*, i. 127–30; *TE*, iv. 109, v. 278–9.
10. 'Epilogue to the Satires', Dialogue I, 5–8; *TE*, iv. 297.
11. *Essay on Criticism*, 135–40.
12. Pope to Caryll, 16 February 1729; *The Correspondence of Alexander Pope*, ed. George Sherburn, 5 vols (Oxford: Clarendon, 1956), iii. pp. 18–19.
13. *TE*, v. 33–5.
14. *TE*, v. 99–101. Pope's note directs the reader to his classical model in Virgil, *Aeneid* book x, but as Sutherland points out, readers might also notice a resemblance to an episode in Swift's *Battle of the Books*.
15. Pope's note to line 120, *TE*, v. 111.
16. Pat Rogers, 'Proper Nouns in *The Dunciad*', in *Essays on Pope* (Cambridge: Cambridge University Press, 1993), pp. 98–128, at p. 118. 'A. Moore' was also the name of a fictitious publisher put on pamphlets to disguise their origin;

and 'Smyth' was the name of Pope's pseudonymous envoy to Curll in the matter of his letters.

17. *TE*, v. 101–2, 209.
18. See further 'A Letter to the Publisher', *TE*, v. 16, 'Martinus Scriblerus of the Poem', *TE*, v. 52; notes to ii. 134 and iii. 147.
19. Guerinot, *Pamphlet Attacks*, pp. 134, 162.
20. Pope to Broome, 2 May 1730; to Bethel, 9 June 1730; *Correspondence*, iii. pp. 106 and 114.
21. Guerinot, *Pamphlet Attacks*, pp. 188–93; James T. Hillhouse, *The Grub-street Journal* (Durham, NC: Duke University Press, 1928), pp. 57–63.
22. For instance, Samuel Butler's 'Satyr Upon Plagiaries' is a virtuoso set of tropes on the criminal, legal and economic possibilities of plagiarism; *A Journal from Parnassus: Now Printed From a Manuscript circa 1688*, edited by Hugh Macdonald (1937) institutes a full court sessions to determine the plagiarisms of Dryden.
23. The attacks began in the January issue (pp. 24–6) and continued through February (pp. 82–5), April (p. 189), June (pp. 285–6), and August (pp. 363–6). See Paul Baines, *The House of Forgery in Eighteenth-Century Britain* (Aldershot: Ashgate, 1999), Chapter 4, and sources cited therein.
24. See especially Lauder, *Essay*, pp. 28, 74, 90, 115, 163.
25. Douglas, *Milton Vindicated*, pp. 26–7, 33–5.
26. See Baines, *House of Forgery*, p. 85.
27. *A Letter to the Reverend Mr. Douglas, Occasioned by his Vindiation of Milton* (1751); for the Pope line see *Dunciad*, iv. 112; *TE*, v. 352.
28. See further Baines, *House of Forgery*, pp. 88–9.
29. Baines, *House of Forgery*, p. 82.
30. Fielding, A*n Enquiry into the Causes of the Late Increase of Robbers and Related Writings*, ed. Malvin R. Zirker (Oxford: Clarendon Press, 1988), pp. 131, 143; Pope, 'A Letter to the Publisher', *Dunciad*, *TE*, v. 15.
31. Fielding, *The Life and Death of Jonathan Wild the Great* (1743). For Pope on Wild, see *Epilogue to the Satires*, Dialogue II, 39–54; *TE*, iv. 315.
32. Fielding, *Enquiry*, p. 154.
33. The overall model here derives from Michel Foucault's contrast between public execution and regulatory timetable in *Discipline and Punish*, trans. Alan Sheridan (Harmondsworth: Penguin Books, 1979).
34. *Letters from a Late Eminent Prelate to One of His Friends*, 2nd edition (London: T. Cadell and W. Davies, 1809), p. 29. Hereafter cited as *Letters*.
35. *Q. Horatii Flacci Ars Poetica. Epistola ad Pisones. With an English Commentary and Notes* (London, 1749).
36. *Epistola* (1749), pp. v, 11–12, 60–1, commenting on Horace, *Epistola ad Pisones*, lines 128–35. Hurd notes that Horace's terms 'communia' and 'publica' are from the Civil Law.
37. *Letters*, pp. 4–5, 9–11; *Epistola* (1749), p. ix.
38. *Q Horatii Flacci Epistola ad Augustum. With an English Commentary and Notes. To which is added, A Discourse Concerning Poetical Imitation* (London and Cambridge, 1751); the 'Discourse' occupies pp. 109–207. Warburton to Hurd, 27 October and 8 November 1750; *Letters*, pp. 32, 48, 65–9.
39. Hurd, 'Discourse', p. 201; and see pp. 180, 199, 202–6.

40. Quoted from the edition by W. J. Bate and Albrecht B. Strauss (*Yale Edition of the Works of Samuel Johnson*, iv, New Haven and London: Yale University Press, 1969), pp. 393–4: Horace, *Epistles* I.iii.19–20, translated by Philip Francis.

41. Lauder, *Essay*, pp. 102, 115; Douglas, *Milton Vindicated*, p. 103. Pope may have been thinking of such a line in stuffing Moore's head with removable feathers.

42. Compare Hurd, 'Discourse', p. 125.

43. Barnard, *Critical Heritage*, p. 386.

44. Barnard, *Critical Heritage*, pp. 408–9, 491, 497.

45. *Q. Horatii Flacci Epistolae ad Pisones, Et Augustum*, 'third edition', 2 vols (Cambridge and London, 1757). The new dissertation, 'A Letter to Mr [William] Mason; On the Marks of Imitation' is separately paginated in volume 2. The 'second edition', combining the commentaries, had appeared in 1753 with a dedication in volume 2 to Warburton, who had by now edited 'our English Horace, the *best* that was ever given of any classic' (i. xvi). Mansfield (a judge, and friend of Pope's) apparently commended the dissertation especially; *Letters*, pp. 230–59.

46. Hurd listed several of Pope's (and Gray's) borrowings in his edition of *Select Works of Mr. A. Cowley*, 2 vols (Dublin, 1772).

47. Young, *Conjectures On Original Composition. In a Letter to the Author of Sir Charles Grandison* (London, 1759); *Critical Heritage*, p. 422, and p. 345; *Letters*, p. 285. The second of Young's two epistles commends originality.

48. Hurd, 'Discourse', p. 206.

49. See *The English Essays of Edward Gibbon*, ed. Patricia Craddock (Oxford: Clarendon Press, 1972), pp. 27–53, 107, 229–313; Capell, *Reflections on Originality in Authors* (1766), pp. 52–3, 62.

50. Hurd, 'Marks of Imitation', pp. 11–12; Whalley, *An Enquiry into the Learning of Shakespeare* (London, 1748), pp. 81–3; Farmer, *An Essay on the Learning of Shakespeare*, second edition (London, 1767), p. 19.

51. *The Genuine Remains In Verse and Prose of Mr. Samuel Butler, Author of Hudibras*, 2 vols (1759), ii. 496–7.

52. Hurd, *Letters on Chivalry and Romance* (London, 1762). Millar also published Fielding's *Enquiry* and Young's *Conjectures*.

53. See Robert J. Griffin, *Wordsworth's Pope: A Study in Literary Historiography* (Cambridge: Cambridge University Press, 1995).

Chapter 12

1. Cited from *The Spectator*, ed. D. F. Bond, 5 vols (Oxford: Clarendon Press, 1965), IV. 438–9.

2. For a discussion of plagiarism before 1700, mostly in connection with drama, see Brean S. Hammond, *Professional Imaginative Writing in England 1670–1740: 'Hackney for Bread'* (Oxford: Clarendon Press, 1997), pp. 83–104; and Paulina Kewes, *Authorship and Appropriation: Writing for the Stage in England, 1660–1710* (Oxford: Clarendon Press, 1998).

3. *Epistle to Arbuthnot* (1735), line 184, and *The Dunciad* (1743), I. 128, in *The Poems of Alexander Pope*, ed. J. Butt and others, 11 vols (London: Methuen, 1939–69), vol. IV, ed. J. Butt, p. 109; and V, ed. M. Mack, p. 279.

4. Joseph Spence, *Observations, Anecdotes, and Characters of Books and Men*, ed. J. M. Osborn, 2 vols (Oxford: Clarendon Press, 1966), no. 745, I. 304.

5. 'Verses on the Death of Dr. Swift, D.S.P.D.', lines 317–18, in *Jonathan Swift: The Complete Poems*, ed. P. Rogers (Harmondsworth: Penguin Books, 1983), p. 493. Swift's lines are themselves borrowed from Sir John Denham's poem 'On Mr. Abraham Cowley', lines 29–30. The best overview of issues to do with plagiarism in the eighteenth century is Roger Lonsdale, 'Gray and "Allusion": The Poet as Debtor', *Studies in the Eighteenth Century IV*, ed. R.F. Brissenden and J. C. Eade (Canberra: Australian National University Press, 1979), pp. 31–55. See also Julie C. Hayes, 'Plagiarism and Legitimation in Eighteenth-Century France', *The Eighteenth Century* 34 (1993), pp. 115–31.

6. I have been influenced in this part of my essay by Quentin Skinner, 'The Idea of a Cultural Lexicon', *Essays in Criticism* 29 (1979), pp. 205–24; see esp. pp. 207–11.

7. I know of no satisfactory treatment of the issue of plagiarism in connection with eighteenth-century prose fiction. I have, though, read and profited from an essay by Paulina Kewes on literary appropriation in the eighteenth-century theatre: ' "[A] Play, which I presume to call *original*": Appropriation, Creative Genius and Eighteenth-Century Playwriting', *Studies in the Literary Imagination*, 34 (2001), pp. 17–47.

8. Nathan Bailey, in his *Dictionarium Britannicum* (1st edn London, 1721; 1736), defines plagiarism as 'the stealing other people's works, and publishing them as one's own'; Johnson (1755) offers 'Theft; literary adoption of the thoughts or works of another'; *OED* has 'The wrongful appropriation, or purloining, and publication as one's own, of the ideas, or the expression of the ideas . . . of another.'

9. For details about Lauder's life, see *DNB*; for treatment of the Lauder controversy, see James L. Clifford, 'Johnson and Lauder', *Philological Quarterly* 54 (1975), pp. 342–56; and Paul Baines, *The House of Forgery in Eighteenth-Century Britain* (Aldershot: Ashgate, 1999), pp. 81–102.

10. See *The Dunciad* (1743), IV. 112.

11. See *Gentleman's Magazine* XX (London, 1750), 535–6.

12. See William Lauder, *An Essay on Milton's Use and Imitation of the Moderns* (London, 1750), 'Preface'.

13. Ibid., pp. 37, 71.

14. Ibid., p. 74.

15. Ibid., p. 163.

16. Cited from the *Yale Edition of the Works of Samuel Johnson*, 13 vols (New Haven, CT: Yale University Press, 1958–), IV, ed. W. J. Bate and A. B. Strauss (1969), p. 394.

17. *The Correspondence of Alexander Pope*, ed. George Sherburn, 5 vols (Oxford: Clarendon Press, 1956), I. p. 19.

18. See Thomas McFarland, 'The Originality Paradox', *New Literary History* 5 (1973–74), p. 471.

19. 'Preface' to 'An Essay on the Different Stiles of Poetry', in *Collected Poems of Thomas Parnell*, ed. Claude Rawson and F. P. Lock (Newark: University of Delaware Press, 1989), p. 48; *Critical Works of John Dennis*, ed. E. N. Hooker, 2 vols (Baltimore: Johns Hopkins University Press, 1939–43), II. p. 27.

20. Henry Fielding, *Tom Jones* (London, 1749), Book XII, Chapter 1.

21. John Douglas, *Milton Vindicated from the Charge of Plagiarism* (London, 1751), p. 8.
22. *Q. Horatii Flacci Epistola ad Augustum. With an English Commentary and Notes. To which is added A Discourse concerning Poetical Imitation* (London, 1751), p. 177.
23. Ibid., pp. 183, 186.
24. See Richard Hurd, *A Letter to Mr. Mason on the Marks of Imitation* (Cambridge, 1762), pp. 9, 60.
25. *Correspondence of Thomas Gray*, ed. P. Toynbee and L. Whibley, 3 vols (Oxford: Clarendon Press, 1935), II. p. 477.
26. *Yale Edition*, IV. 394–5.
27. Ibid., IV. 399. This understanding of plagiarism as a copying of language (not of stories or ideas) is very similar to the theory of plagiarism in Gerard Langbaine's *An Account of the English Dramatick Poets* (1691); see Kewes, *Authorship and Appropriation*, p. 116.
28. *London Magazine*, no. XXII, in *Boswell's Column*, ed. Margery Bailey (London: William Kimber, 1951), pp. 131–2, 134.
29. *Adventurer* 95, 2 October 1753, in *Yale Edition*, II, ed. W. J. Bate, J. M. Bullitt and L. F. Powell (1963), pp. 425–7.
30. For discussion of Langbaine, see Kewes, *Authorship and Appropriation*, pp. 96–129.
31. *Johnson's Lives of the Poets*, ed. A. Waugh, 6 vols (London: Kegan Paul, 1896), II. p. 255.
32. Ibid., p. 133.
33. Ibid., p. 162–3.
34. *Milton Vindicated*, p. 14.
35. *Yale Edition*, IV. 394.
36. Edward Young, *Conjectures on Original Composition*, ed. Edith J. Morley (Manchester: Manchester University Press, 1918), pp. 10–11. For an interesting discussion, see Joel Weinsheimer, 'Conjectures on Unoriginal Composition', *The Eighteenth Century: Theory and Interpretation* 22 (1981), pp. 58–73.
37. *Conjectures*, p. 11.
38. Sir Joshua Reynolds, *Discourses Delivered to the Students of the Royal Academy*, ed. Roger Fry (London: Seeley, 1905), p. 34.
39. Ibid., p. 165.
40. *Conjectures*, p. 12.
41. Reynolds, *Discourses*, p. 165.
42. Ibid., p. 164.
43. Ibid.
44. For Warton on Pope's plagiarism, see *An Essay on the Genius and Writings of Pope*, fifth edition, 2 vols (London, 1806), I. pp. 94–5.
45. Percival Stockdale, *An Inquiry into the Nature and Genuine Laws of Poetry* (London, 1778), pp. 74, 85. Stockdale's discussion of plagiarism is reproduced virtually *verbatim* in his essay on Pope in *Lectures on the Truly Eminent English Poets*, 2 vols (London, 1807), I. 425–37. A good recent treatment of the eccentric Stockdale is Howard D. Weinbrot, 'Samuel Johnson, Percival Stockdale, and Brick-bats from Grubstreet: Some Later Response to the *Lives of the Poets*', *Huntington Library Quarterly* 56 (1993), pp. 105–34.
46. Stockdale, *Inquiry*, p. 74.

47. Ibid., pp. 75–6.
48. Ibid., p. 77.
49. Ibid., pp. 77–9.
50. See *Gentleman's Magazine* 55 (London, 1785), pp. 544–7, 579–81, 717–20, 784–5, 888. The controversy surrounding Pinkerton's book rumbled on throughout the following year.
51. John Pinkerton [Robert Heron], *Letters of Literature* (London, 1785), p. 356.
52. Ibid., p. 362.
53. Ibid.
54. Ibid., pp. 357–9.
55. *Adventurer* 95, in *Yale Edition*, II. 425.

Chapter 13

1. For a discussion of Holwell, see G. Moorhouse, *India Britannica* (London: Harvill, 1983), p. 50.
2. For discussions of the role of information in the British colonial state, see C. A. Bayly, *Empire and Information: Intelligence Gathering and Social Communication in India 1780–1870* (Cambridge: Cambridge University Press, 1996) and B. S. Cohn, *Colonialism and its Forms of Knowledge: The British in India* (Princeton, NJ: Princeton University Press, 1996).
3. For an important account of linguistic scholarship in British India, see Cohn, *Colonialism*, pp. 16–56. However, Cohn does not discuss the relationship between the individual and the collective in this context.
4. The first edition was published in 1772 and the second in 1774.
5. J. Gilchrist, 'Preface' [to *Hindoostanee Philology*] (Calcutta: The Mirror Press, 1798), p. v, footnote.
6. Gilchrist, 'Preface' presents an account of the author's early years in India and of the making of the dictionary and grammar.
7. G. Hadley, *Grammatical Remarks on the Practical and Vulgar Dialect of the Indostan Language commonly called Moors* (London: Cadell, 1772), pp. 12–30.
8. J. Gilchrist, *A Grammar of the Hindoostanee Language; or, Part Third of Volume First, of a System of Hindoostanee Philology* (Calcutta: Chronicle Press, 1796), p. 99.
9. Gilchrist, *Grammar*, p. 143.
10. J. Wilkins, *Essay towards a Real Character and a Philosophical Language* (London: Gellibrand and Martyn, 1668), p. 446.
11. For an illustrated account of the Daniells' 'picturesque travels' in India, see J. Mahajan, *Picturesque India: Sketches and Travels of Thomas and William Daniell* (Delhi: Lustre, 1983).
12. Gilchrist, 'Preface', pp. xliv–xlv.
13. Ibid., p. xlv.
14. The fables were published under the title, *The Hindee Moral Preceptor: and Persian Scholar's Shortest Road to the Hindoostanee Language; or Vice Versa.*
15. Gilchrist, 'Preface', p. xlv.
16. J. Gilchrist, *The Oriental Linguist* (Calcutta: Ferris and Greenway, 1798), p. i.
17. Ibid., p. ii.
18. Ibid.

19. M. P. Tilley, *A Dictionary of the Proverbs of England in the Sixteenth and Seventeenth Centuries: A Collection of the Proverbs Found in English Literature and the Dictionaries of the Period* (Ann Arbor: University of Michigan Press, 1950), p. 106.
20. Gilchrist, *Oriental Linguist*, p. ii.
21. For a discussion of early grammars of Wolof, see J. E. Irvine, 'Mastering African Languages: The Politics of Linguistics in Nineteenth-Century Senegal', *Social Analysis*, 33 (1993), pp. 27–46.
22. J.-F. Roger, *Recherches philosophiques sur la langue ouolofe, suivies d'un vocabulaire abrégé français–oulof* (Paris: Dondey-Dupré, 1829), p. 6. Translations are my own.
23. Roger, *Recherches philosophiques*, pp. 13–14.
24. J. Dard, *Grammaire wolofe* (Paris: Imprimerie Royale, 1826), p. 13.
25. Roger, *Recherches philosophiques*, p. 30.

Afterword

1. Zsuzsa Baross, 'The (False) Gift of Writing', *New Literary History*, 31 (2000), 441, 447; Joseph Gibaldi, *MLA Handbook for Writers of Research Papers*, 5th edn (New York, 1999), p. 30.
2. Ron Scollon, 'Plagiarism and Ideology: Identity in Intercultural Discourse', *Language in Society*, 24 (1995), p. 1.
3. Ibid., pp. 25–6.
4. Paulina Kewes, *Authorship and Appropriation: Writing for the Stage in England, 1660–1710* (Oxford: Clarenden, Press, 1998).
5. Max W. Thomas, 'Eschewing Credit: Heywood, Shakespeare, and Plagiarism before Copyright', *New Literary History*, 31 (2000), p. 279.
6. *Aubrey's Brief Lives*, ed. Oliver Lawson-Dick (London: Mandarin Paperbacks, 1992), p. xciii, font romanized. I thank Anne Goldgar for pointing me to this passage.

Index

Bacon, Sir Francis   106, 108, 110, 112,
  234, 236
Baconian   68
Badian, E.   236
Bailey, Margaret   249
Bailey, Nathan   209
  Dictionarium Britannicum   248
Baines, Paul   17, 224, 229, 246, 248
Bainton, R. H.   230
Baker, Sir Richard
  *A Chronicle of the Kings of
  England*   234
Baldwin, T. W.   129, 239
ballad, ballads   14
Ballard, Pierre   143ff., 148, 242, 243
ballet   138, 143, 241
*Ballet de la prospérité des armes de la
  France*   138, 241
Barber, G.   223
Barnard, John   245, 247
Baross, Zsusa   215, 251
Barrow, Isaac   155, 163
Barthes, Roland   134
Bate, Jonathan   224
Bate, Walter Jackson   247, 248, 249
Bathyllus   29
Baxter, Richard   161
Bayly, C. A.   250
Beckett, Samuel
  Waiting for Godot   44
Bedingfield, Edward   190
Behn, Aphra   72–3
Belgioioso, Baldassarino de
  Le balet comique de la reine   143, 146
Bellany, Alastair   244
Bengal   202
Bennett, J. A. W.   236
Bentley, G. E.   69, 70, 71, 73
Bentley, J. H.   230
Bentley, Richard   83, 129
Berkeley   57, 58
Berlin   84
Bethel, Hugh   168, 171, 246
Bible   93ff., 156, 163, 175
  authorship of   93ff., 104, 105
  translations of xiii, 13, 94ff., 223,
    230, 244
bibliography   12
Biden, Senator Joseph   226

Bietenholz, P. G.   231
Bishops' Bible   104
Blair, Rhonda L.   237
blank verse   49
Blount, Martha   166
Blount, Thomas
  Glossographia   222
Bodin, Jean
  De Republica libri sex   107
Bodleian Library   125
Boileau, Nicholas Despreaux   177,
  198
Bolgar, R. R.   235
Bolingbroke, *see* St John, Henry,
  Viscount Bolingbroke
Bombay   203
Bond, D. F.   247
Bond, H. L.   236
book, books   7ff., 22, 72, 84, 88, 124,
  129, 135ff., 185, 187, 202, 211
  market   8, 51, 96, 97, 135
  see also codex; commonplace books;
    manuscript; pamphlet; print;
    roll; scribal publication
Book of Common Prayer   154
bookseller, booksellers   10, 11, 76,
  78–9, 151, 169, 181
  see also publisher, publishers
borrowing   2, 4, 8, 14, 23, 30, 31, 42,
  45, 47, 50, 52, 55, 67, 79, 80, 85,
  107ff., 120ff., 146, 158ff., 167,
  170, 177, 181, 182, 187ff., 198,
  209, 234, 237, 247, 248
Bos, Jean Baptiste, Abbé du
  Réflexions critiques   188
Boston   22
Boston University   35, 39
Boswell, James   198
  Life of Johnson   228
  'On Similarity among
    Authors'   190–1
Bouchard, Donald F.   240
Bowers, Neal
  plagiarized author   21–2, 34–5, 40
Bowersock, G. W.   236
Bowle, John   77, 173
  *Reflections on Originality in
    Authors*   228
Boyle, James   25

258 *Index*